LIFE IN CHRIST

A Catechism for Adult Catholics

Frs. Gerard Weber and James Killgallon

HarperSanFrancisco
An Imprint of HarperCollinsPublishers

Nihil Obstat
Reverend John J. McDonnell, S.T.D.
Censor Deputatus
April 4, 1995

Imprimatur
+ Most Reverend Raymond E. Goedert, M.A., S.T.L., J.C.L.
Vicar General
April 7, 1995

The *Nihil Obstat* and *Imprimatur* are official declarations that a book is free of
doctrinal and moral error. No implication is contained therein that those who
have granted the *Nihil Obstat* and *Imprimatur* agree with the content, opinions,
or statements expressed.

Permissions appear on page 313.

Reprinted by arrangement with ACTA Publications, 4848 N. Clark Street,
Chicago, IL 60640.

FIRST EDITION

Library of Congress Cataloging-in-Publication Data

Weber, Gerard P.
    Life in Christ / Frs. Gerard Weber and James Killgallon.
    Text revised by Michael Place and Sammie Maletta.
    Includes bibliographical references and index.
    ISBN 0-06-069318-5 (pbk.)
    1. Catholic Church—Doctrines—Miscellanea.   2. Catholic Church—
Customs and practices—Miscellanea.   I. Killgallon, James J.,
1914- . II. Place, Michael.   III. Maletta, Sammie.   IV. Title.
BX1754.3W43   1996
238'.2—dc20   95–52131

96 97 98 99 00 OFF 10 9 8 7 6 5 4 3 2 1

Contents

PART IV: CHRIST'S ABIDING PRESENCE: THE SACRAMENTS

PART V: LIFE IN CHRIST

Introduction

Centuries ago, St. Augustine wrote: "Our hearts are restless, until they rest in you, O Lord." How many of us have felt that same restlessness in our own lives? We look in various places for answers, but we never find real and lasting happiness.

For those of us who believe, however, we do find rest in Jesus of Nazareth, the Christ, the "anointed one." For us, Jesus is both the messenger and the message of God, whom Jesus taught us call our Father. Jesus is the Word of God, who alone can satisfy the hungers of the human heart. Jesus sent us the Holy Spirit, to comfort and strengthen us on our journey, and he established his Church, the Pilgrim People of God, to help us on our way.

This catechism is an attempt to help the reader learn how to attain "life in Christ"—a life filled with peace and joy. Following the path indicated here, one can find complete fulfillment in knowing, loving and serving Jesus, the Son of God, who became truly human, lived an died among us, was raised from the dead and ascended into heaven where he now sits at the right hand of the Father.

The best way to learn about Jesus is to begin by prayerfully reading the Bible (also called the Scriptures). If we want to encounter Jesus today, we must read the Bible and pray as we do so. That is why *Life in Christ* contain so many excerpts and references to the Bible. We also encourage the reader to have a copy of the Bible available as you study this catechism and to read and refer to it often.

The teachings of the Catholic Church are not only based on the Bible but also on the 2,000 year tradition of Church teaching. This catechism is therefore designed to help readers become familiar with some of the statements of the saints, popes and Church councils, and especially the documents of the Second Vatican Council and the new *Catechism of the Catholic Church*.

You are invited to experience *Life in Christ*, a catechism that has led millions of people to the Catholic faith. May you join them and us in discovering the love of Jesus and his community of followers.

Introduction
to the New Edition

Interest in the new *Catechism of the Catholic Church* surprised many people. It should not have. For 2,000 years, people of good will everywhere have sought to understand the meaning and the teachings of Jesus Christ. So the new official catechism of the universal Church, the first since the Council of Trent, was welcomed throughout the world.

The Church's new catechism is meant to give direction to those attempting to teach others the Catholic faith, and so it should be read by every priest, religious, catechist and religious educator. The catechism, however, was not designed for the average person. That is where *Life in Christ* comes in. Since 1958, *Life in Christ* has been used by more than 2,000,000 million adults as their basic introduction to Catholicism. Originally written by Frs. Gerard Weber and James Killgallon and later revised by Msgr. Leonard Ziegmann, *Life in Christ* has now been completely revised and updated in accordance with the new *Catechism of the Catholic Church* by Frs. Michael Place and Sammie Maletta, with Fr. Weber himself approving the revision.

This new edition contains over 25% new material, including many direct references to the *Catechism of the Catholic Church* itself. (The paragraph numbers in the new catechism from which direct quotes are taken are given immediately following each quote, e.g., CCC 1234.)

At the end of each section, there is an updated section called "Practice" that explains various Catholic practices related to the topic being discussed. Also included for the first time in *Life in Christ* is a special section containing many of the most familiar Catholic prayers. At the end of the book is an index of specific topics. Sources of quotes from Church documents are included with the text, with a list of these references given before the index.

Part I: THE GIFT OF LIFE

Section 1 **Happiness**

> *In times past, God spoke in partial and various ways to*
> *our ancestors through the prophets; in these last days, he*
> *spoke to us through a son, whom he made heir of all*
> *things and through whom he created the universe,*
> > *who is the refulgence of his glory,*
> > > *the very imprint of his being,*
> > *and who sustains all things by his mighty word.*
> > *When he had accomplished purification from sins,*
> > *he took his seat at the right hand of the Majesty*
> > > *on high— Heb 1:1-3.*

SOME TWO THOUSAND YEARS AGO there lived one whose influence on the world is unique in history. He did not live in one of the great centers of civilization, but in a remote corner of the world. He was not born with the material advantages that wealth and social position can give; he was born in a stable. He did not have a long career, nor one which carried him into many countries; his life span was only thirty-three years; his activity was confined to an area of a few hundred miles. His life did not end on a note of triumph; he suffered the shameful death of crucifixion.

Yet today, twenty centuries later, this man is worshiped by hundreds of millions in every country of the world as the Savior of the human race. Through the centuries since his death millions have gladly renounced all that the human heart holds dear— home, family, riches and friends—to carry his name to other corners of the earth. He is loved throughout the world as no other person has been loved. His cross, once a symbol of a criminal death, is now displayed triumphantly atop churches throughout the world, a symbol of hope and love. His teachings have humanized and ennobled people and nations.

What is it that makes Jesus Christ unique among all people in history and accounts for the influence he has had and still has on the world?

The answer is, of course, that Jesus Christ was not merely a great teacher and religious leader; he is the Son of God. He is the Redeemer promised by God, who brought salvation to the human race, who ransomed all people by his death on the cross.

Jesus Christ is a true human being. He is the mediator between God and people of every age and time. No one can come to the Father except through him. Jesus Christ is also God. His teachings, therefore, are the word of God revealed to us.

Jesus Christ is *"the way, and the truth, and the life"*—Jn 14:6. It is by union with Jesus that people receive the life of grace. It is through the acceptance of Jesus' teachings that we find salvation. It is by submission to Jesus' rule that we find freedom as children of God.

Jesus said to his disciples, *"And behold, I am with you always, until the end of the age"*—Mt 28:20. Although he ascended into heaven, and we can no longer see and hear him as did his contemporaries, Jesus in his great love for us remains with us in his Church. He continues to give life and truth and guidance to those who are joined to him.

1. What does Jesus Christ promise to those who love him?

Jesus Christ promises eternal happiness to those who love him. *"I came so that they might have life and have it more abundantly"*—Jn 10:10.

2. Does Jesus Christ promise us happiness in this life?

Jesus Christ promises us happiness in this life. When Jesus became human he not only revealed himself as the image of the invisible God, he also restored to humanity that which had been lost to sin, the full beauty and majesty of our dignity as creatures made in God's image. True happiness is the result when we live up to the dignity of the human person.

3. In what words did Christ tell us how to attain happiness in this life?

In the Sermon on the Mount, which contained what are known as the Beatitudes, Jesus said:

Blessed are the poor in spirit,
 for theirs is the kingdom of heaven.

Blessed are they who mourn,
 for they will be comforted.

Blessed are the meek,
 for they will inherit the land.

Blessed are they who hunger and thirst for righteousness,
 for they will be satisfied.

Blessed are the merciful,
 for they will be shown mercy.

Blessed are the clean of heart,
 for they will see God.

Blessed are the peacemakers,
 for they will be called children of God.

Blessed are they who are persecuted for the sake
  of righteousness,
 for theirs is the kingdom of heaven—Mt 5:3-10.

In the above passage Jesus promises us happiness. In fact the word "blessed" means "happy." The Beatitudes are at the core of Christ's teaching. They fulfill the promise made to the Jewish people by pointing beyond earthly happiness to the eternal happiness of heaven. The reward promised in each of the Beatitudes is primarily heaven.

The Beatitudes reveal the goal of human existence, the ultimate purpose of human acts; God calls us to his own beatitude. This vocation is addressed to each individual personally, but also to the Church as a whole, the new people made up of those who have accepted the promise and live from it in faith—CCC 1719.

If we live according to this plan of Christ we shall have a foretaste of the happiness of heaven in this life. Christ tells us that we will be happy by doing for his sake the very things which we may think will make us unhappy. Christ tells us that we must not set our hearts on money, whereas many people appear to want even more money than they already have. Christ tells us that we must forgive our enemies and love them, whereas many people seem to want to "get even with" or at least avoid those who hurt them. Christ tells us that we must avoid all sin, that we must be willing to take a lower place, that we must suffer for him, etc. These are conditions which might seem to make us unhappy, but the Lord's words tell us otherwise.

4. How is it possible for us to live according to these high standards set by Christ?

Christ has not only told us how to live; he has shown us by his example. What is more, he gives us all the help we need to follow his example. If we love Christ and try to follow his example we shall receive the strength he promised when he said:

I am the vine, you are the branches. Whoever remains in me and I in [them] will bear much fruit, because without me you can do nothing—Jn 15:5.

Practice

▲ In recent years the Church has revived the ancient Order of Christian Initiation (sometimes referred to as the Rite of Christian Initiation of Adults or R.C.I.A.) by which individuals can become full members of the Catholic Church. Attendance at Sunday worship is an integral part of the initiation process. Weekly attendance at Sunday Mass not only familiarizes the candidates with the order of service and the various practices and gestures of the Mass, but it also introduces them to the parish community. In the context of prayer the candidates are welcomed to the Church as they learn Church teaching and tradition. Usually at the close of the Liturgy of the Word the candidates are invited to leave the assembled body of worshipers to more carefully dwell upon the Word. Even if the candidates do not participate in this formal dismissal and remain for the Liturgy of the Eucharist, they may not receive Holy Communion until they are admitted to full communion with the Church.

Part I: THE GIFT OF LIFE

Section 2 **God, Our Father**

*"I am the way and the truth and the life. No one comes
to the Father except through me. If you know me, then
you will also know my Father. From now on you do know
him and have seen him. . . . Whoever has seen me has
seen the Father. How can you say, 'Show us the Father'?
Do you not believe that I am in the Father and the Father
is in me? The words that I speak to you I do not speak on
my own. The Father who dwells in me is doing his works.
Believe me that I am in the Father and the Father is in me,
or else, believe because of the works themselves"—Jn
14:6-7, 9-11.*

THROUGHOUT HISTORY religions of different cultures
and times have expressed their understanding of God as "Father."
Moses told the Jewish people that God was not only their Creator
but also their Father. The Israelites saw God's fatherly love
present most particularly to the poor, orphaned and widowed.
Likewise, Jesus called God "Father," but he did so in an entirely
new way. Jesus announced that God is not only our Father as
creator but that God is also Father eternally in relation to the Son,
just as the Son is always in relation to the Father.

This is Christ's great message: God is not a remote power
who rules the universe from afar. He is our loving Father, who sent
his only Son into the world in order that he might share his life
with us.

God wants to unite us to himself. Therefore we must know
him. We must know him not merely by observing the world about
us, the work of his hands, but by hearing what he has told us of
himself.

1. How can we speak of God?

When we speak of God we are necessarily forced to use human language. We can never have more than partial knowledge of God's omnipotence and, since human knowledge of God is limited, so too is our language about him. For example, we cannot name God except in relation to creatures, because of our limited human means of thinking and knowing. But because God transcends all creatures, we must continually purify our language of anything limited, too imaginative or imperfect, so as to avoid distorting our image of God by expressions that fall short of God's mystery.

2. Why is God called "the Father"?

God is the Father of all human persons because God has created all people. *"God created [humans] in his image; /in the divine image he created [them]; /male and female he created them"—Gn 1:27.*

3. What does it mean to call God "Father"?

When we call God "Father" we are using the language of faith. To call God "Father" does not mean to limit God to the male sex. God is neither male or female, God transcends such categories. In fact, God has also been likened to a mother. In the Book of Isaiah God assures Israel: *"As a mother comforts her son, /so will I comfort you"—Is 66:13.* Likewise, David encourages Israel to hope in God *"like a weaned child on its mother's lap"—Ps 131:2.*

The language of faith attempts to express meaning, and in this case we should understand that when we call God "Father" it is to help us appreciate the parental love God shows to us in several ways:

a) God provides for the needs of his children:

"Therefore I tell you, do not worry about your life and what you will eat, or about your body and what you will wear. For life is more than food and the body more than clothing. Notice the ravens: they do not sow or reap; they

*have neither storehouse nor barn, yet God feeds them.
How much more important are you than birds! Can any of
you by worrying add a moment to your life-span? If even
the smallest things are beyond your control, why are you
anxious about the rest? Notice how the flowers grow. They
do not toil or spin. But I tell you, not even Solomon in all
his splendor was dressed like one of them. If God so
clothes the grass in the field that grows today and is
thrown into the oven tomorrow, will he not much more
provide for you, O you of little faith? As for you, do not
seek what you are to eat and what you are to drink, and
do not worry anymore. All the nations of the world seek
for these things, and your Father knows that you need
them. Instead, seek his kingdom, and these other things
will be given you besides—Lk 12:22-31.*

b) God loves us so much that he sent his Son to save us:

*For God so loved the world that he gave his only Son, so
that everyone who believes in him might not perish but
might have eternal life. For God did not send his Son into
the world to condemn the world, but that the world might
be saved through him—Jn 3:16-17.*

c) God has shared his life with all people:

*See what love the Father has bestowed on us that we may
be called the children of God. Yet so we are. The reason
the world does not know us is that it did not know him.
Beloved, we are God's children now; what we shall be
has not yet been revealed. We do know that when it is
revealed we shall be like him, for we shall see him as he
is. Everyone who has this hope based on him makes
himself [or herself] pure, as he is pure—1 Jn 3:1-3.*

4. How do we know that God exists?

We know that God exists from our observation of the world
around us and by the use of our rational faculties as human
persons.

a) Observation. Everywhere in nature we find beauty and order. To try and explain this beauty and order as a result of chance is foolish. The incredible beauty of the world and its intricate order are obvious signs of an intelligence at work. The magnificence of a sunset coloring up an evening sky is at once beautiful to behold and yet fascinating to comprehend—the various gases of our atmosphere combined with heat, moisture and altitude all harmoniously working together for a few moments of glory. The awesome grandeur of the Grand Canyon, Niagra Falls or the Rocky Mountains, leaves us speechless, while the details of their coming into being boggles our minds. Because of our observation of beauty and order in nature, we conclude that only a living, intelligent being could have created the universe.

b) Reason. Only the human person among all of God's creatures has the ability to reason. This special attribute also allows us to know of God's existence. Our desire for truth, our sense of moral righteousness, the call of our own consciences leads us to reason that there is more to our existence and to life in general than meets the eye. Through this openness we perceive signs of our spiritual souls.

Thus through both observation and reason we are able to discern that we are part of an existence far greater than ourselves. Humans throughout history have identified the existence of a source, a force, a being that knows no time, is not defined by our limits, and is both the cause and final goal of all life. In the Judeo-Christian tradition, we have consistently called this being God.

5. Has God told us of his existence?

God has told us of his existence in the Bible, the Sacred Scriptures. Through the author of the Book of Genesis, for example, we learn that God revealed himself to humankind from the very beginning. In the story of Adam and Eve, God invited our first parents to know him as a loving Father.

In the story of Noah, God made a covenant never to destroy the human race, and in the story of Abraham, God made the Hebrews his "chosen people."

When God spoke to Moses in the book of Exodus, commanding him to lead his people out of Egypt and into the promised land, he even told Moses his name: "Yahweh" or "I Am":

> *"But," said Moses to God, "when I go to the Israelites and say to them, 'the God of your [ancestors] has sent me to you,' if they ask me, 'What is his name?' what am I to tell them?" God replied, "I am who am." Then he added, "This is what you shall tell the Israelites: I AM sent me to you"—Ex 3:13-15.*

God has also revealed his existence through his only Son, Jesus Christ:

> *In times past, God spoke in partial and various ways to our ancestors through the prophets; in these last days, he spoke to us through a son, whom he made heir of all things and through whom he created the universe—Heb 1:1-2.*

7. What has God revealed about himself?

God is a spirit. He is the one limitless, almighty, all-knowing spirit. He does not need anything or anyone outside of himself. He depends on nothing and on no one, but all things depend on him. Yet God cares for and sustains all the things which he has created. And he calls people to become his adopted children.

Although in many ways God is incomprehensible to human beings, from the various authors of the Bible, whom God inspired, we do learn the following:

a) God is love:

> *We have come to know and to believe in the love God has for us. God is love, and whoever remains in love remains in God and God in [them]—1 Jn 4:16.*

b) God is all good. He created the world in order to show

forth his glory and to share his happiness with the beings he created:

"Holy, holy, holy is the LORD of hosts!" they cried one to another. "All the earth is filled with his glory!" —Is 6:3.

c) God shares his divine life with us:

He has bestowed on us the precious and very great promises, so that through them you may come to share in the divine nature, after escaping from the corruption that is in the world because of evil desire—2 Pt 1:4.

d) God loves all people and wills that we be saved:

With age-old love I have loved you;
so I have kept my mercy toward you—Jer 31:3.

For God so loved the world that he gave his only Son, so that everyone who believes in him might not perish but might have eternal life. For God did not send his Son into the world to condemn the world, but that the world might be saved through him—Jn 3:16-17.

. . . who wills everyone to be saved and to come to knowledge of the truth—1 Tm 2:4.

e) God is all-merciful, and he shows his mercy most clearly in his readiness to forgive any sinner who repents:

Merciful and gracious is the LORD, /slow to anger, abounding in kindness. . . . /As the heavens tower over the earth, /so God's love towers over the faithful. . . . /But the LORD'S kindness is forever, /toward the faithful from age to age—Ps 103:8, 11, 17.

"I tell you, in just the same way there will be more joy in heaven over one sinner who repents than over ninety-nine righteous people who have no need of repentance"—Lk 15:7.

f) God is all knowing:

No creature is concealed from him, but everything is

*naked and exposed to the eyes of him to whom we must
render an account—Heb 4:13.*

*He plumbs the depths and penetrates the heart;
  their innermost being he understands.
The Most High possesses all knowledge,
  and sees from of old the things that are to come:
He makes known the past and the future,
  and reveals the deepest secrets—Sir 42:18-20.*

g) God is just:

*A faithful God, without deceit,
  how just and upright he is!—Dt 32:4.*

*Eternal life to those who seek glory, honor, and immor-
tality through perseverance in good works, but wrath and
fury to those who selfishly disobey the truth and obey
wickedness—Rom 2:7-8.*

h) God is infinite, there is no limit to his life:

Great is the Lord and worthy of his praise—Ps 145:3.

*Your throne stands firm from of old;
  you are from everlasting, Lord—Ps 93:2.*

i) God is unchangeable:

*All good giving and every perfect gift is from above,
coming down from the Father of lights, with whom there
is no alteration or shadow caused by change—Jas 1:17.*

j) God is eternal, he had no beginning and will have no
    end:

*Before the mountains were born, /and the earth and the
world brought forth, /from eternity to eternity you are
God. /A thousand years in your eyes /are merely a
yesterday—Ps 90:2, 4.*

". . . before Abraham came to be, I AM"—Jn 8:58.

The Lord shall reign forever and ever—Ex 15:18.

k) God is all-powerful:

O LORD, great are you and glorious, /wonderful in power and unsurpassable. /Let your every creature serve you; /for you spoke, and they were made, /You sent forth your spirit, and they were created; /no one can resist your word—Jdt 16:13-14.

l) God is everywhere:

Where can I hide from your spirit?
  from your presence, where can I flee?
If I ascend to the heavens, you are there;
  if I lie down in Sheol, you are there too.
If I fly with the wings of dawn,
  and alight beyond the sea,
Even there your hand will guide me,
  your right hand will hold me fast.
If I say, "Surely the darkness shall hide me,
  and night shall be my light"—
Darkness is not dark for you,
  and night shines as the day.
  Darkness and light are but one—Ps 139:7-12.

Practice

▲ Now that we have learned why God can properly be called our Father, we can pray the Lord's prayer with more understanding and meaning. The beauty of the "Our Father" is that it not only describes but also expresses our relationship with God.

▲ Two other prayers which Catholics use regularly are the "Hail Mary" and the "Act of Contrition." These traditional prayers have a beauty and simplicity that can help in developing a solid prayer life. However, Catholics are not limited to such traditional forms of prayer; rather we are also encouraged to study and meditate on Sacred Scripture as well as offering our personal prayer from within our hearts.

Part I: THE GIFT OF LIFE

Section 3 **The Gift of Divine Life**

For God so loved the world that he gave his only Son, so that everyone who believes in him might not perish but might have eternal life. For God did not send his Son into the world to condemn the world, but that the world might be saved through him—Jn 3:16-17.

SALVATION BEGINS BY REBIRTH into the life of Christ. When Jesus says, *"I came that they might have life, and have it more abundantly" —Jn 10:10*, he is speaking of divine life, that gift of God which allows us to share in the very life of Christ.

By the power of the Holy Spirit we begin the process of rebirth by an inner conversion. We reject our sinful ways and embrace God's life by accepting his gift of grace. Joined to the death of Jesus we die to our former ways, thereby gaining a share in his resurrected glory. We are reborn to a new life as adopted children of God and become members of his Body, the Church.

Throughout this rebirth and because of it, we are justified— that is, our sins are forgiven and we are renewed in holiness. Justification enables us to actualize our true human freedom by cooperating with God's grace in building up the Body of Christ. The gift of divine life restores us to our original role in God's plan for creation.

1. What does God want for us?

God wants what we want—for us to be happy. This natural desire for happiness was placed in the human heart at the time of creation. God placed it there in order that we might be drawn toward him, who is the only one that can truly satisfy our desire. In other words, God calls each of us to God's own happiness. This ultimate happiness is sometimes described as being God's "beatitude." It is our entering into or sharing in God's glory, in God's divine life.

2. Does the divine life make us divine?

The divine life makes us divine in the sense that we share God's life. It does not make us divine in the sense that we become God or "part of God." Such an idea would be absurd. Even in heaven, seeing and loving God face to face, we shall never lose our identities, our individuality, our complete dependence on God.

3. Why is this ultimate happiness called supernatural?

It is called supernatural because we cannot merit or earn it; it is a gift from God. This kind of happiness it is not anything we can understand or imagine. It is *super*-natural, that is, above the natural.

4. How does a sinner gain such happiness?

It is the Holy Spirit who makes it possible for a sinner to realize this ultimate gift. Through the grace of the Holy Spirit sinners are "justified." Justification is the result of God's offer of mercy which takes away sin and sanctifies the entire person. The sinner, through God's invitation, is made holy and becomes an adopted child of God.

5. What does "adopted child" of God mean?

As creatures we are made in the image and likeness of God. Through the divine life of grace, however, we are transformed from within and take on an inner likeness to God.

6. What is this grace of the Holy Spirit?

"Grace" is a simple word that describes a beautiful but

complex reality. First of all grace is a gift—a favor—that is freely given by God. Grace is something that we never earn or deserve. Second, grace is a participation in God's very life. It is our sharing in the intimacy of the Trinity. Third, grace is the source of our becoming holy or sanctified. Through the divine life of grace we are empowered to live as God lives, that is, to know God as he knows himself and to love him as he loves himself.

7. Does that mean we have no choice about being holy?

God's offer of his love requires our free response for it to be effective, for us to be sanctified.

8. How do Christians experience the mystery of grace?

While grace which justifies and sanctifies is present everywhere and at all times, it is true that God's life of love is experienced in a unique way in the sacramental life of the Church and in special gifts (or charisms) which are gifts of the Spirit for the good of the Church and the salvation of the world.

9. Are we able to know whether we "have grace"?

Grace is supernatural it is not something we can know or experience like other aspects of our life. While we can never be certain of grace, by observing our own good actions and those of others we can learn to trust in the presence of God's grace.

Practice

▲ Grace is part of everyday life. At home, school, or at work—alone or with others—God seeks to break through our mundane senses and reveal his will to us. These moments of insight and special strength can be understood as grace. The better we become at recognizing these moments for what they truly are, the better will we be able to take advantage of God's gift of grace.

▲ One special way of developing a better awareness of grace is to meditate. Prayer can be expressed in words, but it also can be the gathering of our hearts and minds in silence, allowing our pretenses to fall and experiencing God's presence. Such unstructured prayer is not always easy but in the long run it is worth the effort.

Part I: THE GIFT OF LIFE

Section 4 **The Gift of Revelation**

*In times past, God spoke in partial and various ways to
our ancestors through the prophets; in these last days, he
spoke to us through a son, whom he made heir of all
things and through whom he created the universe—Heb
1: 1-2.*

THE HUMAN PERSON can know certain aspects of God's
existence through observation of nature and by the use of natural
reason. However, the mystery of God's plan, which no human
can independently comprehend, is made manifest in God's gift of
divine revelation. This mystery of God's plan is most clearly and
fully seen in the incarnation, life and resurrection of his son, our
Lord, Jesus Christ.

Because God has revealed himself to us we are better able to
know and love him. Consequently, we are better able to respond
to his loving invitation to live in Christ.

The gradual method that God chose to reveal himself was
through the thoughts, feelings and experiences of his people. The
rich deposit of God's self-revelation is found in two independent
but related sources—the Sacred Scriptures (the Bible) and Tradition.

1.   What is revelation?

Human reason, by itself, cannot learn all we need to know
about God. So God himself has chosen to reveal himself to us. He
did so gradually by inspiring holy writers and teachers through
the centuries. These men and women reflected on the events

around them and wrote down the revelation God wanted us to know. However, these inspired authors were free to compose in their own style, using their own words.

2. Must we accept revelation?

We must accept God's revelation because God is truthful and cannot deceive or be deceived.

3. Where can a person find the contents of revelation?

One part of revelation is called the Sacred Scriptures (or the Bible). This is a collection of sacred books written by human beings under the inspiration of God himself. Thus God is the true author.

The Bible is divided into two main sections. The first part is called the Old Testament and contains the inspired writings written before the time of Jesus. These forty-six books contain God's revelation to the Jews.

The second and shorter portion of the Bible is the New Testament. It contains the record of the life of Jesus and the writings of some of the early followers of Jesus. When Jesus died there was no written New Testament. People could learn about Jesus only by listening to his followers teaching his message. Eventually the followers began to write down what they remembered about Jesus. Keep in mind the twenty-seven books of the New Testament have at least eight different authors. The first books were not written immediately after the death of Jesus. At least one was not written until almost sixty years had passed. St. John reminds us:

> Now Jesus did many other signs in the presence of [his] disciples that are not written in this book. But these are written that you may [come to] believe that Jesus is the Messiah, the Son of God, and that through this belief you may have life in his name—Jn 20:30-31.

The other part of revelation is called "Tradition." It is the body of truths about God handed down within the Church. The truths of tradition can be found in the doctrines of the Church, the decrees of the popes and councils and in the compositions of the early teachers of the Church, the "fathers" and "doctors" of the Church.

4. Who are the fathers and doctors of the Church?

The fathers of the Church are certain leaders of the early centuries of Christianity who were characterized by orthodoxy of doctrine and holiness of life.

St. Hilary, St. Athanasius and St. Augustine are examples of the fathers of the Church. St. Gregory the Great, who died in 604 A.D., is generally considered to be the last of the fathers of the Western Church. St. John Damascene, who died about the middle of the eighth century, is the last father of the Eastern Church.

The doctors of the Church are theologians and teachers of later centuries who possess the same qualities of orthodoxy and holiness. St. Thomas Aquinas, who lived in the 13th century, is considered by many the greatest of the doctors of the Church. St. Teresa of Avila of the 16th century is a doctor of the Church who is an example of the many women who have served the Church as teachers and theologians.

5. Since the Bible was written over a period of many years by different authors in different countries, who collected them into one book?

Over the years, there were many books presented to the Church, all claiming to be divinely inspired. But were they? Who could decide? Only a council of Church leaders could answer such a question. A local council in Carthage in 397 A.D. compiled a list, accepting 73 books of the Bible and rejecting others. They sent the list to Pope Siricius, who in turn approved it. Thus we have an authentic list (or canon) of divinely inspired books.

6. Should the average person read the Bible?

The Church has always used the Scriptures in its sacred liturgy or public worship. It encourages all members to read a portion daily in their private devotions. Unfortunately, this has not always been as widespread a custom as the Church has desired. The Bible is not easy reading.

7. What are literary forms?

The reason some people have difficulty in understanding the Bible is that it is composed in many different literary forms.

The term "literary forms" refers to the different types or styles of literature which can be distinguished from each other. There are many types of literary styles used in the Scriptures. Thus, the Bible is not a book of simple prose statements of fact. Some sections of the Scriptures are written in poetic form while other parts are prophecy. To properly understand each section the reader must be aware of the type of literature being used as well as the rules of interpreting that type of literature.

8. How does a person read the Sacred Scriptures?

Because the Bible has many different literary forms we need assistance in determining the meaning of any particular passage. The Second Vatican Council has given us guidance in this regard. First, one needs to be attentive to the overall content and unity of the Scriptures. One part or section cannot be read apart from the whole. Second, the Bible must be read in the context of the entire Tradition of the Church. And finally, the reader must keep in mind what is known as the "analogy of faith." In other words, the integrity found within the truths of faith and the entire plan of salvation must be respected when reading the Scriptures.

9. What is the difference between a Protestant Bible and a Catholic Bible?

Actually, very little. Some of the older editions of the so-called Protestant Bible omit some of the books from both the Old

Testament and the New Testament. The books which Protestant Bibles sometimes omit today include 1 and 2 Maccabees, Tobit, Judith, Sirach, Wisdom, Baruch, plus parts of Daniel and Esther. Most recent Protestant editions, however, now contain all 73 books.

Practice

▲ The Church has been entrusted with the task of safeguarding God's revelation by offering authentic interpretation of both the Bible and Tradition from generation to generation. Roman Catholics are encouraged to familiarize themselves to the both sources of revelation.

▲ It is a good practice to read the Scriptures daily. Many parishes have Bible Study classes in which you may want to participate.

▲ Your parish staff can also recommend various writings of the Church Fathers and Doctors which you might want to read. You should also familiarize yourself with the documents of the Second Vatican Council (Vatican II) as well as other Church documents.

▲ There are many excellent Catholic newspapers and magazines that regularly explore the Bible and Tradition. Consider subscribing to one or more of them.

Part I: THE GIFT OF LIFE

Section 5 **The Gift of the Sacred Scriptures**

In the beginning was the Word,
and the Word was with God,
and the Word was God—Jn 1:1.

THE BIBLE TELLS OUR STORY as the people of God. We hear of our human origins when we read the story of Adam and Eve. We learn of Israel's struggle to become God's chosen people through their obedience and faithfulness. The drama of individuals like Abraham, Jacob, Moses, Ruth and David teach us how God calls everyone to a life of holiness and service. The warnings of the prophets remind us of the consequences we bring upon ourselves when we stray from God's righteous path. The Gospels fill us with excitement and hope as the life of Jesus Christ—God's living word—is made manifest to all people. We gain wisdom as we study the implications of the Letters (or Epistles) and the story of the early Church's journey toward unity and holiness found in the Acts of the Apostles and the Book of Revelation.

As a Church we find our strength and nourishment in the content of the Scriptures. It is our belief as Roman Catholics that each book of the Bible, even though written at different times and by different people, people of different languages and cultures, is really God's revelation expressed in human language.

1. What is the Old Testament (the Hebrew Scriptures)?

The Old Testament (or the Hebrew Scriptures) is a collection of the sacred books of the Hebrew people. It tells the story of their relationship with God. It is usually presented as forty-six books, which vary in length and literary form. There are twenty-one books of History, eighteen books of Prophecy and seven books of Wisdom literature.

These books are to be understood in the light of the literary style and the mentality of the times in which they were written, although recent archeological studies have in many cases indicated their geographical and historical roots. The books of the Old Testament were written by many authors over a long period of time. The traditions of the Hebrew people recounted in the first five books of the Bible certainly go back to the time of Moses (1400-1200 B.C), while the story of the Maccabees, told in the last two books of the Old Testament, was written about 100 B.C.

2. Why is this collection of books called the Old Testament?

These books are called a "testament" because they are an account of the covenant (agreement) entered into by God with his chosen people through Moses on Mount Sinai. For Christians, this testament or covenant is called "old" to distinguish it from the new one which God entered into with all people through Jesus on Mount Calvary. The prophet Jeremiah foretold the transition from the old to the new testament five hundred years before the birth of Christ:

> The days are coming, says the LORD, when I will make a new covenant with the house of Israel and the house of Judah. It will not be like the covenant I made with their [ancestors] the day I took them by the hand to lead them forth from the land of Egypt; for they broke my covenant and I had to show myself their master, says the LORD. But this is the covenant which I will make with the house of Israel after those days, says the LORD. I will place my law within them, and write it upon their hearts; I will be their God, and they shall be my people. No longer will they have need to teach their friends and kinsmen how to know the LORD. All, from least to greatest, shall know

me, says the LORD, for I will forgive their evildoing and remember their sin no more—Jer 31:31-34.

More recently, some or all of these books of the Bible have been referred to as the "Hebrew Scriptures" to emphasize that they are the story of the Hebrew (Jewish) people.

3. What kind of history is recorded in the Old Testament?

The Old Testament is a theological history of God's dealings with his chosen people. Consequently, it is an interpretative history and does not intend to give a thorough account of all the secular events of the time.

a) The Old Testament is the history of God's kingdom on earth. The Hebrews (or Jews) were God's people. He was their king, who exercised his authority through the prophets, judges and kings. God separated the Jews from all other people and promised them large families, good harvests, peace and his continual presence and protection if they were faithful to him. He threatened them with war, famine, plague and exile if they were unfaithful. The Jews frequently turned from God. In each case God chastised them, forgave them and accepted them again as his chosen people.

b) The Old Testament tells the story of only one people, the Hebrews. Other people are mentioned only incidentally. It does not give a complete history of even the Jewish people, but treats of only those events which have direct bearing on the plan of God. There are gaps of hundreds of years in the narrative, and only people who have a direct impact on the plan of salvation figure prominently in it.

c) The Old Testament anticipates the coming of the Messiah. It tells of the historical events leading up to his coming. It records the prophecies which Jesus Christ was to fulfill.

4. What is the importance of the Hebrew people in God's plan of salvation?

The Hebrews were the people through whom the one true God was revealed during the centuries before Christ. God's ancient revelation was given to the Jews. It was they who preserved it and handed it down. When the Son of God became a man, he was born a Jew.

The Jews, therefore, are the spiritual ancestors of all Christians. Christianity is the Jewish religion brought to its fulfillment and opened up to the whole world. It should be noted, however, that the Jews remain God's chosen people, since God's covenant with them has never been revoked.

(The Hebrews were not called "Jews" until later in their history. For the purpose of clarity, however, "Jews" or "Jewish people" is used interchangeably with "Hebrews" throughout this book.)

5. Who was Abraham?

Abraham, who it is believed lived around 1850 B.C., was called by God to be the founder of the Hebrew people. God entered into a covenant with Abraham and through that covenant God made Abraham's descendents his "chosen people." It was to this people that God revealed himself.

6. Who was Moses?

Moses was the great leader and law-giver whom God chose to lead the Hebrews out of captivity in Egypt into the land he had promised them. It was to Moses that God gave the ten commandments on Mount Sinai when he renewed his covenant with the Jews.

7. What is a prophet?

A prophet is a person sent by God to reveal to the people the will of God. The prophets of the Old Testament strove continually to keep the Hebrew people faithful to God; they reminded the Jews of God's promises to them, of his past benefits and of their future glory if they remained faithful to him. Some of the prophets also foretold future events such as the destruction of the kingdom of Israel. Many of the prophets spoke of the coming of the Messiah and of his kingdom:

> *The word of the LORD came to me thus:*
> *Before I formed you in the womb I knew you,*
> *before you were born I dedicated you,*
> *a prophet to the nations I appointed you.*
> *"Ah, Lord GOD !" I said,*
> *"I know not how to speak; I am too young."*
> *But the LORD answered me,*
> *Say not, "I am too young."*
> *To whomever I send you, you shall go;*
> *whatever I command you, you shall speak—Jer 1:4-7.*

8. What things were foretold by prophets concerning Christ and his kingdom?

Many individual traits of the person, character, kingdom and rule of the Messiah were foretold by the prophets. These facts were revealed over a long period of time and were never gathered into one place in any book of the Old Testament. Many of the prophecies were obscure. Most likely the prophets themselves did not understand exactly how their prophecies would be fulfilled. In fact, various prophecies seemed to contradict one another. One group showed a victorious king ruling in justice over a peaceful people, while another group foretold the humiliation, the rejection, the suffering and the violent death of the Messiah. Many of the prophecies were not clearly understood until after Christ came and by his life and actions fulfilled them—even those which had seemed to be contradictory. For example:

> *But you, Bethlehem—Ephrathah,*
> *too small to be among the clans of Judah,*
> *From you shall come forth to me*
> *one who is to be ruler in Israel—Mi 5:1.*

After they had crucified him, they divided his garments by casting lots—Mt 27:35.

They stare at me and gloat;
*   they divide my garments among them;*
*   and for my clothing they cast lots—Ps 22:18-19.*

9.   What is the New Testament?

The New Testament is a collection of writings that were composed at various times by different authors after the death of Jesus. They were not assembled together until the end of the second century, and it was not until the end of the fourth century that the Church concluded definitively which books belonged to the New Testament. There are three types of writings in the New Testament: Gospels, Letters (or Epistles), and the apocalyptic writings of John.

10.   How were the Gospels composed?

There were three stages in the formation of the Gospels. First there was the actual life and teachings of Jesus. The foundation of the Gospels is in that historical reality. Second, there is the oral communication by which the apostles and disciples of Jesus passed on what they had seen and experienced. Third, there are the written Gospels. These final texts brought together the oral tradition and already existing written texts. Each of the authors (or Evangelists) was faithful to the truth of revelation, but each sought to communicate this truth in a manner that addressed different situations of the early Church. Because the final version of each Gospel was a form of preaching and not meant to be the presentation of literal history, there is some divergence of style and sequence between the Gospels. Christians believe that these differences are merely literary and that the truth of the revelation of God through Jesus Christ was protected from error by the guidance of the Holy Spirit.

Practice

▲ St. Jerome said, "To be ignorant of Scripture is to be ignorant of Jesus."

▲ The liturgical celebration of the Church has been divided into three cycles (A, B and C), which rotate every three years. Cycle A focuses on readings from the Gospel of Mark, Cycle B on Matthew, and Cycle C on Luke. Readings from the Gospel of John are interspersed throughout the three liturgical cycles. This insures that all the major parts of the four Gospels and a variety of other readings from the Old and New Testaments are read publicly every three years.

▲ A variety of approved translations of the Bible are now available to Catholics. These include the New American Bible (NAB), the New Revised Standard Version (NRSV) and the New Jerusalem Bible (NJB).

Part I: THE GIFT OF LIFE

Section 6 **The Creation of the World**

> *In the beginning was the Word,*
> *and the Word was with God,*
> *and the Word was God.*
> *He was in the beginning with God.*
> *All things came to be through him,*
> *and without him nothing came to be—John 1:1-3.*

ALTHOUGH WE OFTEN REFER to God the Father as Creator, the Scriptures teach that we cannot separate the creative action of the Son and Spirit from that of the Father.

As difficult as it is for us to fathom the mystery of the creative work of the Holy Trinity, the original plan of creation was beautifully simple. God gave his children the gift of divine life at the instant he created them and placed them in the world in order that he might prepare them for heaven. We were to be born in possession of the divine life and were to keep it always. There was to be no disorder, no sickness, no death—provided we remained faithful to God and did not rebel against him by sinning. But, as told in the story of creation, those who began our race failed God and us, their descendants. They sinned and thereby lost humankind's most precious possession, the divine life, which makes us children of God.

The story of God's creation of the world and of our first parents, Adam and Eve, of their elevation to the divine life and their rebellion against God is told in the first book of the Bible, the Book of Genesis.

> *In the beginning, when God created the heavens and the*
> *earth, the earth was a formless wasteland, and darkness*

covered the abyss, while a mighty wind swept over the waters.

Then God said, "Let there be light," and there was light. God saw how good the light was. God then separated the light from the darkness. God called the light "day," and the darkness he called "night." Thus evening came, and morning followed—the first day.

Then God said, "Let there be a dome in the middle of the waters, to separate one body of water from the other." And so it happened: God made the dome, and it separated the water above the dome from the water below it. God called the dome "the sky." Evening came, and morning followed—the second day.

Then God said, "Let the water under the sky be gathered into a single basin, so that the dry land may appear." And so it happened: the water under the sky was gathered into its basin, and the dry land appeared. God called the dry land "the earth," and the basin of the water he called "the sea." God saw how good it was. Then God said, "Let the earth bring forth vegetation: every kind of plant that bears seed and every kind of fruit tree on earth that bears fruit with its seed in it." And so it happened: the earth brought forth every kind of plant that bears seed and every kind of fruit tree on earth that bears fruit with its seed in it. God saw how good it was. Evening came, and morning followed—the third day.

Then God said: "Let there be lights in the dome of the sky, to separate day from night. Let them mark the fixed times, the days and the years, and serve as luminaries in the dome of the sky, to shed light upon the earth." And so it happened: God made the two great lights, the greater one to govern the day, and the lesser one to govern the night; and he made the stars. God set them in the dome of the sky, to shed light upon the earth, to govern the day and the night, and to separate the light from the darkness. God saw how good it was. Evening came, and morning followed—the fourth day.

Then God said, "Let the water teem with an abundance of living creatures, and on the earth let birds fly beneath the dome of the sky." And so it happened: God created the great sea monsters and all kinds of swimming creatures with which the water teems, and all kinds of winged birds. God saw how good it was, and God blessed them, saying, "Be fertile, multiply, and fill the water of the seas; and let the birds multiply on the earth." Evening came, and morning followed—the fifth day.

Then God said, "Let the earth bring forth all kinds of living creatures: cattle, creeping things, and wild animals of all kinds." And so it happened: God made all kinds of wild animals, all kinds of cattle, and all kinds of creeping things of the earth. God saw how good it was. Then God said: "Let us make [humans] in our image, after our likeness. Let them have dominion over the fish of the sea, the birds of the air, and the cattle, and over all the wild animals and all the creatures that crawl on the ground."

God created [humans] in his image;
   in the divine image he created [them];
   male and female he created them.

God blessed them, saying: "Be fertile and multiply; fill the earth and subdue it. Have dominion over the fish of the sea, the birds of the air, and all the living things that move on the earth." God also said: "See, I give you every seed-bearing plant all over the earth and every tree that has seed-bearing fruit on it to be your food; and to all the animals of the land, all the birds of the air, and all the living creatures that crawl on the ground, I give all the green plants for food." And so it happened. God looked at everything he had made, and he found it very *good. Evening came, and morning followed—the sixth day.*

Thus the heavens and the earth and all their array were completed. Since on the seventh day God was finished with the work he had been doing, he rested on the seventh day from all the work he had undertaken. So God blessed the seventh day and made it holy, because on it he rested from all the work he had done in creation—Gn 1:1-31, 2:1-3.

The story of creation as it is given in the Bible was based on the oral traditions of the ancient Hebrew people. It was written with these people in mind. It is, of course, inspired by God. It is not, however, a scientific account. We must not expect in it answers to scientific questions. It is up to human learning and research, for example, to determine the age of the earth and the question of evolution. The Bible was not intended to answer such questions.

1. What does this biblical account of creation teach?

This account teaches certain important religious truths:

a) There is only one God.

b) God is the creator of everything.

c) God created everything effortlessly, merely by his word.

d) All things created by God are good and are independent.

e) All that exists depends on God.

f) The world was created for the glory of God.

g) Humanity is the summit of God's work in the visible world.

2. Does the biblical account of creation teach us that the world was made in six days?

The six days are a purely literary device, i.e., a manner of speaking that made it easier for the audience to understand and remember.

Thus God is described as creating "places" on the first three days and the inhabitants of these "places" on the second three days. For example, the "work" of the first and the fourth day is described as the separation of light and darkness first and creation of the heavenly bodies which regulate light and darkness later. The "work" of the second and fifth days is described as the separation of the waters first (the Hebrews thought that there were waters above the sky and under the earth) and then the creation of the fish which live in the waters and the birds which live in the air separating the waters.

The "work" of the third and sixth days is described as the creation of the earth and plant life first and of animals and humans next.

3. Why did the author of Genesis use literary devices?

If the author had known what science now knows about the origin of the world and had stated this information in scientific terms, the people would have been bewildered and would not have understood the religious message.

Instead the author sought to convey to the reader certain important truths by the use of literary devices. The inspired author was attempting to express " . . . the truths of creation—its origin and its end in God, its order and goodness, the vocation of [humanity], and finally the drama of sin and the hope of salvation"—New Catechism 289.

4. Does this biblical account rule out evolution?

This account of creation reveals that God is the creator of all things. The manner in which creation took place is not revealed in the Bible. Modern science teaches us the evolution of plant and animal life. As long as this teaching does not exclude God as the creator and director of the process of evolution, it does not contradict revelation.

5. How did God create the world?

We can't possibly know how God created the world but we believe that creation occurred according to God's wisdom. From God's free will all of creation has its origin and therefore shares in his goodness and wisdom. We further believe that God needed no help or used any pre-existing thing in his creative act. God freely created everything our of nothing.

Creation means more than making something out of nothing. When God creates something he also keeps it in existence. If he did not, it would return to nothing.

6. Was it necessary that God create?

God is absolutely free. He need not have created anything. God has no need of anything outside of himself.

7. Why, then, did God create the world?

God created the world to show forth his glory and to share his goodness with the beings he created. God's glory is the manifestation and communication of his goodness to all of creation.

God accomplishes this by showing his existence with the whole of creation, which mirrors him in various degrees of clarity.

God has created images of himself in the spiritual world, angels; and in the visible world, humans. In his infinite goodness God has willed to give to angels and humans as an utterly free and undeserved gift a share in his nature, the divine life.

8. What are angels?

Angels are spiritual beings created by God. They, like human beings, are created in the image of God, more clearly in

God's image than humans because they are completely spiritual, having no need of bodies or anything material.

9.   How do angels differ from God?

Angels are creatures, i.e., they were created by God. They depend absolutely upon God's sustaining hand for their existence and activity. Although of a higher nature than humans, they, too, are limited beings.

10.   What is the story of the elevation and fall of the angels?

The moment he created angels God gave them divine life. Since they are beings with free will they, too, had to prove their fidelity to God before being admitted to heaven. A vast multitude of the angels rebelled against God and fixed their powerful wills forever on evil. These evil spirits live now in hell and are called "devils."

The angels who remained faithful to God enjoy the vision of God in heaven.

11.   Do angels play any part in our lives?

Our guardian angels protect and help us. The devils tempt us and try to lead us into sin. Satan, the leader of the devils, tempted and led our first parents into sin.

Practice

▲ Everything in the world was created to give glory to God. We, the greatest of his earthly creatures, must praise him with our minds, our hearts, our whole being. The worship of God is our first, our most important, and our most exalted function.

▲ The celebration of the Eucharist (the Mass) is central to the belief and practice of the Catholic faith. No other form of worship can better express God's love for us and our response to that love than when the community of believers gathers around the Lord's table. Because the Eucharist is so essential to our belief as Catholics, the Church obliges all to regularly participate at the Mass every Sunday and holy day of obligation.

Part I: THE GIFT OF LIFE

Section 7 **The Creation of Humans**

God created [humans] in his image;
 in the divine image he created [them];
 male and female he created them—Gn 1:26-28.

GOD, IN CREATING MEN AND WOMEN, exalted human nature by giving humans the divine life of sanctifying grace. Then by a great tragedy which occurred at the very beginning of the human race, humans lost the divine life and the means of attaining heaven. God, therefore, chose to share in our humanity in order that we might come to share in his divinity, i.e., might receive from him the divine life, which had been lost in the sin of Adam and Eve. Through Jesus, God has made our restoration to the divine life more wonderful than the original gift. *"I came so that they might have life and have it more abundantly"—Jn 10:10.*

1.   What are the main points which God teaches us in the Genesis account of the creation of the human race?

The main points which God teaches are these:

a) God has a special love and care for human beings, above all the beings he created. This is because we are made in the image and likeness of God.

b) Both women and men share the same human nature. The two sexes therefore complement each other and are interdependent, and they are of equal dignity in the sight of God.

c) The soul of each individual is created directly by God.

d) Because of our common origin there is fundamental equality among all the peoples of the human family.

2. Could the origin of human beings be explained by the theory of evolution?

The Bible does not give us the answer to this question. The theory of the evolution of the human body could fit the story as we have it in the Bible, provided, of course, that we understand by evolution a process directed by God, not by chance.

Revelation makes it very clear, however, that the *souls* of Adam and Eve were created directly by God, as is the soul of every human being.

3. What is a human being?

The human person has been created by God as both a bodily and spiritual being. The unique spiritual dimension of human personhood is what is meant when we speak of the human "soul." The soul is the spiritual principle within each human person that is created directly by God and is immortal. While the soul is that by which we share in a most special way in the very likeness of God, the human body also shares in the dignity of God. In fact, there is a fundamental unity to the human person.

4. Has the soul a life of its own?

The soul is an immortal and living thing that is of the greatest value to the human person. The soul's existence does not come about by human parents, but is created by God alone. The soul is the source of our human dignity in that it most clearly reflects the divine image. Even when separated from the body the soul does not cease to exist and will be reunited to the glorified body at the final resurrection.

5. What was the greatest gift God gave to our first parents?

The greatest among the many gifts God gave humans was the gift of divine life. Thus our first parents enjoyed a close friendship with God and shared in what is described as original holiness and justice.

6. How are we to interpret the "fall" as described in the Genesis account?

In this part of the Scriptures figurative imagery is used to affirm that at the beginning of human history an event transpired in which a freely chosen fault was committed that has marked all of human history.

7. How can we understand the sin of Adam and Eve in the story of creation?

The exact nature of the sin has not been clearly revealed to us. From the figures of the tree of the knowledge of good and evil and the words of the tempter, *". . . your eyes will be opened and you will be like gods who know what is good and what is bad"*— *Gn 3:5,* it appears to have been a sin of disobedience and a refusal to trust in God's goodness. This sin is called original sin.

8. How were Adam and Eve affected by their sin?

Therefore, just as through one person sin entered the world, and through sin, death, and thus death came to all, inasmuch as all sinned . . . . —Rom 5:12.

By far the most tragic consequence was the human loss of the divine life. But Adam and Eve also lost other gifts. Although the union of spirit and matter that is the human person is one in which there would seem to be some conflict by its very nature, there was no such conflict in the case of our first parents. All the inclinations of their bodies were under the perfect control of their souls; all the powers of their souls were oriented to God. By their sin our first parents lost this special gift. They suffered disharmony within themselves. Their bodies were no longer completely subject to their souls; their souls no longer oriented to God. Because of this, they became subject, too, to sickness, suffering and death.

9. How are we affected by the sin of our first parents?

Because of the sin of our first parents we come into the world deprived of the divine life and subject to death, sickness and the inclination to sin.

Original sin—the fact that we come into the world without the divine life—must not be confused with actual or personal sin, which we ourselves commit. Actual sin may be either mortal or venial. Mortal sin is an offense against God which is so serious that it destroys our divine life and breaks our friendship with God. Venial sin is an offense against God which does not destroy the divine life, but which weakens our will and paves the way for mortal sin.

10. What was God's response to the sin of Adam and Eve?

God did not restore their lesser gifts, such as freedom from death. What is much more important, however, is that God promised that his own Son would become human in order to redeem us and restore the divine life to all.

When the Son of God became human he took the name Jesus, which means savior.

11. What did Jesus mean when he said that he came that we might have "life more abundantly"?

Since God has become human we have been honored and exalted more than the angels. We have Jesus Christ as our head, teaching us and sanctifying us through the Church. We have the sacraments, in which we receive the divine life. We eat and drink the body and blood of Christ in the Eucharist.

We have as our mother and model the greatest of all God's

creatures, the only human person who was conceived without original sin, Mary, the Mother of God.

Despite the tragic sin of Adam and Eve and the struggle for salvation in which we must now engage; and despite the suffering and evil which are in the world as a consequence of that sin, the Church still exults in this most striking and beautiful song, which is sung in the Easter Vigil service:

Father, how wonderful your care of us! How boundless your merciful love! To ransom a slave you gave away your Son. O happy fault, O necessary sin of Adam, which gained for us so great a Redeemer!

Practice

▲ The story of Adam and Eve's sin helps us understand our own tendency toward evil and our need to diligently guard against submission to that inclination. At times our actions and attitudes can be influenced by pride and selfishness. Catholics believe that even our natural desires, good in themselves, can easily get out of control and lead us to excessive behavior. Notwithstanding our innate goodness we all must deal with the reality of our weaknesses.

▲ The Catholic tradition has taught that we can strengthen our resolve to do good and avoid evil by practices of self-denial or charitable actions. For example, Catholics are still urged to either forego meat on Fridays or to perform some other act of sacrifice. This type of exercise can strengthen us spiritually as it reminds us that we need God's help in avoiding sin.

▲ The Our Father, the prayer that Jesus himself taught us, asks God to "lead us not into temptation, but deliver us from evil."

Part II: CHRIST THE LIFE

Section 8 **Jesus Christ: God-Man**

*"Everything that the Father gives me will come to me,
and I will not reject anyone who comes to me, because I
came down from heaven not to do my own will but the
will of the one who sent me. And this is the will of the
one who sent me, that I should not lose anything of what
he gave me, but that I should raise it [on] the last day.
For this is the will of my Father, that everyone who sees
the Son and believes in him may have eternal life, and I
shall raise [that person] [on] the last day"—Jn 6:37-40.*

WHEN, "IN THE FULLNESS OF TIME," God sent the long
promised Redeemer, he sent not merely a human empowered to
teach and act in his name, but his only-begotten Son. Jesus Christ
is no mere human; he is God-become-human that he might be the
mediator between God and us.

Jesus Christ expressed the threefold office he holds as the
God-Man in these words, *"I am the way and the truth and the
life"* —Jn 14:6

Jesus is the life—our priest, who redeemed us by his death
on the cross, who shares with us his divine life.

Jesus is the truth —our teacher, who reveals to us by word
and example the eternal truths of the kingdom of heaven.

Jesus is the way—our king, who came to draw all people to
himself in a spiritual kingdom, begun here on earth in his Church
and to be completed in his everlasting kingdom in heaven.

It was as a human that the Son of God fulfilled these three
offices. It was as a human being that Jesus first revealed himself.
Later he openly proclaimed and proved his divinity. But first he

won the love and trust of those around him by showing them his true humanity. In studying the life of Christ, therefore, we shall approach the God-Man as he revealed himself first, through his human nature.

1. Who is the mother of Jesus?

The Blessed Virgin Mary is the mother of Jesus.

2. How did the Blessed Virgin become the mother of Jesus?

In the sixth month, the angel Gabriel was sent from God to a town of Galilee called Nazareth, to a virgin betrothed to a man named Joseph, of the house of David, and the virgin's name was Mary. And coming to her, he said, "Hail, favored one! The Lord is with you." But she was greatly troubled at what was said and pondered what sort of greeting this might be. Then the angel said to her, "Do not be afraid, Mary, for you have found favor with God. Behold, you will conceive in your womb and bear a son, and you shall name him Jesus. He will be great and will be called Son of the Most High, and the Lord God will give him the throne of David his father, and he will rule over the house of Jacob forever, and of his kingdom there will be no end." But Mary said to the angel, "How can this be, since I have no relations with a man?" And the angel said to her in reply, "The holy Spirit will come upon you, and the power of the Most High will over-shadow you. Therefore the child to be born will be called holy, the Son of God. And behold, Elizabeth, your relative, has also conceived a son in her old age, and this is the sixth month for her who was called barren; for nothing will be impossible for God." Mary said, "Be-hold, I am the handmaid of the Lord. May it be done to me according to your word." Then the angel departed from her—Lk 1:26-38.

3. Why did the angel greet Mary, "Hail, favored one! The Lord is with you"?

The angel greeted Mary thus because, since she was destined to be the Mother of God, Mary is the most highly privileged of all God's creatures. She is the only human person who was preserved from all stain of original sin at the first moment of her conception. We call this her "Immaculate Conception." Moreover, so perfectly did Mary cooperate with God's plan for her that she is the holiest of all his creatures. Throughout all her life she was never guilty of the slightest sin or failure to do God's will.

4. What is meant by the words, "The holy Spirit will come upon you, and the power of the Most High will overshadow you"?

These words mean that Jesus would be conceived in the womb of Mary miraculously, without the aid of a human father. We call this announcement the Annunciation.

5. Why was Jesus born of a virgin?

Jesus was born of a virgin because his Father willed it. It would have been possible for Christ to have had a human father; but it was eminently fitting that his mother be a virgin and his conception miraculous. Throughout the centuries of preparation for the coming of Christ, God had worked wonders in the conception of his servants who prepared the way for the coming of his Son. Abraham received a son from Sarah only when she was old and past the child-bearing period. Elizabeth, who had been sterile, in her old age miraculously conceived John the Baptist, the precursor of Christ. It is only right, therefore, that an even greater miracle should mark the conception and birth of the Redeemer himself. God determined that Jesus should have no earthly father. He would be God's own Son. It was fitting too, that the womb that bore the Son of God should not thereafter bear a mere human child. Therefore Mary, the Mother of God and the Spouse of the Holy Spirit, remained a virgin after the birth of Christ.

6. Who was St. Joseph?

St. Joseph was the husband of Mary and the foster father of Jesus. We know that Joseph was of the House of David (cf. Mt 1:16), that he was a carpenter (cf. Mt 13:55), and that he was obedient to God, who spoke to him through angels (cf. Mt 1:19-25; 2:13-15, 19-23). Joseph is venerated as the patron saint of all workers and fathers.

7. Who are the "brothers of Jesus" mentioned in the Bible?

They are not brothers but relatives. The word brother was commonly used at that time to express any blood relationship. The word "first-born" likewise does not imply that Mary and Joseph had any other children. It is a term referring to the first-born male, who had to be offered to God under Jewish law (cf. Ex. 13:2).

8. What is the story of the birth of Christ?

In those days a decree went out from Caesar Augustus that the whole world should be enrolled. This was the first enrollment, when Quirinius was governor of Syria. So all went to be enrolled, each to his own town. And Joseph too went up from Galilee from the town of Nazareth to Judea, to the city of David that is called Bethlehem, because he was of the house and family of David, to be enrolled with Mary, his betrothed, who was with child. While they were there, the time came for her to have her child, and she gave birth to her firstborn son. She wrapped him in swaddling clothes and laid him in a manger, because there was no room for them in the inn—Lk 2:1-7.

9. Where did Jesus live most of his life?

After his birth in Bethlehem and exile in Egypt (to escape King Herod, who sought to kill him) Jesus lived in the little town of Nazareth in Galilee of Judea, a section of what is now the country of Israel, until he was about thirty years of age.

10.   Why did Jesus spend thirty years in a hidden life?

Jesus did so in order to give us an example of how to live a holy, ordinary human life. Most people cannot imitate Christ in his life of preaching and teaching. But everyone can imitate him in the quiet family life of Nazareth.

11.   Did Jesus feel and act as other people do?

In becoming human he took to himself all that belongs to human nature, sin and ignorance alone excepted.

12.   What are some of the incidents in the Gospels which show us the humanity of Jesus?

Throughout his boyhood the behavior of Jesus was that of a normal boy, so much so that when as a man he proclaimed himself to be the Messiah the people of his own town refused to believe him (cf. Lk 4:16-30).

Within the canon of Scripture there is only one unusual episode during the childhood of Jesus and that is when he taught in the temple at the age of twelve (cf. Lk 2:42-51).

We also know that Jesus felt hunger, thirst, fatigue (cf. Lk 4:2; Jn 19:28; Jn 4:6).

He was fond of children (cf. Mk 10:13-16).

He felt sorrow and wept (cf. Jn 11:32-36; Lk 19:41-44).

He knew loneliness (cf. Mt 26:37-46).

He enjoyed human companionship (cf. Jn 2:1-12).

He visited the homes of his friends (cf. Lk 19:1-10).

He felt keenly the betrayal of Judas and the denial of Peter (cf. Lk 22:39-62).

He experienced the agony of his passion and death. The very anticipation of it caused him such mental suffering that he sweat blood (cf. Lk 22:41-44).

The tender love of Jesus for all people is evident continually throughout the Gospels. In no place is it so beautifully shown as in his discourse to the apostles at the Last Supper. This discourse and prayer of Christ for his apostles takes up four chapters of St. John's Gospel (cf. Jn 14-17).

13. When did Jesus begin his public life?

Jesus began his public life when he was about thirty years of age. At that time he left Nazareth and went about preaching, teaching and working miracles.

Practice

▲ The Catholic faith teaches us that Jesus Christ is true God and true Man—not "really" one or "really" the other. This doctrine of the Incarnation also tells us that Jesus is not some mixture of part divine and part human. We express this mystery of the incarnation by stating that the divinity of Jesus "assumed" the humanity of Jesus. This fundamental Christian belief is clearly stated in the Nicene Creed, which was written in the third century A.D. and is still recited at Mass.

▲ One seasonal custom which can be observed in church and at home is the "Advent Wreath." A laurel made of an evergreen-type material is placed in a prominent place in the church and/or home. Four candles are equally spaced around the wreath. At the beginning of each week of Advent a candle is lit to signal the approaching coming of Christ. Advent, the season of anticipation, prepares us to celebrate Christmas, the feast of the Incarnation. Christmas begins with Mass at midnight.

▲ There are three different Masses for Christmas, the midnight Mass, the Mass at dawn and the Mass later in the morning. At the midnight Mass the emphasis is on the eternal generation of the Word of God before all time. In the dawn Mass the emphasis is on Christ as the light of the world. The third Mass emphasizes that God has sent his Son into the world to save all people. All who hear him and follow him are made sons and daughters of God.

▲ On the great feast of the Epiphany we celebrate the manifestation of Christ to the gentiles (all those who are not Jewish) with the story of the Magi (the wise men or astrologers or kings) who came from the East to pay homage to the Christ Child.

Part II: CHRIST THE LIFE

Section 9 Jesus Christ: Supreme Teacher

And he spoke to them at length in parables, saying: "A sower went out to sow. And as he sowed, some seed fell on the path, and birds came and ate it up. Some fell on rocky ground, where it had little soil. It sprang up at once because the soil was not deep, and when the sun rose it was scorched, and it withered for lack of roots. Some seed fell among thorns, and the thorns grew up and choked it. But some seed fell on rich soil, and produced fruit, a hundred or sixty or thirtyfold" —Mt 13:3-8.

CHRIST WAS SENT into the world by his Father to tell the fallen human race of God's saving love for them and of the coming of God's kingdom. It was to the Jews that Jesus preached, because it was to the Jews that God had promised the Redeemer. Our Lord spent the three years of his public life seeking out the chosen people to proclaim this good news.

He preached in the towns and in the country, in the streets and on the hillsides, in the temple and in the homes of the people. In John's Gospel, when Jesus' life had but one day left to run, he summed up how he had taught when he said:

"I revealed your name to those whom you gave me out of the world. They belonged to you, and you gave them to me, and they have kept your word. Now they know that everything you gave me is from you, because the words you gave to me I have given to them, and they accepted them and truly understood that I came from you, and they have believed that you sent me"—Jn 17:6-8.

Jesus was a courageous teacher. He did not modify his doctrine to please the leaders of the people or the people themselves. He knew that many of his words would fall upon deaf ears, but he also knew that each person who receives his words with joy *"bears fruit and yields a hundred or sixty or thirtyfold"*—Mt 13:23 and would carry his message to the ends of the earth.

1.   What did Our Lord teach the people?

Our Lord taught the people that salvation and redemption were at hand and that the kingdom of God had come. St. Mark says that he was heralding the joyful tidings of God's kingdom (cf. Mk 1:14). St. Matthew says that Jesus went about *"proclaiming the gospel of the kingdom"*—Mt 4:23.

Jesus fulfilled the Old Law of the Hebrews. He took each part of the old revelation of doctrine, moral law and worship, and brought it to completion in a new, more perfect revelation of doctrine, moral law and worship. *"Do not think that I have come to abolish the law or the prophets. I have come not to abolish but to fulfill"*— Mt 5:17.

In preaching his gospel Jesus told us of the infinite love of God for all, of the mystery of the Trinity, of his own divinity, of his Church and of the sacraments.

2.   How did Jesus teach?

Jesus taught in various ways. Some of his teachings, for example the law of love, he stated simply and directly. Some of his teachings he gave by means of parables, stories such as that of the sower who sowed good seed (cf. Mt 13:18-23). Although Jesus taught in words which carried great authority and worked miracles which amazed people, he taught most effectively by his example. St. Augustine, referring to the example of Christ, says, "He did not say, 'Learn from me how to build a world and raise the dead' but 'Learn from me; I am meek and humble of heart.' "

3. What is a parable?

A parable is an illustration of a truth by means of an example or a story. By using parables Jesus was able to present great religious truths in a form which allowed them to be grasped and remembered by all, the unlearned as well as the learned.

For example, Jesus taught:

a) the necessity for good works, in the parable of the barren fig tree (cf. Lk 13:6-9);

b) the virtues of humility and contrition, in the parable of the Pharisee and the publican (cf. Lk 18:9-14);

c) the necessity of being prepared for death at any moment, the need of being in possession of the divine life at all times, in the parables of the wise and foolish virgins (cf. Mt 25:1-13) and the marriage of the king's son (cf. Mt 22:1-14);

d) the necessity of forgiving one's enemies, in the parable of the unmerciful servant (cf. Mt 18:23-35);

e) the necessity of loving one's neighbor, in the parable of the good Samaritan (cf. Lk 10:30-37);

f) the love and mercy of God, in the parable of the prodigal son (cf. Lk 15:11-32).

4. What are some of the doctrines which Jesus taught by his example as well as by his words?

Our Lord exemplified all his teachings in his life, particularly those on the love of God and one's neighbor, prayer, submission to the will of God and poverty and detachment.

5. How did Jesus teach love?

"You have heard that it was said, 'You shall love your neighbor and hate your enemy.' But I say to you, love your enemies, and pray for those who persecute you, that you may be children of your heavenly Father, for he

*makes his sun rise on the bad and the good, and causes
rain to fall on the just and the unjust. For if you love
those who love you, what recompense will you have? Do
not the tax collectors do the same? And if you greet your
brothers [and sisters] only, what is unusual about that?
Do not the pagans do the same? So be perfect, just as
your heavenly Father is perfect"—Mt 5:43-48.*

Jesus exemplified this teaching by freely laying down his
own life for all. *"No one has greater love than this, to lay down
one's life for one's friends"— Jn 15:13.*

On the cross he prayed for those who crucified him. *"Father, forgive them, they know not what they do"—Lk 23:34.*

Most of his miracles were worked out of compassion for the
sick and the suffering:

a) the cure of the centurion's servant (cf. Mt 8:5-13);

b) the raising from the dead: of Jairus' daughter (cf. Mt
9:18-26), of the widow's son (cf. Lk 7:11-16) and
Lazarus (cf. Jn 11:1-44);

c) the cure of the paralytic at the pool of Bethsaida (cf. Jn
5:1-9);

d) the cure of the man who had been born blind (cf. Jn 9:1-
38).

6.   How did Jesus teach prayer?

Jesus taught the true spirit of prayer, insisting on sincerity
and simplicity, and denouncing hypocrisy and wordiness in
prayer (cf. Mt 6:5-9).

The whole life of Jesus was lived in constant union with his
Father. All his actions were in perfect accord with the will of the
Father. His whole life, therefore, was one continual prayer.

But Jesus also spent long periods absorbed in prayer. The
Gospels frequently state that he spent the whole night in prayer.

He prefaced his public life by retiring to the desert, where he
spent forty days and nights in prayer and fasting (cf. Lk 4:1-2).

When he was about to choose his disciples, Jesus spent the whole night in prayer (cf. Lk 6:12).

A great many of his miracles were preceded by prayer, e.g., the healing of the deaf mute (cf. Mk 7:34); the raising of Lazarus from the dead (cf. Jn 11:41); the multiplication of the loaves (cf. Mt 14:19).

He began his passion with prayer at the Last Supper (cf. Jn 17, entire chapter).

He prayed during his agony in the garden (cf. Mt 26:36-44).

He prayed as he hung on the cross (cf. Lk 23:34,46).

7. How did Jesus teach perfect submission to the will of God?

"I do nothing on my own, but I say only what the Father taught me. The one who sent me is with me. He has not left me alone, because I always do what is pleasing to him"—Jn 8:28-29.

The outstanding characteristic of Jesus is his total, unreserved surrender to the will of God, his mighty burning love for his Father. No other person has ever so completely fulfilled the first commandment of the law, *"You shall love the LORD your God, with all your heart, with all your soul, with all your strength"—Dt 6:5.*

The first recorded words of Jesus, then a boy of twelve, were, *"Did you not know I must be in my Father's house?"—Lk 2:49.* These words he spoke to Mary and Joseph to explain why he had remained in Jerusalem. Yet, having uttered these words, he went down to Nazareth and *"was obedient to them"—Lk 2:51,* because such was the will of his Father.

Every action of Jesus was dictated by his love for his Father. In the anguish he endured in contemplating the sufferings and death he was about to undergo he prayed, *"My Father, if it is possible, let this cup pass from me; yet, not as I will, but as you will"—Mt 26:39.*

8. How did Jesus teach poverty and detachment?

"Therefore I tell you, do not worry about your life, what you will eat [or drink], or about your body, what you will wear. Is not life more than food and the body more than clothing? Look at the birds in the sky; they do not sow or reap, they gather nothing into barns, yet your heavenly Father feeds them. Are not you more important than they? Can any of you by worrying add a single moment to your life-span? Why are you anxious about clothes? Learn from the way the wild flowers grow. They do not work or spin. But I tell you that not even Solomon in all his splendor was clothed like one of them. If God so clothes the grass of the field, which grows today and is thrown into the oven tomorrow, will he not much more provide for you, O you of little faith? So do not worry and say, 'What are we to eat?' or 'What are we to drink?' or 'What are we to wear?' All these things the pagans seek. Your heavenly Father knows that you need them all. But seek first the kingdom [of God] and his righteousness, and all these things will be given you besides. Do not worry about tomorrow; tomorrow will take care of itself. Sufficient for a day is its own evil"— Mt 6:25-34.

"Do not store up for yourselves treasures on earth, where moth and decay destroy, and thieves break in and steal. But store up treasures in heaven, where neither moth nor decay destroys, nor thieves break in and steal. For where your treasure is, there also will your heart be"—Mt 6:19-21.

Jesus exemplified this teaching by his own complete detachment. He was born in a stable. He worked as a carpenter in the tiny town of Nazareth. During the three years of his public life, he had no home and no possessions. He said of himself: *"Foxes have dens and birds of the sky have nests, but the Son of Man has nowhere to rest his head"*—Mt 8:20.

Jesus had special love and concern for the poor. He chose as his disciples, for the most part, those of little means, and required that they give up all things to follow him.

Practice

▲ Jesus still teaches the world. Now he does so through his Church. One of the most effective ways in which Our Lord teaches us today is through the liturgy of the Church. Remind yourself that it is Christ himself speaking and teaching you as you listen to the reading of the Scripture lessons and to the homily at Mass.

▲ Read with care the parables of Jesus found in the four Gospels. The stories that Jesus used should inspire us to tell others our own personal stories of faith.

▲ Every Christian should follow the example of Jesus and pray every day.

▲ The Church promotes Jesus' spirit of poverty and detachment through the example of many of her vowed religious orders, some of whom have special auxiliaries for lay people.

Part II: CHRIST THE LIFE

Section 10 **Christ's Great Teaching: The Blessed Trinity**

"All power in heaven and on earth has been given to me. Go, therefore, and make disciples of all nations, baptizing them in the name of the Father, and of the Son, and of the holy Spirit"—Mt 28:18-19.

JESUS CHRIST HAS REVEALED to us the secrets of the kingdom of heaven. In the greatest of his teachings he has revealed to us the secret of God himself. He has told us of the inmost life of God, the mystery of the Blessed Trinity. The one God, he has told us, is not one Person alone, as we would think, but rather three Persons, Father, Son and Holy Spirit. This may be difficult for us to comprehend or understand but we should remember the words of the prophet Isaiah:

For my thoughts are not your thoughts,
nor are your ways my ways, says the LORD.
As high as the heavens are above the earth,
so high are my ways above your ways
and my thoughts above your thoughts—Is 55: 8-9.

Of all the mysteries of our faith the Blessed Trinity is the deepest of mysteries. Nevertheless God has revealed it to us through his Son, Jesus. He has done so because he wants us to know God as God truly is, to know as much about God as we can in order that we might in some measure return the boundless love God has for us.

1. What did Jesus teach us of the inmost life of God?

Jesus taught, as indeed the Hebrews of his time already knew, that there is only one God—one supreme Creator and Law-giver.

But in revealing the inmost life of God, Jesus taught that in the one God there are three distinct Persons, each absolutely equal to the others. He told us the names of these three Divine Persons: Father, Son and Holy Spirit.

2. How did Jesus tell us that there are three Divine Persons?

Jesus spoke continually of his Father, calling him always by that name. When he drove the money changers from the temple, he said, *"Take these out of here, and stop making my Father's house a marketplace"—Jn 2:16.*

He said to his apostles:

"By this is my Father glorified, that you bear much fruit and become my disciples. As the Father loves me, so I also love you. Remain in my love. If you keep my commandments, you will remain in my love, just as I have kept my Father's commandments and remain in his love—Jn 15:8 -10.

Jesus also revealed that he is the Son, the only-begotten Son of that Father, equal to the Father. Speaking of himself he said, *"For God so loved the world that he gave his only Son, so that everyone who believes in him might not perish but might have eternal life"—Jn 3:16.*

At the Last Supper Jesus prayed to the Father:

"Father, the hour has come. Give glory to your son, so that your son may glorify you, just as you gave him authority over all people, so that he may give eternal life to all you gave him. Now this is eternal life, that they should know you, the only true God, and the one whom you sent, Jesus Christ. I glorified you on earth by accomplishing the work that you gave me to do. Now

glorify me, Father, with you, with the glory that I had
with you before the world began"—Jn 17:1 -5.

He said to his apostles, *"Everything that the Father has is mine"—Jn 16:15.*

In response to Philip's words, *"Master, show us the Father, and that will be enough for us"—Jn 14:8,* Jesus said to him:

"Have I been with you for so long a time and you still do not know me, Philip? Whoever has seen me has seen the Father. How can you say, 'Show us the Father'? Do you not believe that I am in the Father and the Father is in me?"—Jn 14:9 -10.

Finally, Jesus promised to send a third Divine Person, the equal of himself and the Father. At the Last Supper he told the apostles:

"I will ask the Father, and he will give you another Advocate to be with you always, the Spirit of truth, which the world cannot accept, because it neither sees nor knows it"—Jn 14:16 -17.

"The Advocate, the holy Spirit that the Father will send in my name—he will teach you everything and remind you of all that [I] told you"—Jn 14:26.

"When the Advocate comes whom I will send you from the Father . . . he will testify to me—Jn 15:26.

When he sent the apostles to preach the Gospel to the whole world Jesus told them to baptize *"in the name of the Father, and of the Son, and of the holy Spirit"—Mt 28:19.* Here Christ expresses in one short formula the idea of one God (in the name) in three distinct and equal Divine Persons (of the Father, of the Son, and of the Holy Spirit).

3. Why is the First Divine Person called the Father?

The First Divine Person is called the Father because this is the way Jesus spoke of him. It is the Father who begets the Second Divine Person, the eternal Word, who is *"the refulgence of his glory, /the very imprint of his being"—Heb 1:3.*

4. Why is the Second Divine Person called the Son?

The Second Divine Person is called the Son because he is the perfect image of the Father: "God from God, Light from Light, true God from true God, begotten, not made, one in Being with the Father"—Nicene Creed.

5. Why is the Third Divine Person called the Holy Spirit?

The Third Divine Person is called the Holy Spirit because he is the Person of divine love, breathed forth by the Father and the Son. He is "the Lord, the giver of life, who proceeds from the Father and the Son. With the Father and the Son he is worshiped and glorified. He has spoken through the prophets"—Nicene Creed.

6. How do we distinguish between the three Persons in God?

Jesus spoke of the Father as the creator and ruler. The Gospels also show Jesus using the very loving and familiar term "Abba," which can be translated "Daddy," in addressing his Father.

Jesus, the Second Divine Person, became human and lived and died on earth. As God, Jesus is called the Word, the eternal Knowledge of the Father. That is why St. John, speaking of the Second Divine Person, says:

In the beginning was the Word, /and the Word was with God, /and the Word was God. . . . /All things came to be through him /and without him nothing came to be. . . . /The Word became flesh /and made his dwelling among us—Jn 1:1,3,14.

Jesus spoke of the Holy Spirit as the one whom he and the Father would send to enlighten and inspire us. We naturally associate works of love and inspiration with the Holy Spirit, since he is Divine Love.

We know, however, that each of the three Divine Persons are

the one God who is creator, ruler, savior, and spirit of love who dwells in all who possess the divine life.

7. Do we find any manifestations of the Blessed Trinity in the New Testament?

When Jesus was baptized by John in the river Jordan:

After all the people had been baptized and Jesus also had been baptized and was praying, heaven was opened and the holy Spirit descended upon him in bodily form like a dove. And a voice came from heaven, "You are my beloved Son; with you I am well pleased"—Lk 3:21-22.

When Jesus was transfigured before Peter, James and John, the Father spoke from heaven: *"This is my beloved Son. Listen to him"—Mk 9:7.*

On Pentecost the Holy Spirit's coming was manifested by the sound of a mighty wind and parted tongues of fire:

When the time for Pentecost was fulfilled, they were all in one place together. And suddenly there came from the sky a noise like a strong driving wind, and it filled the entire house in which they were. Then there appeared to them tongues as of fire, which parted and came to rest on each one of them. And they were all filled with the holy Spirit and began to speak in different tongues, as the Spirit enabled them to proclaim—Acts 2:1-4.

8. How has the Church spoken of the Trinity?

It is impossible to adequately describe this mystery. Even the great Church Father St. Augustine is reputed to have said that trying to understand the Trinity would be like trying to fit the ocean into a tiny hole in the sand. Over the centuries the Church in its creeds and theology has used terms such as "substance" or "nature" when speaking of the unity of the Trinity. It has also used the term "person" when speaking to the real distinctions or differences among the Trinity as well as the term "relation" to indicate that the three Persons of the Trinity are essentially in relation to each other. These words capture the essential truths of the mystery of the Trinity.

9. How do we honor the Blessed Trinity in the liturgy?

a) The Church usually addresses her prayers to God the Father, through the Son, in union with the Holy Spirit.

b) On the great feast of Pentecost, fifty days after Easter, we celebrate the coming of the Holy Spirit upon the Church.

c) We celebrate Trinity Sunday every year on the first Sunday after Pentecost.

10. How may we pray to the Blessed Trinity?

a) We may pray simply to God, i.e., to the Blessed Trinity.

b) We may pray to any one of the three Divine Persons.

c) We may pray as the Church does most often—to the Father, through the Son, in union with the Holy Spirit. Our Lord promised: *"Amen, amen, I say to you, whatever you ask the Father in my name he will give you"*— Jn 16:23.

Practice

▲ The equality of the Persons of the Blessed Trinity, their oneness in nature and their distinctness in person is expressed beautifully in the Athanasian Creed:

Now this is the Catholic faith: that we worship one God in Trinity, and Trinity in unity; neither confusing the persons nor distinguishing the nature.

The person of the Father is distinct; the person of the Son is distinct; the person of the Holy Spirit is distinct.

Yet the Father and the Son and the Holy Spirit possess one God-head, equal glory and co-eternal majesty.

As the Father is, so is the Son, so also is the Holy Spirit.

The Father is uncreated, the Son is uncreated, the Holy Spirit is uncreated.

The Father is infinite, the Son is infinite, the Holy Spirit is infinite.

The Father is eternal, the Son is eternal, the Holy Spirit is eternal.

Nevertheless there are not three eternals, but one eternal; even as there are not three uncreateds but one uncreated, and one infinite.

So likewise the Father is almighty, the Son is almighty, the Holy Spirit is almighty. And yet they are not three almighties, but one almighty.

So also the Father is God, the Son is God, the Holy Spirit is God. And yet they are not three Gods, but only one God.

So, too, the Father is Lord, the Son is Lord, the Holy Spirit is Lord. And still there are not three Lords, but only one Lord.

For just as we are compelled by Christian truth to profess that each Person is individually Lord and God, so also are we forbidden by the Catholic religion to hold that there are three Gods or Lords.

The Father was made by no one, being neither made nor created nor begotten.

The Son is from the Father only, being neither made nor created, but begotten.

The Holy Spirit is from the Father and the Son, being neither made nor created nor begotten, but proceeding.

Consequently, there is one Father, not three Fathers; there is one Son, not three Sons; there is one Holy Spirit, not three Holy Spirits.

Furthermore, in this Trinity there is no "before" or "after," no "greater" or "less"; for all three Persons are co-eternal and co-equal.

In every respect, therefore, as has already been stated, unity must be worshiped in trinity, and trinity in unity. . . .

▲ Because we possess divine life, the Blessed Trinity dwells within us. It is important that we remain aware of this presence of God within us. St. Paul tells us:

Do you not know that your body is a temple of the holy Spirit within you, whom you have from God, and that you are not your own? For you have been purchased at a price. Therefore glorify God in your body—1 Cor 6:19-20.

No matter where we are we should remember these words and act accordingly. Over-indulgence in food and alcoholic beverages, use of illegal drugs and abuse of legal drugs, lack of sleep and poor personal hygiene may harm our bodies and therefore diminish our ability to share the inner presence of the triune God with others.

▲ Every time we begin and/or end a prayer using the Sign of the Cross we profess our faith in and make an act of adoration to the Blessed Trinity.

Part II: CHRIST THE LIFE

Section 11 **Jesus Christ: Our Redeemer**

> *But when the fullness of time had come, God sent his
> Son, born of a woman, born under the law, to ransom
> those under the law, so that we might receive adoption.
> As proof that you are children, God sent the spirit of his
> Son into our hearts, crying out, "Abba, Father!" So you
> are no longer a slave but a child, and if a child then also
> an heir, through God—Gal. 4: 4-7.*

AT THE CENTER of our faith, and of any catechetical
transmission of the faith, is our belief in Jesus of Nazareth. Jesus
is the Word made flesh, the One sent by the Father. Born of a
woman, he died for us and by his bloody death he has redeemed
us from our sins. The history of Jesus and the meaning of that
history is the matrix upon which the Catholic faith has been built.
It is important then for us to know and understand the key points
of his life.

1.   What do the names Jesus and Christ mean?

Our English word "Jesus" is a derivative of the Hebrew name
"Joshua" or "Yeshua" which means "God saves." "Christ" means
"anointed" or the "anointed one" After the Resurrection these
names came to have deeper significance for the Christian community, as did the phrase "Son of God" and the title "Lord."   In
various ways they express the belief that Jesus, Son of the Father,
was sent (anointed) to be our savior and is truly divine.

2. Why did the Son of God take on a human nature?

The Word became flesh to save us, to reveal God's love to us, to be a model of holiness for us and to enable us to participate in the very nature of God.

3. What does it mean when we affirm that Jesus Christ is true God and true man?

Fundamental to the Christian faith is the belief in the Incarnation: the Son of God became human in order to save us. During the early centuries of its existence the Church struggled to understand how Jesus was fully human while remaining God. In time it came to use the language of Greek philosophy to describe this mystery: namely, that there is one Person, the Son of God, who has two natures, one human and one divine. Because Jesus is, therefore, truly human, his human intellect and will are limited. It was necessary for him—like all other human beings—to acquire that which can only be learned from experience. *"And Jesus advanced [in] wisdom and age and favor before God and man"—Lk 2:52.*

4. What is the history of the passion and death of Jesus?

Jesus began his passion by eating the Last Supper with his twelve apostles. At this meal he instituted the Holy Eucharist and ordained the apostles priests:

> *Then he took the bread, said the blessing, broke it, and gave it to them, saying, "This is my body, which will be given for you; do this in memory of me." And likewise the cup after they had eaten, saying, "This cup is the new covenant in my blood, which will be shed for you"—Lk 22:19-20.*

He underwent a night of agony in the garden of Gethsemane:

> *Then Jesus came with them to a place called Gethsemane, and he said to his disciples, "Sit here*

*while I go over there and pray." He took along Peter
and the two sons of Zebedee, and began to feel sorrow
and distress. Then he said to them, "My soul is sorrowful
even to death. Remain here and keep watch with me." He
advanced a little and fell prostrate in prayer, saying,
"My Father, if it is possible, let this cup pass from me;
yet, not as I will, but as you will"—Mt 26:36-39.*

He was betrayed by Judas and taken prisoner:

*While he was still speaking, Judas, one of the Twelve,
arrived, accompanied by a large crowd, with swords and
clubs, who had come from the chief priests and the
elders of the people. His betrayer had arranged a sign
with them, saying, "The man I shall kiss is the one;
arrest him." Immediately he went over to Jesus and said,
"Hail, Rabbi!" and he kissed him—Mt 26:47-49.*

He was taken before the high priests, where he professed
that he was God:

*Then the high priest said to him, "I order you to tell us
under oath before the living God whether you are the
Messiah, the Son of God." Jesus said to him in reply,
"You have said so. But I tell you:*

> *From now on you will see 'the Son of Man
>   seated at the right hand of the Power'
>   and 'coming on the clouds of heaven.' "*

*Then the high priest tore his robes and said, "He has
blasphemed! What further need have we of witnesses?
You have now heard the blasphemy; what is your
opinion?" They said in reply, "He deserves to die!"—Mt
26:63-66.*

He was denied by Peter:

*Now Simon Peter was standing there keeping warm. And
they said to him, "You are not one of his disciples, are
you?" He denied it and said, "I am not." One of the
slaves of the high priest, a relative of the one whose ear*

Peter had cut off, said, *"Didn't I see you in the garden with him?"* Again Peter denied it. And immediately the cock crowed—Jn 18:25-27.

He was taken before Pilate, the Roman governor. He was scourged, mocked, crowned with thorns and condemned to death:

Then Pilate took Jesus and had him scourged. And the soldiers wove a crown out of thorns and placed it on his head, and clothed him in a purple cloak. . . . When the chief priests and the guards saw him they cried out, "Crucify him, crucify him!" Pilate said to them, "Take him yourselves and crucify him. I find no guilt in him." The Jews answered, "We have a law, and according to that law he ought to die, because he made himself the Son of God." . . . When Pilate heard these words he brought Jesus out and seated him on the judge's bench in the place called Stone Pavement, in Hebrew, Gabbatha. It was preparation day for Passover, and it was about noon. And he said to the Jews, "Behold, your king!" They cried out, "Take him away, take him away! Crucify him!" Pilate said to them, "Shall I crucify your king?" The chief priests answered, "We have no king but Caesar." Then he handed him over to them to be crucified—Jn 19:1-2,6-7,13-16.

He was crucified between two thieves:

When they came to the place called the Skull, they crucified him and the criminals there, one on his right, the other on his left—Lk 23:33.

After three hours' agony on the cross he died:

It was now about noon and darkness came over the whole land until three in the afternoon because of an eclipse of the sun. Then the veil of the temple was torn down the middle. Jesus cried out in a loud voice, "Father, into your hands I commend my spirit"; and when he had said this he breathed his last—Lk 23:44-46.

5. Was it necessary for Jesus to suffer and die in order to redeem us?

It was not absolutely necessary for Jesus to suffer and die in order to redeem us. Any action or prayer of Christ would have been of such great value that it could have redeemed any number of worlds.

6. Why did Jesus submit to his suffering and death?

By dying on the cross—a terrible death by any standard—Jesus showed us that there was no limit to God's love, no suffering he was unwilling to endure to redeem humankind. *"No one has greater love than this, to lay down one's life for one's friends"—Jn 15:13.*

The passion and death of Christ teaches us, above all, the immense mercy and love of God. We do not deserve to be saved. We do not merit salvation. Rather, it is God who never ceased to love us despite our sinfulness. *"God proves his love for us in that while we were still sinners Christ died for us."—Rom 5:8.*

The passion and death of Our Lord teaches us the enormity of sin. It was sin which caused Christ to suffer such agony and to die. All the efforts of the world to minimize or to glamorize sin fail before the image of the crucified Savior.

7. How was Jesus put to death?

In addition to being scourged mercilessly Jesus was forced to carry his heavy cross through the city to the place of crucifixion. His condition during this journey was such that his enemies feared that he would die before reaching Calvary. Hence they forced Simon of Cyrene to help carry the cross (cf. Mt 27:32).

Jesus was nailed to the cross and hung there for three hours. At the moment of his death there was a sign from heaven:

> But Jesus cried out again in a loud voice, and gave up his spirit. And behold, the veil of the sanctuary was torn in two from top to bottom. The earth quaked, rocks were

*split, tombs were opened, and the bodies of many saints
who had fallen asleep were raised. And coming forth
from their tombs after his resurrection, they entered the
holy city and appeared to many—Mt 27:50-53.*

The Roman soldiers broke the legs of the two thieves who
were crucified with Jesus in order to hasten their death. But when
they came to Jesus they saw that he was already dead; there is no
need to break his legs. One of the soldiers, however, took a lance
and opened up Jesus' side, piercing his heart (cf. John 19:31-37).

8. What were the circumstances of Jesus' burial?

The body of Jesus was placed in a tomb by his friends, and
a heavy stone was rolled against the opening to seal the tomb. But
his enemies, taking every precaution, and mindful of Jesus'
prediction that he would rise on the third day, placed a guard of
soldiers around the tomb (cf. Mt 27:62-66).

9. Who is responsible for the death of Jesus?

The guilt of those who participated in the trial of Jesus is
known to God alone. We do know he forgave those who had
persecuted him on the cross. We also know that what was done
during Jesus' passion "cannot be imputed indiscriminately to all
Jews living at that time or to Jews today . . . . Jews must not be
portrayed as rejected or accursed by God, as if it followed from
Sacred Scripture"—Declaration on the Relation of the Church to
Non-Christian Religions.

Practice

▲ One traditional Roman Catholic devotion which is used
throughout the year to commemorate the salvific acts of Jesus is
the Stations (or Way) of the Cross. It is for this reason that all
Catholic Churches have a series of fourteen pictures depicting
various scenes or "stations" in the Passion and death of Jesus.
These pictures are in sequence, beginning at the front of the

Church and continuing down one side wall and up the other. To make the way of the cross all one has to do is to walk from picture to picture meditating on the Passion of Christ. One may "make the stations" privately at any time; the devotion often is held publicly in churches on the Fridays of Lent.

The fourteen traditional stations are:

1) Jesus is condemned to death.
2) Jesus accepts the cross.
3) Jesus falls the first time.
4) Jesus meets his mother.
5) Simon helps Jesus carry the cross.
6) Veronica wipes Jesus' face.
7) Jesus falls the second time.
8) Jesus speaks to the women of Jerusalem.
9) Jesus falls the third time.
10) Jesus is stripped of his garments.
11) Jesus is nailed to the cross.
12) Jesus dies on the cross.
13) Jesus is taken down from the cross.
14) Jesus is laid in the tomb.

▲ It is in the liturgy of Holy Week that the entire Church officially remembers and celebrates the mysteries of our redemption.

• On Passion Sunday, the Sunday before Easter, sometimes called Palm Sunday, palms are blessed and distributed. Carrying these palms, we walk in procession singing, *"Hosanna to the Son of David"—Mt 21:9,* as did the children of Jerusalem at Christ's triumphal entry into the Holy City as he came to begin his Passion. At the Mass which follows, the whole story of the Passion and death of Christ is recounted as the Passion of Our Lord according to St. Matthew, or St. Mark, or St. Luke.

• On Holy Thursday we begin the Sacred Triduum. On that evening we celebrate the anniversary of the Last Supper by a Mass which expresses both our joy and gratitude for the great gifts of the Eucharist, our common call to service, and our deep mourning at the Passion of Christ, which began on that night. Many parishes re-enact Jesus washing the feet of his apostles during this liturgy.

• The service on Good Friday is not a Mass, not the unbloody sacrifice of Christ; it is a service which concentrates, rather, on the bloody death of Christ on the first Good Friday. The service consists of readings, prayers, the reading of the Passion according to St. John, veneration of the cross and Holy Communion. After the services of Good Friday night the church is left empty and silent; the altar is bare. From then until the Easter Vigil service on Holy Saturday night, we relive the time when the dead body of Christ lay in the tomb.

Part II: CHRIST THE LIFE

Section 12 **The Resurrection of Jesus**

*If Christ has not been raised, your faith is vain; you are
still in your sins. Then those who have fallen asleep in
Christ have perished. If for this life only we have hoped
in Christ, we are the most pitiable people of all.*

*But now Christ has been raised from the dead, the
firstfruits of those who have fallen asleep. For since
death came through a human being, the resurrection of
the dead came also through a human being. For just as
in Adam all die, so too in Christ shall all be brought to
life—1 Cor 15:17-22.*

THE RESURRECTION OF JESUS CHRIST has both
historical and theological import. Historically, his appearance to
eye witnesses stirred his followers conviction that Jesus wasn't
merely a great teacher but was indeed the Messiah, the Son of
God. Theologically, Jesus' resurrection demonstrated his ultimate power over evil as epitomized by death. Further, the fact
that Jesus conquered death has provided all those united to him
by Baptism with the shared belief that they too will share his glory
and remain undefeated by death's awful grip.

For the individual believer these historical and theological
tenets merge to provide us with the basis of our personal faith.
Empowered by this belief we stand firm in a world where despair
and apparent failure control the actions of many. For the
Christian, confident in the historical fact of the Resurrection and
assenting to the theological consequences, there is always hope.
Armed with that hope the forces of evil can never overcome our
faith in Jesus Christ.

1. Did Jesus Christ claim to be God?

At his trial the Jews recognized that Jesus was claiming to be the Son of God, the equal of God the Father, and they condemned him to death precisely for making that claim (cf Mt 26:62-66).

On various other occasions, too, Jesus claimed to be God. For example, he had announced to a paralyzed man that his sins were forgiven. The Pharisees, who had heard him, thought in their hearts, *"Who is this who speaks blasphemies? Who but God alone can forgive sins?"—Lk 5:21*. Jesus, giving expression to their thoughts, worked a miracle that all could see showing that he could, indeed, forgive sins, i.e., that he was God.

Jesus even applied to himself the very title for the Almighty, "I am."

> *So the Jews said to him, "You are not yet fifty years old and you have seen Abraham?" Jesus said to them: "Amen, amen, I say to you, before Abraham came to be, I AM"—Jn 8:57-58.*

2. Is it not possible that when he said he was the Son of God Jesus was merely claiming to be a prophet sent by God?

In the first place such a claim would not have been taken as blasphemy. Moreover Jesus called God "my Father" in a way in which no mere person could speak of God. On one occasion he said openly, *"The Father and I are one"—Jn 10:30.* The Jews thereupon took up stones to cast at him, saying, *"You, a man, are making yourself God"—Jn 10:33.*

In speaking to Philip, Jesus said, *"Do you not believe that I am in the Father and the Father is in me?"—Jn 14:10.*

And again at the Last Supper he prayed to the Father: *"Now glorify me, Father, with you, with the glory I had with you before the world began—Jn 17:5.*

3. Does not Jesus at times speak as if he were inferior to the Father and at other times as if they were equal?

Yes. For example, he said, *"The Father is greater than I"*—Jn 14:28, but also, *"Everything that the Father has is mine—Jn 16:15.*

Jesus Christ is one person. But that one person is both divine and human. At the time of the Incarnation that divine Person took a human body and soul. As God, the Second Divine Person, he always existed. The Second Divine Person, therefore, now possesses two natures, a human and a divine. In the Gospels his actions and words sometimes emphasize his human nature, and sometimes his divine nature. When he said "The Father is greater than I," he was emphasizing his humanity; when he said "Everything that the Father has is mine," he was emphasizing his divinity.

4. Did Jesus say that he would rise from the dead?

On many occasions Jesus said that he would rise from the dead.

> At this the Jews answered and said to him, *"What sign can you show us for doing this?"* Jesus answered and said to them, *"Destroy this temple and in three days I will raise it up."* The Jews said, *"This temple has been under construction for forty-six years, and you will raise it up in three days?"* But he was speaking about the temple of his body. Therefore, when he was raised from the dead, his disciples remembered that he had said this, and they came to believe the scripture and the word Jesus had spoken—Jn 2:18-22.

> Then some of the scribes and Pharisees said to him, *"Teacher, we wish to see a sign from you."* He said to them in reply, *"An evil and unfaithful generation seeks a sign, but no sign will be given it except the sign of Jonah the prophet. Just as Jonah was in the belly of the whale*

three days and three nights, so will the Son of Man be in the heart of the earth three days and three nights—Mt 12:38-40.

5. What is the story of Jesus' Resurrection?

Early Sunday morning several women, followers of Jesus, went to the tomb with the intention of anointing the body of Jesus. When they arrived they were amazed to find the stone rolled away and the tomb empty. An angel announced to them that Jesus had risen and instructed them to tell Peter and the other apostles that he would meet them in Galilee (cf. Lk 24:1-13).

Peter and John, upon hearing the news, ran to the tomb to see for themselves. They, too, found the tomb empty (cf. Jn 20:3-10).

6. Did the disciples of Jesus expect that he would rise from the dead?

Despite Jesus' prediction that he would rise on the third day his friends did not expect the resurrection and at first refused to believe that Jesus had risen.

Mary Magdalene, seeing the empty tomb, immediately concluded that the body had been stolen. When Jesus appeared to her she thought he was the gardener (cf. Jn 20:1-18).

That evening Jesus appeared to two of his disciples on a road outside of Jerusalem. They also had not believed the rumors of the Resurrection and did not recognize Jesus until he broke bread with them (cf. Lk 24:13-35).

That same evening Jesus entered the room where most of the apostles were gathered. Instead of rushing to meet him they cowered in a corner, believing him to be a ghost. Jesus ate food in order to convince them that he was alive (cf. Lk 24:36-43).

One of the apostles, Thomas, who had not been present the first time Jesus appeared to the others, refused to believe that Jesus had risen. He said that unless he could examine the wounds in Jesus' body he would not believe. Later Jesus again appeared and insisted that Thomas see for himself (cf. Jn 20:24-29).

7. What did Jesus' Resurrection teach the disciples?

Jesus' resurrection taught the disciples that he was not only the promised Messiah but God himself, the eternal Son of God. After the Holy Spirit came upon them on Pentecost they fully understood the fact that Christ was God and grasped the meaning of his death as the act by which he redeemed the world.

8. How is the Resurrection of Jesus the source of our hope?

The resurrection of Jesus shows us that Jesus has conquered sin and death. He conquered sin by his death on the cross. He conquered death by his resurrection. Death is a result of original sin. Jesus' victory over death is his pledge that he will raise us up on the last day.

> For if we believe that Jesus died and rose, so too will God, through Jesus, bring with him those who have fallen asleep. . . . For the Lord himself, with a word of command, with the voice of an archangel and with the trumpet of God, will come down from heaven, and the dead in Christ will rise first—1 Thes 4:14,16.

9. What happened after the death of Jesus?

The early tradition of the Church presupposed that between the death of Jesus and his resurrection he "descended to the dead." By this they meant that like all people Jesus truly died. They also meant that he joined all those who were dead and brought redemption to those who had died before him.

10. Did the Resurrection really happen?

As Christians we believe that the resurrection of Jesus is a real, historical event. We further believe that the resurrected body of Jesus was seen by many of the disciples. The faith of the early Church was based on the witness of the apostles and others who saw the risen Lord.

11. What is the importance of the Resurrection?

The Resurrection has several important consequences:

a) validating all that Jesus said and did;

b) fulfilling the teaching of the Old Testament;

c) confirming the divinity of Jesus;

d) restoring us to God's grace and making us adopted children of God.

11. What was the Ascension of Jesus?

The ascent of Jesus to heaven was the last stage of his mission on earth. It marks the "definitive entrance of Jesus' humanity into God's heavenly domain"—CCC 665.

12. What did Jesus do at the time of his Ascension?

Jesus delegated his powers to his apostles and their successors. He gave them the commission to teach, sanctify and rule in his place.

13. Did the apostles begin their work immediately after the Ascension of Jesus?

The apostles did not begin their work immediately. Jesus had instructed them to remain in Jerusalem in prayer. He had promised that the Holy Spirit would come to strengthen them and give them understanding of all that he had taught, which happened on Pentecost.

14. Will Christ come again?

At the end of time Christ will come and there will be the final judgment of the living and the dead. Before the second coming there will be many signs and wonders. There will also be religious deception, the culmination of which will be the manifestation of the Anti-Christ. A final battle will shake the foundations of this world, but God will triumph (cf. Mt 24: 3-44; Rev. 21:1-8).

Practice

▲ The resurrection of Christ and its profound meaning in our lives is brought home to us in the liturgy of Easter. The Easter services begin with the Easter Vigil, which is held on Holy Saturday night, preferably late in the night, so that the first Easter Mass may begin about midnight. This service is one of the most beautiful and meaningful of the liturgical year. In it we enact in word, ceremony and song the story of our redemption, our passage from death to life by means of water and the Holy Spirit. Christ, the Light of the World, represented by the new Easter fire, comes among us once more, risen from the dead, a guarantee of our future resurrection, provided we live in him and by him. The ceremony begins with the dramatic blessing of the new fire. This is followed by the lighting of the paschal candle, which represents Christ, and the singing of a glorious hymn praising this holy night and the wonder of our redemption. A series of instructions or readings is then sung. This provides an instruction for all, but particularly for those who are to be baptized during the ceremony. After praying the Litany of the Saints the baptismal water is blessed. Then those who have participated in the process of the Order of Christian Initiation are fully admitted to the community, some by Baptism, others by a profession of faith. Everyone present is invited to renew his or her baptismal vows. Then follows the first Mass of Easter, celebrated with fullest solemnity.

▲ On Ascension Thursday we celebrate Our Lord's triumphal ascension into heaven and begin a nine day's period of prayer to the Holy Spirit in preparation for the glorious feast of Pentecost.

▲ Read the account of the Lord's resurrection and of his appearances to his apostles and disciples in John 20:1-30 and Luke 24:1-49.

Part II: CHRIST THE LIFE

Section 13 **Christ's Promise: The Gift of the Spirit**

When the time for Pentecost was fulfilled, they were all in one place together. And suddenly there came from the sky a noise like a strong driving wind, and it filled the entire house in which they were. Then there appeared to them tongues as of fire, which parted and came to rest on each one of them. And they were all filled with the holy Spirit and began to speak in different tongues, as the Spirit enabled them to proclaim—Acts 2:1-4.

THE CHURCH TRADITIONALLY EXPLAINS that the Holy Spirit as the third person of the Holy Trinity eternally "proceeds" from the Father and the Son. It is through the power of the Holy Spirit that God is revealed to us by enabling us to know the Father and to understand the Father's Word. It was the coming of the Holy Spirit that Jesus promised his disciples. It was the Holy Spirit who enabled the apostles to preach on Pentecost. It was by the Holy Spirit's inspiration that the Scriptures were written. And it is the Holy Spirit who continues to guide the life and mission of the Church.

1. Who is the Holy Spirit?

The Holy Spirit is the Third Person of the Blessed Trinity. References to the Spirit are found in the Scriptures, the liturgy and our theological tradition. Other titles given to the Third Person are "Paraclete," "Advocate," "Spirit of God," and "Spirit of Christ."

2. Why is it we know so little about the Holy Spirit?

The Holy Spirit along with the Father and the Son has been part of the plan of salvation from the very beginning. We only came to truly know of the Spirit, however, through the Word of God made flesh, Jesus, in whom the Spirit abides and whom we know consecrated Christ as the Messiah. While Jesus spoke of the Spirit in various times and in various ways, it was only toward the end of his life on earth that he promised the coming of the Spirit. Through our resurrection faith we also know that the work of salvation is the joint work of the Son and the Holy Spirit.

3. When did the Holy Spirit come?

It was at Pentecost that the Holy Spirit descended in the form of tongues of fire upon the apostles and others who had gathered in Jerusalem (cf. Acts 2:1-4). With the coming of the Spirit the paschal mystery was completed and the mystery of the Trinity made manifest. The Church, which was born from the pierced side of Christ as he died on the cross, was made manifest to the world on that day. Also, the kingdom (or reign) of God was inaugurated on Pentecost Sunday, though it has not yet been completed.

4. What was the effect of the coming of the Holy Spirit upon the disciples?

After the Holy Spirit had come upon them, the disciples were no longer timid or uncertain. They then understood the teachings which Jesus had patiently taught them for three years. They went forth fearlessly, preaching, healing and baptizing in the name of Jesus Christ.

The apostles remained for a time in their own country, using Jerusalem as a base. Later they went forth to the various parts of the world. Saints Peter and Paul eventually made their way to Rome, of which city St. Peter became bishop.

5. What are the gifts of the Holy Spirit?

The Holy Spirit remains today with the Church and infuses each Christian in a special way in the sacrament of Confirmation.

We have spoken traditionally of seven gifts of the Holy Spirit that help us live as Jesus taught us. They are wisdom, understanding, counsel, fortitude, knowledge, piety and fear of the Lord.

6. What is the relationship of the Holy Spirit and the Church?

The Church is spoken of as being the Body of Christ and the Temple of the Holy Spirit. Christ gives to the fellowship of believers the Holy Spirit who "builds, animates and sanctifies the Church"—CCC 747. In fact, it can be said that "the Church's mission is not in addition to that of Christ and the Holy Spirit, but is its sacrament: in her whole being and in her members, the Church is sent to announce, bear witness, make present and spread the mystery of the communion of the Holy Trinity"—CCC 738. It is the Holy Spirit who works to enable this mission of the Church and who is communicated to the faithful through the sacraments.

Practice

▲ The Solemnity of Pentecost celebrates the gift of the Holy Spirit to God's people. The beginning of the Eucharistic Prayer for Pentecost elegantly attributes the beginning of the Church to the coming of the Holy Spirit upon the disciples on the first Pentecost Sunday:

> Today we celebrate the great beginning of your
>   Church
> when the Holy Spirit made known to all peoples
>   the one true God,
> and created from the many languages
> one voice to profess one faith.

▲ In recent years there has been a renewed interest in the Holy Spirit. In the late 1960's a movement, known as the charismatic renewal, began among Roman Catholics and did much to emphasize the role of the Holy Spirit in our daily lives.

▲ The new *Catechism of the Catholic Church* stresses the Holy Spirit and in a particular way emphasizes the Church's relationship to the Third Person of the Trinity.

Part III: CHRIST'S ABIDING PRESENCE: THE CHURCH

Section 14 **The Mystery of the Church**

For as in one body we have many parts, and all the parts do not have the same function, so we, though many, are one body in Christ and individually parts of one another. Since we have gifts that differ according to the grace given to us, let us exercise them: if prophecy, in proportion to the faith; if ministry, in ministering; if one is a teacher, in teaching; if one exhorts, in exhortation; if one contributes, in generosity; if one is over others, with diligence; if one does acts of mercy, with cheerfulness—Rom 12:4-8.

THE WORD MYSTERY can be misleading and has often been misused when referring to God's Church. To say that the Church is a mystery is not a way of ending a discussion. It is, rather, an invitation to begin a new and more profound discussion.

When our way of understanding relies solely on the human intellect, then "the mystery" of the Church can appear contrary to human reason. In fact, mystery merely transcends—not contradicts—reason, making our human method of comprehension merely inadequate.

Doubt and uncertainty, however, can be transformed by faith. Our focus in learning about the Church need not be on unanswered questions but on the richness and wonder of the reality we experience. Mystery is not a problem we need to analyze and solve but an opportunity to discover God and in the process give our lives true meaning.

1. What is the starting point for understanding the mystery of the Church?

Because the Church carries on the mission of Christ through the power of the Holy Spirit, it cannot be fully appreciated apart from our faith in Christ and the Spirit. It is this faith that provides the context for our belief in the Church. The Church is both an institution with a hierarchical structure given to it by Christ and a spiritual community filled with the gifts of the Holy Spirit.

2. What does the word "Church" mean?

The origin of the word "Church" is to be found in the Greek Old Testament, where it meant an assembly, God's assembly. Today the word is used in various ways. In common usage it often refers to a building where worship is conducted. More properly it refers to a congregation gathered in liturgical prayer, to the local community of believers, and, finally, to the universal Church. These later three meanings ought not be separated, because the Church is all three.

3. What is the origin of the Church?

The origin of the Church is the salvific work of the Blessed Trinity. In a particular way it is founded in the words and deeds of Jesus Christ. Like Christ, the Church is both human and divine. As a human and divine community the Church is on a pilgrimage toward the perfection that will be found only at the end of time. In the "in-between," which is now, the Church is, as it were, a sacramental or instrumental sign of our intimate union with God and the unity of all humanity.

4. How did Jesus speak of Church?

Jesus spoke of his Church:

a) As his bride, referring to himself as the bridegroom: *"Can the wedding guests mourn as along as the bridegroom is with them? The days will come when the bridegroom is taken away from them, and then they will fast"*—Mt. 9:15.

b) As his flock, of which he is shepherd:

"I am the good shepherd, and I know mine and mine know me, just as the Father knows me and I know the Father; and I will lay down my life for the sheep. I have other sheep that do not belong to this fold. These also I must lead, and they will hear my voice, and there will be one flock, one shepherd"—Jn 10:14-16.

c) As his kingdom, the kingdom (or reign) of God: *"The kingdom of heaven is also like a net thrown into the sea, which collects fish of every kind"*—Mt 13:47.

d) As a vine and its branches, a living organic union between himself and the members of his Church: *"I am the vine, you are the branches"*—Jn 15:5.

5. How and what did Jesus teach about this kingdom?

Jesus used parables in an effort to teach the people about his kingdom. It was to be a spiritual kingdom that extended beyond the Jewish people to the whole world. A prayerful reading of the following parables will help us appreciate the mystery of the kingdom of God:

a) the sower (cf. Mt 13: 3-9, 18-23);
b) the wheat and the cockle (cf. Mt 13:24-30, 37-43);
c) the mustard seed (cf. Mt 13:31-32);
d) the leaven (cf. Mt 13:33);
e) the fishing net (cf. Mt 13:47-50);
f) the laborers in the vineyard (cf. Mt 20:1-16);
g) the vine-dressers (cf. Mt 21:33-41);
h) the marriage of the king's son (cf. Mt 22:1-14).

6. How is the Church spoken of today?

Church teaching and theologians often speak of the Church in three ways—as the people of God, the Body of Christ, and the Temple of the Holy Spirit. Each of these images provide us with profound insights into the mystery of the Church:

a) As God's people the Church participates in Christ's priestly, prophetic and royal office.

b) As the Body of Christ the Church is intimately united to Christ, who is its head and its members, within their diversity, are one with each other.

c) As the Temple of the Holy Spirit the Church is animated by the Spirit's gifts that make possible the building up of the human family, as well as the renewal and development of the Church itself.

7. Why is the image "Pilgrim People of God" helpful?

The Second Vatican Council used the image of the Church as a pilgrim people. This image is helpful because it enables us to understand many different aspects of this mystery that is the Church. The term "pilgrim" indicates the members are travelers from this present life moving toward union with God in a life that will never end. Because we can never fully reach our goal in this life we journey always as pilgrims—always in movement, never arrived at our destination in this world.

The term "people" is less clear but very important. A "people" is a group that shares three things, namely (a) common ancestry, (b) common experiences, and (c) common goals.

The common ancestry of the Church is twofold: Baptism and redemption. By Baptism we are children of God, and by Jesus' sacrifice we are redeemed. This creates a family within the Church.

The common experiences we share are the liturgical actions of the Church. On any given Sunday throughout the world the same Scripture lessons are experienced by being read and explained in the homily. Even though separated by distance and language we share the same religious experience. We also share the same seven sacraments, the sources of divine life. In these sacraments God does come to each of us, even though at different times and different places.

The common goals we experience within the Church are to live the Christian message and share it with all of humanity. We also hope to bring all people with us to eternal happiness in heaven.

The expression "people of God" also stresses the value of each individual member. Each person has opportunities and obligations within the Church. Each has the responsibility to live and share the gift of faith with all. This response is not just the work of priests or bishops or even just the pope. Rather, it is the common work of all the members of the Church.

8. How do we as God's people manifest the love and unity which is ours as a community of faith?

Another way to speak of Church is as a "communion" or community of faith. As a fellowship of believers we manifest our love and unity:

a) by gathering to celebrate the Eucharist, the Mass, and within that celebration by sharing in Holy Communion, in which we receive the bread of life and the cup of salvation, which both symbolizes and effects our unity;

b) by praying for each other;

c) by helping each other in need;

d) by supporting with our prayers and alms all the members of Christ who are laboring in the missions;

e) by working together to *"renew the face of the earth"*— *Ps 104:30* by associating and cooperating with one another in the work of the diocese and the parish to which we belong, and in social, economic and civic life.

9. Are there distinguishing marks by which the Church can be identified?

The Nicene Creed speaks of four essentially interrelated features of the Church and its mission. Often times they are spoken of as the "marks" of the Church. "We believe in one, holy, catholic and apostolic church"—Nicene Creed.

Practice

▲ The Church was founded by Jesus Christ and is therefore intimately united with him. Because of this relationship the Church is a type of sign or sacrament of our union with God. This mystery is celebrated in various ways and is present in many aspects of Church life.

▲ Key feast days that celebrate the mystery of the Church are Pentecost Sunday, when the Church received the Holy Spirit; Christ the King, which focuses on the inauguration of the kingdom (or reign) of God; and All Saints, where all the faithful throughout history are remembered.

▲ Many Catholics still take actual pilgrimages to holy sites: the places associated with the life of Jesus throughout Israel; Rome, the spiritual center of the Church; or thousands of other places of special importance to the Church. Such pilgrimages can be an occasion of special grace and can also serve to reinforce the fact that we are all on a pilgrimage—even in our daily lives.

Part III: CHRIST'S ABIDING PRESENCE: THE CHURCH

Section 15 **The Church Is One**

"I pray not only for them, but also for those who will believe in me through their word, so that they may all be one, as you, Father, are in me and I in you, that they also may be in us, that the world may believe that you sent me. And I have given them the glory you gave me, so that they may be one, as we are one, I in them and you in me, that they may be brought to perfection as one, that the world may know that you sent me, and that you loved them even as you loved me"—Jn 17:20-23.

THIS PRAYER OF CHRIST is realized today in the oneness which is present amid a remarkable diversity among the followers of Christ. The members of Christ's Body live in every country of the world and belong to every race on earth. Even though they have different cultures, different tastes, different political opinions and speak different languages, they are one in the great unity of the Body of Christ.

There are, however, millions of men and women who love Christ and worship him as their Savior and their God who are separated from full unity with the Church. The prayer of Christ for unity among his members is a prayer also for their complete reunion.

1.   What are the bonds of the Church's unity?

The ultimate foundation for the unity of the Church is love. It also is assured by the affirmation of one faith, by the common life of divine worship and by the apostolic succession given to the Church through the sacrament of Holy Orders.

2. Can there be more than one true Church of Christ?

There cannot be more than one true Church of Christ because the Church is Christ. Christ cannot be divided. There is but *"one body and one Spirit, as you were also called to the one hope of your call; one Lord, one faith, one baptism; one God and Father of all, who is over all and through all and in all"*—Eph 4:4-6.

It follows that among all the nations of the earth there is but one People of God, which takes its citizens from every race, making them citizens of a kingdom which is of a heavenly and not of an earthly nature.

All are called to be part of this catholic unity of the People of God, a unity which is a harbinger of the universal peace it promotes. And there belong to it or are related to it in various ways the Catholic faithful as well as all who believe in Christ, and indeed the whole of (humankind). For all are called to salvation by the grace of God— Constitution on the Church.

. . . all those justified by faith through baptism are incorporated into Christ. They therefore have a right to be honored by the title Christian, and are properly regarded as brothers (and sisters) in the Lord by the (daughters and) sons of the Catholic Church.

Moreover some, even very many, of the most significant elements or endowments which together go to build up and give life to the Church herself can exist outside the visible boundaries of the Catholic Church: the written word of God; the life of grace; faith, hope and charity; along with the interior gifts of the Holy Spirit and visible elements. All of these, which come from Christ and lead back to Him, belong by right to the one Church of Christ—Decree on Ecumenism.

3. How has the unity of the Church been weakened?

From the very beginning the Church has experienced disputes that brought division and resulted in large communities being separated from full communion with the rest of the Church. Because of our shared faith in the Lord Jesus the members of these communities are fellow Christians and are our sisters and brothers. Because they share in various ways in elements of God's salvific efforts, Christ's Spirit is able to make use of these separated ecclessial communities "as means of salvation, whose power derives from the fullness of grace and truth that Christ has entrusted to the Catholic Church. All these blessings came from Christ, lead back to him and are calls to Catholic unity"—CCC 819. Thus, the movement to restore the full unity of the Christian family is truly the work of the Holy Spirit.

4. What is the ecumenical movement?

The ecumenical movement is an attempt on the part of many leaders of various Christian denominations to work toward the union envisioned and prayed for by Jesus at the Last Supper. Since the Second Vatican Council efforts have concentrated on exploring the common heritage of the various Christian communities. Some are very similar in ritual and doctrine while others have basic and fundamental differences. These difficulties will have to be resolved before true union can be achieved.

The Second Vatican Council reminded us that all Christians have an obligation to pray for and work for this unity. We do not seek a new Church of only the fewest common articles of faith. Rather, we pray together and study the total Christian message so all those enlightened by the Holy Spirit will through Jesus come to know their common true Father in heaven.

Ecumenism means we recognize that our separated brethren possess and share with us many elements of the Christian revelation.

5. What is a rite?

A rite is a system of ritual and prayer used in the worship of God and the administration of the sacraments.

The Latin rite, the one used by Rome and all the West, is the largest. The next largest rite is the Byzantine, which has many national subdivisions. There are also Alexandrian or Coptic, Syriac, Armenian, Maronite and Chaldean rites, which are used in various countries.

6. How did these various rites originate?

Originally each bishop said Mass and administered the sacraments in his own way. Gradually the customs of certain important cities influenced the surrounding countryside. Rome was the most influential in Western Europe, Constantinople in Greece, Antioch in Asia Minor, Jerusalem in the Holy Land, and Alexandria in North Africa. In the course of centuries the liturgies of these cities became the basic part of a "rite," and even sub-rites developed and still exist.

7. What are some of the differences between the Eastern and Western rites?

a) The ceremonies used at Mass and in the administration of the sacraments are different.

b) In some of the Eastern rites a married man may become a priest (no man may marry after ordination; bishops and monks are unmarried or widowers). In the Western rite priests and bishops are unmarried.

c) Some of the Eastern rites always have Communion under both species and use leavened instead of unleavened bread. In recent years members of the Western rite, who had previously received Holy Communion only under the form of bread, have begun to receive Holy Communion under both forms on special occasions or even regularly.

d) In the Eastern rite people do not genuflect but bow profoundly. They also make the Sign of the Cross from right to left instead of from left to right, as is the practice in the Western rite.

e) Eastern rites have some Church laws different from those of the Western Church.

There are other similar examples of the differences between the Eastern and Western rites. The Church is wise in preserving all these customs. The Eastern rites are as old as or older than the Western rite. Hence they are not an exception in the Church but an example of how unity can exist with diversity.

8. Do all these rites still exist within the Catholic Church?

In the course of time various groups such as the Orthodox Eastern Churches (Greek, Russian, Georgian, etc.) broke with the Roman Church. This is known as the Eastern Schism. The causes of division are many and varied, usually including some differences in interpretation of doctrine. Throughout the centuries some of these peoples have returned to union with Rome. When they did so they were allowed to keep their own particular rite. The Church is very solicitous about preserving these rites. Ordinarily one must obtain permission from Rome to change from one rite to another, but a woman may transfer to the rite of her husband without any special permission.

9. What other peoples have separated themselves from the unity of the Church?

Next to the Eastern Schism, the greatest split began in the sixteenth century when Martin Luther broke with Rome and began the Protestant Reformation.

10. Why did Protestants leave the Roman Catholic Church?

The conditions which brought about the Protestant Reformation were very complex. No adequate treatment of the subject could possibly be given here. The following points, however, can be noted:

a) There were real and serious evils in the Church in the sixteenth century. Many of the clergy were not faithful to their vows. There was an overemphasis on externals and a neglect of the inner religious spirit. Responsible elements in the Church had long been calling for a real reformation to correct these abuses.

b) The spirit of nationalism was growing at that time. There was a strong desire in many countries to rebel against any authority— such as the Church—higher or more universal than that of the individual state.

11. What effect did the Protestant Reformation have on the Church?

The Protestant Reformation divided Christianity in Europe, taking millions away from the unity of the Body of Christ, just as the Eastern Schism had done earlier.

On the other hand, the Protestant Reformation forced the Roman Church to reform itself from the inside. Great saints rose up within the Church—such as St. Charles Borromeo and St. Ignatius Loyola. The Catholic Church emerged weaker in numbers but stronger internally.

The division among Christians that exists today is deeply distressing to all who love Christ. People of good will both within the Catholic Church and among the separated Eastern and the Protestant churches pray for the reunion of all the followers of Christ. We can only hope and pray that through love and mutual understanding, the day will come when all who believe in Christ will once more be united.

Practice

▲ Attending an Eastern rite liturgy can be an interesting and impressive experience. Some of the ceremonies are different and can seem foreign from those of the Western rite, yet they are essentially the same.

▲ Latin rite Catholics may fulfill their Sunday obligation by attending at Mass in a Catholic Eastern rite church. A Latin rite Catholic may, of course, receive Holy Communion in one of these rites.

▲ Today there are many individuals committed to various ecumenical efforts. In many areas ministers and laity from different churches meet regularly to plan activities and share in fellowship. Such groups promote better understanding and religious tolerance through organized meetings and prayer services.

▲ Each year many dioceses and parishes celebrate a special week for Christian unity, often with Protestant and Orthodox churches in their areas.

▲ Despite these ecumenical efforts, it is still not permitted for Catholics to receive Holy Communion in Protestant services or for Protestants to do so at a Catholic Mass.

Part III: CHRIST'S ABIDING PRESENCE:
            THE CHURCH

Section 16 **The Church Is Holy And Catholic**

*"I have told you this so that my joy might be in you and
your joy might be complete. This is my commandment:
love one another as I love you. No one has greater love
than this, to lay down one's life for one's friends. You
are my friends if you do what I command you. I no
longer call you slaves, because a slave does not know
what his master is doing. I have called you friends,
because I have told you everything I have heard from my
Father. It was not you who chose me, but I who chose
you and appointed you to go and bear fruit that will
remain, so that whatever you ask the Father in my name
he may give you. This I command you: love one another—John 15:11-17.*

HOLINESS HAS BEEN DESCRIBED in many different
ways. When we speak of the Church as holy we refer to the fact
that Christ's love for the Church makes it holy. Holiness means
that love becomes the motive and goal of the entire Church. As
members of the Church we are to love each other as Christ loves
his Church. Further, since the Son of God came as the visible
expression of God's love for all people, Jesus' mission can rightly
be described as universal—or "catholic" with a small "c." The
Church's love cannot be limited to just one family or group but
must be offered to all.

1. How is the Church holy?

Because of its unique relationship to the Blessed Trinity the Church is "indefectibly" holy. This means that, having been sanctified by Christ, the Church also shares in Christ's power to sanctify others. This holiness, however, is imperfect in that we, the members of the Church, have not yet reached perfect holiness. For this reason it is true to say that we are a Church of sinners and that the Church is always in need of penance and renewal.

2. How does the Church help people achieve holiness?

a) The liturgical and sacramental life of the Church offers a unique way in which the holiness of God is experienced in a particularly effective way.

b) The teachings of the Church are a powerful means of sanctification. The Church gives us the recipe for holiness in its doctrine. Anyone who truly lives according to the teachings of the Church is bound to lead a holy life.

c) The individual examples of holiness which the Church holds out to us provide an incentive for imitation. In every age there have been great saints whom the Church presents to us as models.

d) In addition to liturgical services, Catholic parishes conduct a variety of devotions which are an added means of sanctification. The Church also encourages a variety of forms of private prayer and meditation to suit individual needs.

e) The laws of the Church are a means of sanctification because they oblige us to perform necessary acts of worship, penance and sacrifice that we might otherwise neglect. This is why the Church obliges us to assist at Mass on certain days, to fast and abstain at certain times and to receive the sacrament of Reconciliation once a year if mortal sin has been committed and Holy Communion at least once a year during the Easter season.

Those who fear the LORD seek to please him,
those who love him are filled with his law.
Those who fear the LORD prepare their hearts
and humble themselves before him—Sir 2:16-17.

f) The many religious orders and apostolic movements within the Church provide different ways of life that help many people attain holiness.

3. How is the Church Catholic?

The word "catholic" means "universal" in the sense of "having the character of totality or wholeness." There are two aspects to this catholicity. First, there is the catholicity that comes from the fact that the Church possesses the full and complete means of salvation bestowed upon it by Jesus Christ. In addition, there is the universality that comes from the Church's mission to the entire human family.

4. How can the Church be universal and local at the same time?

The Second Vatican Council reminded us that the Church is really present in all lawful local communities of the faithful. In fact, it is in those local or particular Churches, which we call dioceses or eparchies, that the Catholic Church exists. To insure their legitimacy, however, it is necessary that these dioceses or eparchies be in communion with the Church of Rome, which is the foundation of all local Churches because of its connection with its first bishop, St. Peter (cf. Mt 16:18).

It is especially important to realize that when one speaks of these different aspects of catholicity that the universal Church is not the sum of, or a federation of local Churches. Rather, each local Church is an expression of the universal Church that is one, holy, catholic and apostolic.

5. What is a diocese or an eparchy?

A diocese (called an eparchy in the Eastern rites) is a local Church in a particular area with established boundaries that is pastored by a diocesan bishop. Today the diocesan bishop in most instances is appointed by the Holy Father, the bishop of Rome, who is the pastor of the universal Church. As a member of the college of bishops, who are the successors of the apostles, the diocesan bishop pastors the Church he serves by teaching, ruling and sanctifying. He is assisted in this ministry by the priests, who pastor and minister in that local Church. He also shares responsibility for the pastoral life of the universal Church with other bishops. This responsibility is carried on under the direction and guidance of the Holy Father, the pope.

6. What is a parish?

"A parish is a definite community of the Christian faithful established on a stable basis within a particular Church; the pastoral care of the parish is entrusted to a pastor as its own shepherd under the authority of the diocesan bishop"—Code of Canon Law.

7. What is the role of a parish?

The role of the parish is the same as that of the Church itself:

a) It proclaims the Word of God to individuals and the community. This is done through the liturgy, in the parish's catechetical and religious educational programs, and by the daily efforts of all members of the parish.

b) It gives praise to God through its liturgical and sacramental life and in this way brings sanctification to individual believers and the entire community.

c) It witnesses to and participates in the transformation of the world through its programs of social action and by nurturing the baptismal responsibilities of all believers.

8. What is the role of the pastor?

The pastor carries on the ministry of the diocesan bishop in the parish he is called to serve. He is assisted in his ministry by other parish ministers—both clergy and lay. The pastor's responsibilities are also shared with the members of the parish through consultative bodies like the parish pastoral council and the parish finance council.

9. What is the role of the people of the parish?

The Second Vatican Council has reminded us that all of the baptized share in the responsibility of carrying on the mission which Jesus Christ left to his Church. Consequently every member of a parish should cooperate with the pastor in the total life of the parish. The laity's is a role of taking an active part in the worship of the parish, of belonging to and working together in the various parish organizations, of supporting the parish financially and of carrying the teaching and sanctifying action of the Church into the community in which they live and work.

10. Who is the center of the parish?

The center of the parish and the source of its life is Christ. He is physically present in the Eucharist. He is present among us as we read the Sacred Scriptures. He is present in the individuals who possess the divine life. He is present, too, among the community of Christians who meet with him in their midst. Through their meeting with one another in a spirit of love the people of the parish give evidence of Christ's presence among them, the sign by which the world can recognize them as members of Christ's kingdom. *"For where two or three are gathered together in my name, there I am in the midst of them"*—Mt 18:20.

11. What is meant when it is said that "outside the Church there is no salvation"?

This statement originated in the teachings of the early Christians. They affirmed the fact that Christ, who is the head of the Church, is the source of all salvation. To know this and to refuse to participate in the life of the Church, which is the body of Christ, would be to separate oneself from that salvation. On the other hand, the Church clearly teaches that all others, who through no fault of their own do not know of this aspect of God's plan of salvation, can certainly achieve salvation. This fact, however, does not free the Church from the obligation to continue to proclaim the Good News of Jesus to all people. This is why we say that the Church is "missionary." It is always eager to carry the message of Jesus to those who have yet heard it and to invite all who believe to participate in the full life of his Church.

Practice

▲ Catholics should become familiar with their local parish. For example, they should get to know the many persons and organizations that comprise the parish, such as the pastor, possibly an associate pastor, the school, the religious education program, and the youth group, women's organization, men's club, etc.

▲ The parish structure fits into a larger structure known as a diocese, which is headed, of course, by the diocesan bishop. The diocese is part of a Province comprised of several dioceses, which is overseen by a Provincial, who is an Archbishop. In the United States, each Province is part of a Region, which represents a particular geographical area of the country.

▲ Every country (or in some instances several countries together) has a Conference of Catholic Bishops to which all bishops of that country belong. Some areas of the canon law mandate that the Conferences establish particular regulations which the local bishops must follow. In terms of relationship to the Holy Father, Conferences are seen as representative of the bishops but never take the place of direct contact between the pope and individual bishops.

▲ The pope can call some or all of the bishops together at any time for a Synod of Bishops on a specific topic. The pope may also call a council of the Church, such as the Second Vatican Council, that can address a variety of issues.

▲ The pope can name cardinals of the Church. These are usually bishops, although they do not have to be. The "College of Cardinals" are the pope's special advisors. When a pope dies, all cardinals under the age of eighty meet in a "conclave" to elect a new pope.

▲ At the head of the Church is the pope, also known as the Holy Father, who is the bishop of Rome and the head of the Vatican (the name of the world headquarters of the Church). The pope as the successor to St. Peter, the first bishop of Rome, is the supreme pastor of the Church. Since the Vatican is also an independent, though very small country, the pope also heads the Vatican City-State in Rome, Italy.

Part III: CHRIST'S ABIDING PRESENCE: THE CHURCH

Section 17 **The Church Is Apostolic**

So then you are no longer strangers and sojourners, but you are fellow citizens with the holy ones and members of the household of God, built upon the foundation of the apostles and prophets, with Christ Jesus himself as the capstone—Eph 2:19-20.

THE APOSTLES were twelve men who responded to Jesus' individual call to follow him in a special way. These men were present throughout Jesus' public ministry. They were first-hand witnesses to the Lord's teaching, preaching and miracles. Jesus took special care to instruct and train the apostles, because they were to be charged with the responsibility of bringing the gospel to the rest of the world. It was on these apostles that Christ founded his Church. He said to Peter, whom he chose to be the head of the apostles, *"I say to you, you are Peter, and upon this rock I will build my church"—Mt 16:18.*

The Church of Christ, even in its infancy, was the Church of the apostles. The apostles are among us today in the persons of their legitimate successors, the bishops of the Catholic Church. Peter, the first pope, is among us in the person of his successor, our Holy Father, the pope. Thus, Christ is still among us, teaching, sanctifying and ruling through the hierarchy of the Catholic Church.

1. Who were the apostles?

The apostles were ordinary people. Most of them were fishermen; one was a tax collector. One of them, Judas Iscariot, betrayed Jesus to his enemies and later hanged himself in despair. The other apostles, under the guidance of the Holy Spirit, chose Matthias to replace him. After his ascension into heaven Jesus himself called Saul of Tarsus, whose name he changed to Paul, to be the great Apostle to the Gentiles.

Christ sent the apostles to teach, to sanctify, and to rule.

"Go into the whole world and proclaim the gospel to every creature"— Mk 16:15.

[Jesus] said to them again, "Peace be with you. As the Father has sent me, so I send you." And when he had said this, he breathed on them and said to them, "Receive the holy Spirit. Whose sins you forgive are forgiven them, and whose sins you retain are retained"—Jn 20:21-23.

"Whoever listens to you listens to me. Whoever rejects you rejects me. And whoever rejects me rejects the one who sent me"—Lk 10:16.

2. What do we mean when we say that the Church is apostolic?

When we say that the Church is apostolic we mean that through the ministry of the successors of St. Peter and the other apostles the Church remains in communion with its origins and carries on the mission given to the apostles. In fact, all members of the Church, each in his or her own way, share in this apostolate of spreading the kingdom of God to the entire human family.

3. What is meant by "each in his or her own way" share in this apostolic mission?

Through the waters of Baptism all believers are equal in dignity and share responsibility for the mission of the Church. Within this unity in mission there is, however, diversity in ministry. The Spirit, through gifts known as "charisms," calls persons in individual ways to contribute to the building up of the kingdom of God. Most lay people fulfill these charisms in their work, families, and communities. Some are called to serve the Church as lay ministers. Other people are given the charism to pursue the life of vowed religious sisters or brothers as members of religious communities or institutes. Still others are called to share in the sacramental ministry of the Church through the sacrament of Holy Orders as bishops, priests, or deacons.

4. What is a bishop?

A bishop is a person who through his selection and ordination to the episcopacy becomes a successor of the apostles and is made responsible for pastoring a local Church, a diocese. He oversees the proclamation of the Word of God, the sanctification of the community of faith and its proper ordering. He does this in communion with the pope and the other bishops of the Church.

5. Why is the pope called the head of the bishops?

Jesus called together a group of twelve apostles and St. Peter was appointed by Christ as their head. The successors of the apostles, the bishops, are chosen in a similar way and the pope, as the successor of St. Peter as bishop of Rome, is their head. Indeed the Holy Father is the universal pastor of the entire Church of Christ and is the principle of the Church's unity.

6. Where in Scripture do we read that Jesus made Peter the visible head of his Church?

Jesus, first of all, promised that he would make Peter the visible head of the Church. Later he actually conferred this office upon him. At the time he promised the primacy to Peter, Jesus said to him:

> *"And so I say to you, you are Peter, and upon this rock I will build my church, and the gates of the netherworld shall not prevail against it. I will give you the keys to the kingdom of heaven. Whatever you bind on earth shall be bound in heaven; and whatever you loose on earth shall be loosed in heaven"—Mt 16:18-19.*

It is to be noted that Jesus changed Peter's name from Simon to Peter, which means "rock." At the last Supper, in warning Peter of his coming temptation and denial, Jesus said to him: *"I have prayed that your own faith may not fail; and once you have turned back, you must strengthen your brothers"—Lk 22:32.*

In conferring on Peter the primacy among the apostles, which he had earlier promised to him, Jesus told him, "Feed my lambs." Then he said to Peter, "Feed my sheep." The meaning of these words in the language Our Lord was speaking gives Peter a clear commission to "feed," i.e., "teach and rule" not only the people (the lambs) but also the leaders of the flock, the other apostles (the sheep), who were the first bishops.

> *When they had finished breakfast, Jesus said to Simon Peter, "Simon, son of John, do you love me more than these?" He said to him, "Yes, Lord, you know that I love you." He said to him, "Feed my lambs." He then said to him a second time, "Simon, son of John, do you love me?" He said to him, "Yes, Lord, you know that I love you." He said to him, "Tend my sheep." He said to him the third time, "Simon, son of John, do you love me?" Peter was distressed that he had said to him a third time, "Do you love me?" and he said to him, "Lord, you know everything; you know that I love you." [Jesus] said to him, "Feed my sheep"—Jn 21:15-17.*

7. Why is the pope the successor of St. Peter?

St. Peter was the first bishop of Rome. The man who becomes bishop of Rome, therefore, becomes the successor of St. Peter and pope.

114

8. What special guarantee did Jesus give the apostles to help them teach in his name?

In order to help them teach in his name Jesus sent the Holy Spirit as a guarantee that they would not err in teaching his doctrine. *"You will receive power when the holy Spirit comes upon you, and you will be my witnesses in Jerusalem, throughout Judea and Samaria, and to the ends of the earth"—Acts 1:8.*

9. How is the Church infallible?

The Church as a whole is infallible, that is, the entire Church will never accept a doctrine which is contrary to faith.

The bishops as a whole share in the Church's infallibility when they are gathered in a council of the Church or when they separately all teach the same doctrine.

The pope shares in the Church's infallibility when he exercises the fullness of his apostolic office by acting "ex cathedra" (that is, "from the chair" of Peter) and proposing in a definitive manner a doctrine on faith and morals.

10. How should we respond to that which is taught infallibly?

Because we believe the Church is preserved from error by the Holy Spirit, those matters which the Church proposes as being infallibly taught are to be accepted with the obedience of faith.

11. Where do we read in Scripture that Christ gave the apostles the promise of infallibility?

As he prepared to ascend into heaven, Christ gave to all the apostles the commission to teach, rule and sanctify in his name, saying: *"And behold, I am with you always, until the end of the age"—Mt 28:20.*

The words, "I am with you always" mean, in the language of Scripture, "success in your endeavor." Christ says he will be "with them" in their endeavor, which includes teaching his doctrine. This is a guarantee of success. To teach error in so important a matter would not be success, but failure.

The words, "always, until the end of the age," prove that Jesus gave this guarantee not only to the apostles but also to their successors.

11. What is meant by the infallibility of the pope?

The infallibility of the pope means that by the special protection that Jesus promised to St. Peter and his successors God will not permit the pope to teach error when he is speaking as pope to the whole world on matters of faith or morals.

In making Peter the supreme pastor of his flock Christ endowed Peter with a charism of infallibility in matters of faith and morals. If Peter could teach erroneous doctrines to the Church, he would actually be poisoning the flock rather than feeding it. Since Peter is the foundation and rock upon which the Church of Christ rests and has the keys by which he can allow people to enter or be excluded from the kingdom of heaven, it follows necessarily that he and his successor participate in the authority of Christ, which by its very nature must be infallible.

Infallibility must not be confused with inspiration. The writers of Scripture were inspired to write what they wrote by God himself. Infallibility is rather a protection which prevents the pope from defining as an article of faith something which was not taught by the apostles. The public revelation of God ceased with the death of the last apostle. Nothing new will be revealed to humankind as a whole. Papal infallibility merely assures that the revelation given to the world by Christ will come down to all generations undistorted and entire. Although nothing new has been revealed since the death of the last apostle, there is, of course, an "evolution of dogma." This means that, through study by theologians and the teaching of the Church, more and more can be brought to light which is contained in that revelation. Neither does infallibility mean that the pope cannot sin nor make a mistake in judgment.

12. Must we accept the teachings of the pope even when he does not explicitly use his infallible authority?

Divine assistance is also given to the successors of the apostles, teaching in communion with the successor of Peter, and, in a particular way, to the bishop of Rome, pastor of the whole Church, when, without arriving at an infallible definition and without pronouncing in a "definitive manner," they propose in the exercise of the ordinary Magisterium a teaching that leads to better understanding of Revelation in matters of faith and morals. To this ordinary teaching the faithful "are to adhere to it with religious assent" which, though distinct from the assent of faith, is nonetheless an extension of it—CCC 892.

Practice

▲ One expression of the Church's apostolic nature can be seen in the Creed we pray during Sunday and Holy Day liturgies. The Creed we profess at these times is called the "Nicene Creed" taking its name from the Council of Nicea in 325 A.D. The Nicene Creed was the product of that council's attempt to theologically clarify the meaning of the ancient faith of the Church.

▲ The Apostles Creed, which is used when praying the rosary, is even older than the Nicene Creed and was used as the expression of faith in the earliest Christian communities.

▲ The names of the twelve apostles are: Peter, James, John, Andrew, Philip, Bartholomew, Matthew, Thomas, James, Jude, Thaddeus, Simon and Matthias (who replaced Judas). St. Paul is also counted among the apostles as the Apostle to the Gentiles. There were many other important disciples (or followers) of Jesus mentioned in the Bible, including Mary Magdallen, who first discovered that Jesus had risen, Steven, the first martyr, and Mary, the mother of Jesus.

Part III: CHRIST'S ABIDING PRESENCE: THE CHURCH

Section 18 Mary: Mother of Christ and the Church

In the sixth month, the angel Gabriel was sent from God to a town of Galilee called Nazareth, to a virgin betrothed to a man named Joseph, of the house of David, and the virgin's name was Mary. And coming to her, he said, "Hail, favored one! The Lord is with you." But she was greatly troubled at what was said and pondered what sort of greeting this might be. Then the angel said to her, "Do not be afraid, Mary, for you have found favor with God. Behold, you will conceive in your womb and bear a son, and you shall name him Jesus. He will be great and will be called Son of the Most High, and the Lord God will give him the throne of David his father, and he will rule over the house of Jacob forever, and of his kingdom there will be no end." But Mary said to the angel, "How can this be, since I have no relations with a man?" And the angel said to her in reply, "The holy Spirit will come upon you, and the power of the Most High will overshadow you. Therefore the child to be born will be called holy, the Son of God. And behold, Elizabeth, your relative, has also conceived a son in her old age, and this is the sixth month for her who was called barren; for nothing will be impossible for God." Mary said, "Behold, I am the handmaid of the Lord. May it be done to me according to your work." Then the angel departed from her. Lk 1:26-38

MUCH CAN BE GAINED from studying the manner in which Mary has been understood in the various historical and cultural movements of the Church's tradition. Devotion to Mary has generated a richness in Catholic spirituality. At times, however, excesses in such devotion may have clouded the simple beauty of the young Nazarean maiden whose humble obedience to God's will gave all people their Redeemer. Her "let it be done to me" changed the course of human history by fulfilling salvation history. Mary, small and insignificant in her world's eyes, was mighty and strong in her unfailing faith in God. The first to benefit from the Redeemer's salvation, Mary was conceived without sin and is our model of purity. Mary, as human as us, suffered the pain and anxiety of all parents who can no longer protect or save their children from the evils that prevail upon them. God's choice of Mary as the mother of his son continues to challenge modern society's definitions of success and greatness.

1. Why do we refer to Mary as the Mother of God?

Mary is the Mother of God because it was from her that the Second Divine Person took his human nature. Mary gave to Jesus what every mother gives her child—flesh and blood. But her son is not only human but divine. Jesus Christ, whose mother she is, is God; therefore she is, in fact, the Mother of God, as the Church has always believed.

2. Why does Mary merit the title "Mother of the Church"?

This title, as well as most of Our Lady's other titles, stems from three basic facts:

a) It was she from whom the Second Divine Person took his human nature. She is the mother of Jesus, our brother, and therefore the mother of all people.

b) By her complete identification with and acceptance of the offering Jesus made of himself on the cross Mary cooperated in our redemption, thereby acquiring an added claim to the title of Mother of the Church.

c) All the graces which Jesus won for us by his death on the cross and which he applies to the members of his Church are distributed through her maternal intercession.

3. What do we mean by the Immaculate Conception?

By the Immaculate Conception we mean that, by a privilege which was granted to no other human being, Our Lady was preserved from original sin from the very first instant of her conception in the womb of her mother, St. Anne.

We declare, pronounce and define that the Most Blessed Virgin Mary, at the first instant of her conception was preserved immaculate from all stain of original sin, by the singular grace and privilege of the omnipotent God, in virtue of the merits of Jesus Christ, the Savior of humankind, and that this doctrine was revealed by God, and therefore, must be believed firmly and constantly by all the faithful—Ineffabilis Dei.

4. What is meant by the Assumption of Our Lady?

By the Assumption of Our Lady is meant that at the end of her earthly life Mary was taken, body and soul, into heaven. God did not allow the body from which his Son took human life to suffer corruption, the fate of all those who have been affected by original sin.

We pronounce, declare and define it to be a divinely revealed dogma that the immaculate Mother of God, the ever virgin Mary, having completed the course of her earthly life, was assumed body and soul into heavenly glory—Munificentissimus Deus.

5. Why is Mary called "Queen of Heaven and Earth"?

Certainly, in the full and strict meaning of the term, only Jesus Christ, the God-Man, is king; but Mary, too, as mother of the divine Christ, as his associate in the redemption, in his struggle with his enemies and his final victory over them, has a share, though in a limited analogous way, in his royal dignity—Encyclical on the Queenship of Mary.

Practice

▲ The devotion to Mary which is shared by all Roman Catholics is the Rosary. It is predominantly a mental prayer, a meditation on various mysteries in the life of Our Lord and Our Lady. The prayers that we recite as we meditate are meant to become a sort of chant in the background. In other words, while we say the various decades of the Rosary we attend to the mystery we are contemplating rather than to the words of the Hail Mary, Our Father, or Glory Be.

▲ The entire Rosary is composed of fifteen decades (a decade meaning a series of ten beads) corresponding to fifteen mysteries. The five decade rosaries which one commonly sees are really for praying only one-third of the Rosary at a time.

▲ The mysteries on which we meditate in the Rosary are divided into three sets and present an outline of the life of Jesus, stressing the key points in the drama of our redemption. Frequent reflection on these principal events will assist us as our faith grows and develops.

  a) The Joyful Mysteries:
  • The Angel Gabriel announces to Mary that she is to be the Mother of God.

- Our Blessed Lady visits her cousin Elizabeth, the mother of St. John the Baptist.
- Our Lord is born in Bethlehem.
- Our Lord is presented in the temple.
- The boy Jesus is found in the temple after he had been lost for three days.

b) The Sorrowful Mysteries:

- Our Lord suffers his agony in the garden of Gethsemane.
- Jesus is scourged by the Roman soldiers.
- Jesus is crowned with thorns.
- Jesus carries his cross to Calvary.
- Jesus is crucified.

c) The Glorious Mysteries:

- Jesus rises from the dead.
- Jesus ascends into heaven.
- The Holy Spirit descends upon the infant Church.
- Our Lady is assumed into heaven.
- Our Lady is crowned Queen of Heaven.

▲ The Rosary begins with the recitation of the Apostles' Creed. This prayer is followed by an Our Father, three Hail Marys and the Glory Be said on the beads preceding the five decades. Each decade is preceded by an Our Father, includes ten Hail Marys, and concludes with the Glory Be. The Rosary ends with the Hail Holy Queen.

Part IV: CHRIST'S ABIDING PRESENCE: THE SACRAMENTS

Section 19 **The Sacred Liturgy**

"Do this in memory of me"—Lk 22:19

IN DESCRIBING THE LITURGY the Second Vatican Council relates how Jesus sent the apostles, filled with the Holy Spirit, to preach the gospel to every person. They were to proclaim that the Son of God, by his death and resurrection, had freed us from the power of Satan and from death and had inaugurated the kingdom of his Father. But the apostles were to be more than teachers. They were to exercise the work of salvation for us through the sacred ceremonies of sacrifice and sacraments, i.e., through the liturgy.

> For it is liturgy through which, especially in the divine sacrifice of the Eucharist, "the work of our redemption is accomplished," and it is through the liturgy, especially, that the faithful are enabled to express in their lives and manifest to others the mystery of Christ and the real nature of the true Church—Constitution on the Sacred Liturgy.

The liturgy is an exercise of the priestly office of Jesus. It is through the liturgy that our sanctification is manifested by signs perceptible to the senses and is effected in a way which is proper to each of these signs.

Every liturgical celebration is an action of Jesus, our priest, and of the Church, his Body. No other action of the Church can match the efficacy of the liturgy nor equal it in any way. It is in the liturgy that full public worship is performed by the Mystical Body of Jesus (cf. Constitution on the Sacred Liturgy).

> The liturgy is the summit toward which the activity of the Church is directed. At the same time it is the fountain from which all her power flows. For the goal of apostolic works is that all who are made [children] of God by faith and baptism should come together to praise God in the midst of his Church, to take part in her sacrifice, and to eat the Lord's supper—Constitution on the Sacred Liturgy.

The first function of the Church is to worship God. The second is to teach and sanctify its members. The third is to teach and sanctify the world. In this threefold work of the Church the liturgy plays a vital role. It is through the liturgy that the Pilgrim People give unceasing worship to God. It is through the liturgy that the members of the Church receive the divine life of sanctifying grace that flows from Christ. The liturgy of the Church teaches the world the truths of Jesus most effectively because it appeals to the whole person, to the heart as well as the mind.

1. What is the sacred liturgy?

The sacred liturgy is the official public worship of God by the Church. In the sacred liturgy the Church proclaims and celebrates the mystery of Christ so that the faithful might live it and bear witness to it in the world.

2. What is the essence of liturgy?

Two things must be kept in mind if we are to understand the Church's liturgy. First, although God is mysterious, beyond our knowledge or control, he is experienced in a special way through the celebration of sacramental liturgy. Second, liturgy is our response in faith and love to the many blessings we have received from God.

3. Is the liturgy primarily ritual?

Ritual is essential to the liturgy, but it is by no means the whole of it. Jesus himself criticized those who overemphasized form over content, external actions over internal conversion (cf. Mt 15:1-18).

We must worship God intelligently with our minds and emotionally with our hearts. Before we can do either of these, we must be instructed in the meaning of the ceremonies and symbols used in the Mass and the sacraments so that we will be well disposed to actively participate with the priest and the rest of the community in the liturgical celebrations.

4. How important is active participation in the liturgy?

A person does receive some benefit by mere attendance at liturgical services. But when actively participating a member of the assembled congregation is personally proclaiming approval and acceptance of the sacred doctrines and mysteries being celebrated. Consequently each participant in a liturgy should enthusiastically join the assembly in responding to the celebrant's call to worship. Everyone should listen attentively to the readings from the Scriptures and to the homily.

Prayers offered at a liturgy are always on behalf of the welfare of all of the people of God, but they are offered in a special way for those participating in a particular celebration.

5. Does a person really have an obligation to participate in the liturgy in order to worship God?

Beginning with the Sinai covenant about two thousand years before the birth of Jesus the Jewish people were given exact directions on how and when to worship God. The sacred authors of the two books of Kings record God's displeasure with those who did not follow these prescriptions (cf. 1 and 2 Kgs). In the Acts of the Apostles we read that even from the early days of Christianity people gathered together on the first day of the week for the breaking of the bread (cf. Acts 2:42).

6. What is included in the sacred liturgy?

The sacred liturgy includes:

a) the Eucharistic Sacrifice-Meal, the Mass;

b) the seven sacraments;

c) the liturgy of the hours;

d) sacramentals.

7. What is the liturgy of the hours?

The Liturgy of the Hours is the daily prayer of the Church. It is composed mainly of the Psalms, inspired poems of the Old Testament. This prayer of the Church is prayed every day by all clerics in major orders and by monks and other religious in choir. It follows the cycles of the liturgical year. The two principal sections are the morning hour prayer and evening hour prayer. There are three other sections: the hours of readings, mid-day prayer and night prayer.

The Liturgy of the Hours with its wealth of psalms, prayers and hymns and readings from Scripture and from the early Christian saints is a great treasure. The laity, although not officially deputed to pray it, may pray part or all or the daily prayer of the Church with great profit to themselves. The Breviary is the book containing the text of the liturgy of the hours.

8. What is the liturgical year?

The liturgical year is the means by which the Church relives the life of Christ by celebrating throughout the year the mysteries of his life, death and resurrection.

Throughout the liturgical year the Church not only presents to us the mysteries of Jesus Christ but strives to help us experience them and thereby share more fully in the life of Christ.

a) In the four weeks of Advent the Church recalls the unfortunate condition of humanity from shortly after creation until the coming of Jesus into the world. Advent is a time of longing for the light of Christ which will enlighten all of us. It is also a time of joy for us because we know we are blessed to live in the time after the Incarnation. We no longer need to walk in the darkness of sin.

b) Christmas brings us to the stable at Bethlehem and teaches us that the Son of God became flesh for us and for our salvation. We learn that we must be born again and undergo a complete transformation by becoming more intimately united to the Word of God made flesh.

c) At the solemnity of the Epiphany, we celebrate the call of the Gentiles to the Christian faith. The liturgy exhorts us to give thanks for the blessings of the faith and to seek a deeper faith through prayer and meditation.

d) During the forty days of Lent, beginning on Ash Wednesday, the Church issues a call for us to return to our baptismal innocence. The scriptural lessons of this season exhort to purify our intentions and actions. We are called to detest our sins, expiate them by prayer and penance, and amend our lives.

e) Holy Week begins with a representation of the triumphant entry of Jesus into Jerusalem on Passion (Palm) Sunday. Holy Thursday calls attention to the great gifts of the Holy Eucharist and the priesthood. On Good Friday the sufferings of Jesus are put before us. The Church invites us to follow in the bloodstained footsteps of Our Lord, to carry the cross willingly with him, to reproduce in our hearts his spirit of acceptance and atonement and to die together with him so we can rise with him on Easter.

f) The Easter Vigil service on Holy Saturday night is the primary liturgical event in the life of the Church. We celebrate the resurrection of Jesus Christ and his promise of eternal life. We renew our own baptismal promises and welcome new adult members into the Church through their Baptism and Confirmation. We continue the celebration of the Resurrection through all of the Easter Sunday Masses.

g) The Easter season commemorates the triumph of our Savior over sin and death. The Church reminds us that we should rise with him to a new life of greater fervor and holiness, aspiring only to the things of God.

h) At Pentecost the Church urges us to be more open to the action of the Holy Spirit in our lives, so that we may become holy, as Christ and his Father are holy.

i) The Sundays of Ordinary Time fill in those Sundays not covered by special seasons. We continue to celebrate and worship God for the Good News of Jesus Christ.

During the course of the liturgical year, in addition to the mysteries of Jesus Christ, the feasts of some of the saints are celebrated. These feasts are of a lower and subordinate order. Through them the Church strives to put before us examples of sanctity from every age in order to move us to cultivate in ourselves the virtues of Christ.

Practice

▲ Several parishes have worship boards or liturgical committees who help plan how to enhance the celebration of various liturgical seasons and liturgies for specific occasions. They also assist in the presider's preparations. An active liturgical planning group will have the responsibility of coordinating many areas that touch upon the liturgy, including greeters, liturgical ministers (eg., lectors, servers, eucharistic ministers), music, and art and environment.

▲ St. Augustine said that "whoever sings prays doubly well." Try to participate in the singing at your parish liturgies, even if you don't have a trained or perfect voice.

Part IV: CHRIST'S ABIDING PRESENCE: THE SACRAMENTS

Section 20 **The Seven Sacraments**

He had to pass through Samaria. So he came to a town of Samaria called Sychar, near the plot of land that Jacob had given to his son Joseph. Jacob's well was there. Jesus, tired from his journey, sat down there at the well. It was about noon.

A woman of Samaria came to draw water. Jesus said to her, "Give me a drink." His disciples had gone into the town to buy food. The Samaritan woman said to him, "How can you, a Jew, ask me, a Samaritan woman, for a drink?" (For Jews use nothing in common with Samaritans.) Jesus answered and said to her, "If you knew the gift of God and who is saying to you, 'Give me a drink,' you would have asked him and he would have given you living water." [The woman] said to him, "Sir, you do not even have a bucket and the cistern is deep; where then can you get this living water? Are you greater than our father Jacob, who gave us this cistern and drank from it himself with his children and his flocks?" Jesus answered and said to her, "Everyone who drinks this water will be thirsty again; but whoever drinks the water I shall give will never thirst; the water I shall give will become . . . a spring of water welling up to eternal life" Jn 4:4-14.

OUR LORD JESUS CHRIST is the source of "living water," the divine life. He gives us this life and increases it within us by means of seven channels of grace, which are called the sacraments. Through the sacraments Jesus Christ unites us to himself, ever deepening our union with him, ever increasing our holiness. The sacraments are a most special means through which Christ is present with us throughout our lives to provide us with all the help and strength we need to grow in the divine life.

Through Baptism Our Lord first joins us to his Mystical Body and gives us the divine life. Through the Anointing of the Sick he is there to prepare us for death and eternal life. Through Confirmation, Reconciliation, the Eucharist, Marriage and Holy Orders he strengthens, forgives, nourishes and prepares us for our various vocations or callings.

1. What is at the center of the Church's liturgical life?

The entire liturgical life of the Church revolves around the Eucharist (the Mass) and the other six sacraments.

2. What is a sacrament?

"The sacraments are efficacious signs of grace, instituted by Christ and entrusted to the Church, by which divine life is dispensed to us"—CCC 1131. Sacraments are occasions for communicating divine life (grace) because of the power of God and not because of the goodness of the minister who celebrates the sacrament. Whether a sacrament actually brings about a change in the people receiving it depends on their personal dispositions.

3. What are the seven sacraments?

The seven sacraments are Baptism, Confirmation, Eucharist, Reconciliation (or Penance), Anointing of the Sick, Marriage and Holy Orders.

4. Has the Church always spoken of there being seven sacraments?

Like its understanding of Sacred Scripture and other doctrines of faith, the Church has grown in its understanding until it came to see that among its many liturgical celebrations there are seven sacraments which were in fact instituted by Christ.

5. What do we mean when we say that the sacraments were instituted by Christ?

We mean that Jesus himself gave us the sacraments and that they are instruments by which he is now present with us and through which he shares his divine life with us.

6. What is a sacramental "character" or "seal"?

The Church holds that three of the sacraments—Baptism, Confirmation and Holy Orders—confer a permanent sacramental character or seal in addition to the grace they provide the recipient. Through this seal or character a Christian shares in the priesthood of Christ and assumes a particular place in the life of the Church. This seal is "indelible." That is, it cannot be changed or lost and therefore these sacraments cannot be received more than once.

7. What is the purpose of the sacraments?

The purpose of the sacraments is to communicate divine life and to make people holy. They do this by recalling God's saving actions, in particular the death and resurrection of the Lord, and anticipating the future glory which Christ promised.

8. Who celebrates the sacramental liturgy?

Sacramental liturgy is celebrated by the entire community of faith. They are not private actions and for that reason the Church prefers that, insofar as it is possible, they be celebrated in a communal fashion.

9. How are sacraments celebrated?

In sacramental celebrations the sacred minister (bishop, priest or deacon) and other ministers and lay people perform their proper roles in accord with church discipline. The celebration itself utilizes natural signs and sacred symbols that relate to creation, human life and the history of salvation. The celebration involves our encounter with God that is expressed in word and action and is enriched by singing and music.

10. In what way are the sacraments "sacred signs"?

Signs are things or actions which convey an idea. A smile or a frown is a sign of one's feelings. A flag is a sign of a nation. Words convey ideas and are therefore signs. In the sacraments the words together with the actions constitute the sacred signs.

Sacraments, however, are signs which not only communicate an idea but also produce what they signify. The sacraments not only make us aware of the divine life; they actually produce this life within us.

For example, water, since it is so necessary for life, can be used as a sign of life; hence water is an appropriate sign of the infusion of the divine life. But in the sacrament of Baptism the pouring of the water not only signifies that life; it actually produces it. Oil, for another example, is used to strengthen the body. In Confirmation it is used both to signify the strength we receive from this sacrament and to give us that strength. Oil is also used as a medicine. In the sacrament of the Anointing of the Sick it is used both to signify and to impart health of soul and body.

11. Is there only one way to celebrate the sacraments?

While the Paschal Mystery which is celebrated in the liturgy is one and the same throughout the world, it can be and has been expressed in a variety of ways that are in keeping with the diversity of cultures. While essential unity is always maintained, the Church allows many liturgical traditions or rites to enrich its life and mission. The principle rites are the Latin, Byzantine, Alexandrian or Coptic, Syriac, Armenian, Maronite and Chaldean.

12. How can we best understand the seven sacraments?

"The seven sacraments touch all the stages and all the important moments of Christian life: they give birth and increase, healing and mission to the Christian's life of faith"—CCC 1210. While the Eucharist is best understood as "the Sacrament of sacraments," toward which all the other sacraments are directed, all of the sacraments can be understood as having an organic whole. Within that organic whole one can understand the sacraments under three headings: The sacraments of initiation (Baptism, Confirmation and the Eucharist), healing (Reconciliation and Anointing of the Sick), and service (Holy Orders and Marriage).

Practice

▲ The sacraments are life-giving signs of God's immeasurable love for us. It only makes sense that when we worthily receive the sacraments with humility and love we will appreciate the sacraments all the more. The manner in which we prepare ourselves to receive the sacraments can aid us greatly. A good examination of conscience and a grateful heart for God's gift of grace greatly enhances our experience of the sacraments. However, even when we receive the sacraments with little or no preparation they still confer the sanctifying grace which our spiritual lives need to exist.

▲ The preparation and reception of the sacraments should, as often as possible, take place in the context of community. Whether that community is comprised of family, close friends, or parish members, community strengthens and encourages us in our commitment to the Church and its grace-filled sacraments and to our ultimate goal of salvation.

▲ One of the reasons that the Church began to celebrate the liturgy in the "vernacular" (that is, in the language of the people) was to increase the sense of community and participation in the celebration of the sacraments.

Part IV: CHRIST'S ABIDING PRESENCE: THE SACRAMENTS

Section 21 **Baptism**

*Or are you unaware that we who were baptized into Christ
Jesus were baptized into his death? We were indeed
buried with him through baptism into death, so that, just
as Christ was raised from the dead by the glory of the
Father, we too might live in newness of life.*

*For if we have grown into union with him through a death
like his, we shall also be united with him in the resurrection. We know that our old self was crucified with him, so
that our sinful body might be done away with, that we
might no longer be in slavery to sin—Rom 6:3-6.*

IN THE EARLY DAYS of the Church, new Christians were
baptized by immersion. They entered a pool, stripped off their
clothes and were submerged in its waters. They understood that
this symbolized that they were dying to their former sinful selves
and were being buried in the water to rise as Christ did to a new life.
When they left the water they put on white garments to show that
they were alive with the new life of Christ.

This practice symbolized most strikingly what Our Lord does
for us in Baptism. Through the waters of Baptism he washes away
our sins and gives us new life. By Baptism Christ unites us to the
triune God and gives us a share in the grace he earned by his life,
death and resurrection.

1. What is Baptism?

Holy Baptism is the basis of the whole Christian life, the gate to life in the Spirit . . . and the door which gives access to the other sacraments. Through Baptism we are freed from sin and reborn as [children] of God; we become members of Christ, are incorporated into the Church and made sharers in her mission: "Baptism is the sacrament of rebirth through water in the word"—CCC 1213.

2. How is Baptism celebrated?

From the earliest days entrance into the Church has been accomplished by a journey of initiation in several stages. While this journey is as unique as the individual who makes it, there are certain elements which are essential to each journey: the Word of God being proclaimed, the gospel being accepted, conversion taking place, faith being professed, Baptism being received, the Spirit being poured out and the Eucharist being received.

Recently the Church restored the Order of Christian Initiation for Adults (formerly called the Rite of Christian Initiation for Adults or R.C.I.A.) as the usual way in which an adult goes through these stages of initiation. This process reaches its fulfillment in the Easter Vigil service when the Church celebrates the Paschal Mystery and administers the sacrament of Baptism to those seeking to join the Church.

3. What does Jesus Christ accomplish in us through Baptism?

a) The grace received at Baptism remedies the "graceless" condition of the soul called original sin. Jesus also takes away personal sins for those old enough to have sinned. *"For sin is not to have any power over you, since you are not under the law but under grace"*—Rom 6:14.

b) By Baptism Jesus gives us a new life, the divine life, and makes us adopted children of God. He welcomes us into a life of intimacy with the three Persons of the Blessed Trinity: Father, Son and Holy Spirit. *"See what love the Father has bestowed on us that we may be called the children of God. Yet so we are"—1 Jn 3:1.*

Along with the divine life Christ gives us powers which enable us to act as children of God and grow in the divine life. Among these powers are faith, hope and love.

c) Christ unites us to himself and to the members of his Mystical Body. There is *"one body and one Spirit, as you were also called to the one hope of your call; one Lord, one faith, one baptism; one God and Father of all, who is over all and through all and in all"—Eph 4:4-6.*

After Baptism we can no longer pray or suffer alone. When we pray, we pray to a common Father in heaven, and our prayers are heard because of our union with Christ. Our sufferings have value for the entire Church. *"Now I rejoice in my sufferings for your sake, and in my flesh I am filling up what is lacking in the afflictions of Christ on behalf of his body, which is the church"—Col 1:24.*

d) Baptism joins us to the Holy Spirit in a close relationship. *"Do you not know that you are the temple of God, and that the spirit of God dwells in you? If anyone destroys God's temple, God will destroy that person; for the temple of God, which you are, is holy"—1 Cor 3:16-17.*

e) Christ gives us a share in his priesthood through the baptismal character. It is by means of this sharing in Christ's priesthood that we participate in the Mass, unite our prayers and sacrifice with those of Christ and obtain the right to receive the other sacraments.

4. Is Baptism the only way of receiving the divine life of sanctifying grace for the first time?

Baptism is the normal way of receiving sanctifying grace. But the mercy and love of Jesus is so great that he gives the divine life in an extraordinary manner whenever a person, through no fault of his or her own, cannot receive Baptism.

One who has sorrow for sins out of love of God and sincerely desires Baptism receives the divine life of sanctifying grace by virtue of that desire.

One who does not know of the necessity of Baptism but who has sorrow for sins and desires to do the will of God receives sanctifying grace by virtue of the implicit desire for Baptism.

Unbaptized persons who give their lives for their belief in God are baptized, as it were, in their own blood, thereby receiving the divine life of sanctifying grace.

5. Who can be baptized?

Only an unbaptized person can receive the sacrament of Baptism. In the Church's earliest days only adults were ordinarily baptized, and in areas where the Church is new it is still primarily adults who are baptized. For adults the "catechumenate," which is the program of formation in the Christian life, is the final stage of the Christian initiation process. A catechumen, though not yet baptized, is already joined to the life of the Church.

6. Can children be baptized?

The practice of baptizing infants and children can be clearly traced to the second century and perhaps even to apostolic times. The Church has felt that it would be wrong to deprive children of God's gift of salvation and so allows parents or guardians to profess their children's faith and commitment.

7. What is the sign used in Baptism?

The sign used in Baptism is the washing with water and the saying of the words: "I baptize you in the name of the Father, and of the Son, and of the Holy Spirit."

Water is a most appropriate symbol of the effects of Baptism:

a) Water is used for cleansing. The flowing waters of Baptism symbolize the cleansing of the soul of sin.

b) Water is also life-giving. Irrigation makes a desert bloom. In the book of Genesis water is described as one of the elements from which the life of the world came. "*In the beginning, when God created the heavens and the earth, the earth was a formless wasteland, and darkness covered the abyss, while a mighty wind swept over the waters*"—*Gn 1:1-2.*

8. Why are there "sponsors" or "godparents" for Baptism?

Only the person being baptized can make the profession of faith required (except in the case of infants, where their parents do so on their behalf). Through Baptism, however, a person enters into the community of faith, and the full community of faith shares the responsibility of assisting the baptized, whether a child or an adult, to continue growing in that life of faith. A sponsor (or godparent) is a member of the Church who is willing and able to take on this responsibility on behalf of the rest of the community.

9. Who administers the sacrament of Baptism?

Baptism normally is administered by a priest or deacon. In case of necessity, however, anyone can baptize (even an unbeliever, provided the person performs the actions, says the proper words and has the intention of doing what Christ intended).

10. What are the baptismal promises?

The priest asks the person about to be baptized to reject Satan (the devil or evil), and to renounce the works of sin.

The candidate is then asked to respond to three basic questions about the faith so as to profess acceptance and belief:

a) Do you believe in God, the Father Almighty, creator of heaven and earth?

b) Do you believe in Jesus Christ, his only Son, our Lord, who was born of the Virgin Mary, was crucified, died, and was buried, rose from the dead, and is now seated at the right hand of the Father?

c) Do you believe in the Holy Spirit, the communion of saints, the forgiveness of sins, the resurrection of the body, and life everlasting?

11. What happens to unbaptized infants?

Neither the Bible nor tradition gives a solution to this question. We have to leave the answer to the mercy and justice of God.

The salvation of one who does not have the use of reason depends upon the efforts of others. Therefore, parents have a serious obligation to see that their children are baptized soon after birth. If, however, a child should die before Baptism parents should not fear that their child will not go to heaven but rather should trust in God's infinite love.

12. Why does it sometimes happen that a person who had been baptized a Protestant is baptized again when becoming a Catholic?

Whenever a Christian of another denomination desires to become a member of the Catholic Church and enter into full communion with it he or she is not baptized again if proof of valid Baptism can be produced. If there is doubt about the validity or of the existence of such a Baptism a priest would privately baptize that person on the "condition" that it had not been done validly before.

If someone has been truly baptized—either in the Catholic Church or in another denomination—and wishes to become an active Catholic, then he or she merely makes a profession of faith in the Catholic Church and is thus received by the Church. At that time the candidate would also make a confession of sins and receive the sacrament of Reconciliation before receiving Holy Communion.

Practice

▲ Through the divine life which comes with Baptism, each baptized person is called to develop a new life in Christ. In fact a Christian is expected to rise above a mere observance of the moral law. He or she is expected to imitate Jesus in every way.

▲ The name given at Baptism should have some Christian significance. The Church encourages people to name their children after saints. The rationale behind this practice is that the "patron saint" becomes a model and protector of the child being baptized.

▲ Any practicing Catholic over sixteen years of age who has made his or her First Communion and has been confirmed can be a godparent or sponsor. A non-Catholic Christian cannot be a godparent but can act as a Christian witness. Likewise, a Catholic cannot be a godparent for a non-Catholic but can act as a Christian witness. Only one godparent is necessary but two, one of each sex, are usual.

▲ A dying infant may be baptized by anyone who pours natural water over the child's head and says, "I baptize you in the name of the Father, and of the Son, and of the Holy Spirit." A dying adult must express some desire to be baptized and should believe at least that there is one God in three Persons who rewards good and punishes evil and that Jesus Christ is the Son of God.

▲ "Once a Catholic, always a Catholic" is true in the sense that once we are baptized in the Catholic Church we can become an active Catholic at any time by merely confessing our sins and beginning to practice our faith.

Part IV: CHRIST'S ABIDING PRESENCE: THE SACRAMENTS

Section 22 **Confirmation**

*When the time for Pentecost was fulfilled, they were all in
one place together. And suddenly there came from the
sky a noise like a strong driving wind, and it filled the
entire house in which they were. Then there appeared to
them tongues as of fire, which parted and came to rest on
each one of them. And they were all filled with the holy
Spirit and began to speak in different tongues, as the
Spirit enabled them to proclaim.*

*Now there were devout Jews from every nation under
heaven staying in Jerusalem. At this sound, they gathered
in a large crowd, but they were confused because each
one heard them speaking in his [or her] own language.
They were astounded, and in amazement they asked, "Are
not all these people who are speaking Galileans? Then
how does each of us hear them in [our] own native
language? We are Parthians, Medes, and Elamites,
inhabitants of Mesopotamia, Judea and Cappadocia,
Pontus and Asia, Phrygia and Pamphylia, Egypt and the
districts of Libya near Cyrene, as well as travelers from
Rome, both Jews and converts to Judaism, Cretans and
Arabs, yet we hear them speaking in our own tongues of
the mighty acts of God—Acts 2:1-11.*

AS WITH ALL THINGS IN LIFE there are beginning
points—places where we start. We begin our Christian initiation
with the sacrament of Baptism, by which we are forever marked

as followers of Christ and, therefore, share in his dignity as adopted children of God.

Confirmation seals our relationship with Christ and his Church. It signals our maturity as Christians and empowers us to fulfill our responsibility to proclaim the Gospel in our everyday lives.

Another step in the process of initiation occurs when we receive the body and blood of Christ in the sacrament of the Eucharist. Reception of the Eucharist for the first time signals our spiritual growth and marks our communion with the Blessed Trinity.

We become full members of the Church once we have received the sacraments of Baptism, Confirmation and Holy Eucharist.

1. What is the sacrament of Confirmation?

In the sacrament of Confirmation the baptized "are bound more perfectly to the Church; they are endowed with special strength of the Holy Spirit, are thus more strictly obliged, as true witnesses of Christ, to spread and defend the faith by word and deed"—Dogmatic Constitution on the Church. As one of the sacraments of initiation, Confirmation must be received if the grace of Baptism is to have its complete effect.

2. When was the sacrament of Confirmation established?

The Scriptures do not give us the scene of the actual institution of the sacrament of Confirmation. But Christ's institution of the sacrament is revealed in Scripture by the fact that he promised to send, and actually did send, the Holy Spirit to strengthen the apostles, and by the fact that the apostles did administer this sacrament soon after the Resurrection.

Philip went down to [the] city of Samaria and proclaimed the Messiah to them. . . . Now when the apostles in Jerusalem heard that Samaria had accepted the word of God, they sent them Peter and John, who went down

*and prayed for them, that they might receive the holy
Spirit, for it had not yet fallen upon any of them; they
had only been baptized in the name of the Lord Jesus.
Then they laid hands on them and they received the holy
Spirit—Acts 8:5, 14-17.*

3. What does Jesus Christ accomplish in us through the sacrament of Confirmation?

Through Confirmation Jesus gives us:

a) an increase of the divine life;

b) a new and deeper relationship with the Holy Spirit;

c) the sacramental mark or character of Confirmation;

d) an increase of the strength to profess, defend and spread the faith.

4. What is the sign of the sacrament of Confirmation?

In the Latin rite the sign of the sacrament of Confirmation is the imposition of hands and anointing with chrism. The bishop says, "Be sealed with the gift of the Holy Spirit."

The imposition of hands signifies the conferring of full and perfect adulthood. This is an ancient ceremony, which symbolizes the giving of a special power.

Chrism, the oil used in Confirmation, is a mixture of olive oil or a vegetable oil and a perfume called balm, consecrated by the bishop at the Holy Week Chrism Mass.

5. What is the effect of the distinctive "character" or "seal" given in Confirmation?

The character or seal of confirmation perfects that which was received in Baptism and grants to the confirmed person the power to publicly profess the faith of Christ Jesus, especially in everyday life.

6. What is the role of the Holy Spirit in Confirmation?

Our new relationship with the Holy Spirit after Confirmation is similar to that of the apostles after the first Pentecost. On that day they were enlightened so as to better understand the mysteries of God. They were also strengthened to be able to bear witness to Jesus.

At our Confirmation this same Holy Spirit comes with special sacramental graces to enlighten our minds and strengthen our wills so we will be able to live up to our Christian commitments.

7. What are the powers which enable us to profess, defend and spread the faith?

These powers are the gifts of the Holy Spirit and the graces of the sacrament of Confirmation. These graces enable us to meet the challenges to our faith and to take advantage of the possibilities of spreading the faith in our everyday life. *"When they take you before synagogues and before rulers and authorities, do not worry about how or what your defense will be or about what you are to say. For the holy Spirit will teach you at that moment what you should say"—Lk 12:11-12.*

8. How do the gifts of the Holy Spirit help us?

These gifts open us to the inspiration of the Holy Spirit. In Baptism we receive these gifts in embryo. By Confirmation they become more fully developed. The seven gifts of the Holy Spirit are wisdom, understanding, right judgment, courage, knowledge, piety and fear of the Lord.

9. Why must a confirmed Christian be concerned with world problems and social justice?

In the Gospels Jesus teaches his followers that they must not only show concern for everyone but must actively, as much as possible, work to resolve the issues of social justice. In the parable of the Last Judgment, for example, Jesus promises eternal life to those who feed the hungry, give drink to the thirsty, etc. This is presented as a duty, not an optional activity. Those choosing to ignore and neglecting to perform these basic duties in behalf of others were cast into eternal punishment (cf. Mt 25:31-46).

Responding to the question, "Who is my neighbor?" Jesus tells the parable of the Good Samaritan. Here Jesus teaches us the duty to assist anyone in need—even strangers (cf. Lk 10:25-27).

In another parable, Jesus relates the story of a rich man and a beggar named Lazarus. The rich man did not abuse or directly harm Lazarus. However, he was guilty of neglecting to provide care for the basic needs of a suffering person. The rich man, too, entered into eternal punishment for failure at least to attempt to alleviate human misery and suffering (cf. Lk 16:19-31).

From these teachings of Jesus it is easy to see that it is the duty of all Christians to be concerned with the problems facing any members of the human family. Confirmed Catholics cannot limit their areas of concern and assistance to relatives and those in their immediate circle of acquaintants. At first glance it might seem to be impossible for individuals to do much about the social problems of far distant peoples. This is not necessarily true. Moreover, many of the problems, especially of poverty and starvation, are very real to people living in our own country.

The problems of insuring social justice are many and varied. They include world hunger, peace, distribution of wealth, exchange of goods between nations, education, job opportunities, urbanization, etc. The popes of recent years have issued a series of encyclical letters giving Christian guidelines on how to attempt to resolve these basic injustices that are daily occurrences to many suffering people.

Jesus came to save all people. He loves all people. As long as any one person is a victim of any form of injustice each Christian must cooperate to find ways to alleviate the problem.

10. How do Christians profess and spread their faith?

Christians profess and spread their faith by:

a) praying for all people. *"First of all, then, I ask that supplications, prayers, petitions, and thanksgivings be offered for everyone"—1 Tm 2:1.*

b) professing belief in Christ. *Everyone who acknowledges me before others I will acknowledge before my heavenly Father. But whoever denies me before others, I will deny before my heavenly Father—Mt 10:32-33.*

c) giving good example.

You are the light of the world. A city set on a mountain cannot be hidden. Nor do they light a lamp and then put it under a bushel basket; it is set on a lampstand, where it gives light to all in the house. Just so, your light must shine before others, that they may see your good deeds and glorify your heavenly Father—Mt 5:14-16.

d) doing the works of mercy.

Then the righteous will answer him and say, "Lord, when did we see you hungry and feed you, or thirsty and give you drink? When did we see you a stranger and welcome you, or naked and clothe you? When did we see you ill or in prison, and visit you?" And the king will say to them in reply, "Amen, I say to you, whatever you did for one of these least (sisters or) brothers of mine, you did for me"—Mt 25:37-40.

e) aiding the missions—foreign and domestic—by prayers, alms, the encouragement of vocations to the missions and by actually taking part in the work of the missions.

f) participating in the apostolate of suffering. *"Our hope for you is firm, for we know that as you share in the sufferings, you also share in the encouragement"—2 Cor 1:7.*

g) taking part in the work of the Church, which is to sanctify the members and through them to teach and sanctify the world. Once confirmed we have an obligation to strive to live more perfectly the commandments, the virtues and characteristics of a good Christian as described throughout the pages of the sacred Scriptures.

But how can they call on him in whom they have not believed? And how can they believe in him of whom they have not heard? And how can they hear without someone to preach? And how can people preach unless they are sent? As it is written, "How beautiful are the feet of those who bring [the] good news!"—Rom 10:14-15.

11. Who is the minister of Confirmation?

In the Latin rite the bishop is the ordinary minister of the sacrament of Confirmation. This presence of the bishop highlights the fact that through confirmation a person is united in a deeper fashion to the entire Church and to its apostolic mission. It is possible, however, for a priest to confirm in certain circumstances. In fact, if an adult who has completed the Order of Christian Initiation is baptized on Holy Saturday, he or she is to be confirmed by a priest at the Easter Vigil service.

If an adult who is already baptized is being received into full communion with the Catholic Church, it is possible for him or her to be confirmed by the priest at the same time.

12. When may a person be confirmed?

At the present time there is a great deal of discussion and experimentation about the proper age for confirmation in the Latin rite. The most frequent practice is for confirmation to be celebrated in early adolescence, although many people are confirmed as adults after participating in the Order of Christian Initiation.

Practice

▲   Like the sacrament of Baptism the sacrament of Confirmation is given only once. Thus, only an individual who has not been confirmed may receive the sacrament. Also, as with the sacrament of Baptism, an individual who is to be confirmed is to have a sponsor. (It sometimes helps to make the connection between the two sacraments when the confirmation sponsor is also the person's baptismal sponsor.) The sponsor in Confirmation is to be at least sixteen years old and a practicing Catholic who has been confirmed.

▲ An additional patron saint may be selected at the time of confirmation or the baptismal saint alone may be chosen again.

▲ Every member of the Church is called to be apostolic. We have been called by Jesus first through Baptism and now, strengthened by the Holy Spirit in Confirmation, we share the responsibility of carrying the message of the Gospel to all peoples. For most of us this means to our families, friends and co-workers.

Part IV: CHRIST'S ABIDING PRESENCE: THE SACRAMENTS

Section 23 **The Eucharist**

While they were eating, Jesus took bread, said the blessing, broke it, and giving it to his disciples said, "Take and eat; this is my body." Then he took a cup, gave thanks, and gave it to them, saying, "Drink from it, all of you, for this is my blood of the covenant, which will be shed on behalf of many for the forgiveness of sins. I tell you, from now on I shall not drink this fruit of the vine until the day when I drink it with you new in the kingdom of my Father"—Mt 26:26-29.

THE LOVE OF GOD, our Father, knows no bounds. The greatest expression of the love of God for us is the gift he has given us, his own Son, Jesus Christ. *"For God so loved the world that he gave his only Son, so that everyone who believes in him might not perish but might have eternal life"—Jn 3:16.*

The love of Jesus Christ for us, too, is a love without limit. Christ proved that love by offering his life to his Father for our salvation. *"No one has greater love than this, to lay down one's life for one's friends"—Jn 15:13.*

Christ offered himself one time upon the cross. Such is his love for us, however, that on the night before he died he gave us his greatest gift, himself in the Eucharist. By means of the Eucharist Christ continually reoffers himself to the Father in the sacrifice of the Mass.

At the Mass, our ritual meal, Jesus comes to us as spiritual food for our souls. Through the action of Christ and our worship experience, the Eucharist deepens our spiritual lives as it unites us to God the Father and the Holy Spirit. The Eucharist is the sacramental high point of Christian life. All the other sacraments are essentially related to or flow from the Eucharist.

1. What is the significance of the Eucharist?

The sacrament of the Eucharist completes the sacraments of initiation into the Christian life begun with Baptism and Confirmation. In the Eucharist we "participate with the whole community in the Lord's own sacrifice"—CCC 1322.

2. By what other names is the Eucharist known?

Because the Eucharist is a celebration of a mystery that is multifaceted it is known by various names that call to mind various dimensions of its mystery. It is known as "Eucharist" because in this celebration we give "thanks." It is called the Lord's Supper because it reenacts Jesus's last meal with his disciples the night before he died. It is also referred to as the Sacrifice of the Mass because Christ's sacrifice of himself for us is remembered and in a way repeated or reenacted. In the Eastern rites it is called the Holy and Divine Liturgy because it is center of all liturgy. In the Latin rite the Eucharist also is known as the Mass because of the final words of the Latin text which sends the people forth. Finally, it is called the Blessed Sacrament because it is the "Sacrament of sacraments"—CCC 1330.

3. How can we best understand the mystery of the Eucharist?

In understanding the mystery of the Eucharist it is necessary that we consider it as:

a) thanksgiving and praise to the *Father;*

b) the sacrificial memorial of *Christ* and his Body;

c) the presence of Christ by the power of his word and of his *Spirit*—CCC 1358.

It is inappropriate to place more emphasis on one of these aspects than on another. For example one cannot forget that the first meaning of eucharist is thanksgiving. Similarly, as a memorial which recalls the past and proclaims God's marvels in the present, the Eucharist "re-presents" the sacrifice of the cross. Finally, in the sacrament of the Eucharist, Christ is "really present" to us truly and immediately.

4. What is the sign of the sacrament of the Eucharist?

The sign of the Eucharist is bread and wine over which the words "This is my body" and "This is my blood" are said.

5. When did Jesus institute the Eucharist?

Jesus instituted the Eucharist at the Last Supper.

While they were eating, he took bread, said the blessing, broke it, and gave it to them, and said, "Take it; this is my body." Then he took a cup, gave thanks, and gave it to them, and they all drank from it. He said to them, "This is my blood of the covenant, which will be shed for many"—Mk 14:22-24.

6. What was the significance of the Last Supper?

At the Last Supper Jesus told the apostles that they were to celebrate this sacrificial meal in memory of him. This we do in the Mass. The Mass is the reoffering of that sacrificial meal which makes Jesus' death and resurrection present among us.

7. In what ways are the Last Supper, the crucifixion and the Mass the same?

At the Last Supper Jesus changed bread into his body and wine into his blood. He separated them as a sign of his death which was *"for the forgiveness of sin"*—Mt 26:28.

On the cross once again the body and blood of Jesus were separated and Jesus died for the forgiveness of the sins of us all.

In the Mass Jesus, through a priest, once again changes bread into his body and wine into his blood, separates them and offers them for the forgiveness of sins.

In all three events the body and blood of Jesus are separated, indicating his death. In all three Jesus is the principal agent or priest. And all three are done for the explicit purpose of the forgiveness of sins.

8. How are the Last Supper and the Mass the fulfillment of the ancient Jewish Feast of Passover?

The Passover was the annual ritual meal that celebrated the sparing of the Israelites from the angel of death, their escape from the slavery of Egypt and the covenant which God had made with them through Moses on Mt. Sinai. The Last Supper took place on the Passover observance. The Mass celebrates the new, perfect and everlasting covenant which God made with us through Christ, that covenant which was sealed in the blood of Christ as he died on the cross.

The Passover commemorates the saving actions God worked for his chosen people in the Old Testament. The Last Supper introduces the New Testament rite of redemption, the Mass. It was most appropriate that while observing the Passover commemoration Jesus should introduce the new covenant sacrifice.

9. How do we know that Christ is truly present in the Eucharist?

The words "This is my body ... this is my blood" were spoken in fulfillment of a promise Jesus had made that he would give his flesh to eat and his blood to drink. When he made this promise he said, *"The one who feeds on me will have life because of me"*— Jn 6:57.

The people to whom Jesus spoke these words took them literally. Jesus, who could read their minds, did not correct them. Rather he let them go away in disbelief and would have allowed even the apostles to leave unless they would accept his words literally (cf. Jn 6:61-70).

156

St. Paul, speaking of the Holy Eucharist, says:

"This cup is the new covenant in my blood. Do this, as often as you drink it, in remembrance of me." For as often as you eat this bread and drink the cup, you proclaim the death of the Lord until he comes.

Therefore whoever eats the bread or drinks the cup of the Lord unworthily will have to answer for the body and blood of the Lord. A person should examine himself [or herself], and so eat the bread and drink the cup. For anyone who eats and drinks without discerning the body, eats and drinks judgment on [herself or] himself. That is why many among you are ill and infirm, and a considerable number are dying. If we discerned ourselves, we would not be under judgment—1 Cor 11:25-31.

It has been the constant, infallible teaching of the Church that in the Eucharist the body and blood, soul and divinity of Jesus Christ are truly present, contained under the appearances of bread and wine.

9. To whom did Jesus give the power of changing bread and wine into his body and blood?

Jesus gave this power to the apostles at the Last Supper. He gives it to his priests in the sacrament of Holy Orders (cf. Lk 11:14-20).

10. What happens when the priest pronounces the words "This is my body . . . this is my blood" over the bread and wine?

At these words the actual bread and wine cease to exist. In their place is the body and blood, soul and divinity of Jesus Christ. St. Thomas Aquinas called this the miracle of "Transubstantiation."

11. Does anything remain of the bread and wine after the words of consecration have been spoken?

Only the appearances of bread and wine remain. That is, the looks, taste, smell, etc. remain, although the bread and wine themselves have been changed into the body and blood of Jesus Christ.

12. Are both the body and blood of Christ present under the appearances of bread alone?

It is the living Christ who is present in the Eucharist. Under the appearance of bread alone (and under the appearance of wine alone) both the body and blood of Christ are present. In the Latin rite, the Eucharist is often received only under the form of bread, although it may be received under both forms (or "species") at any time

Practice

▲ In addition to Holy Thursday we celebrate another great feast in honor of the Eucharist on the Sunday after Trinity Sunday, the feast of Corpus Christi, "the body and blood of Christ."

▲ In every Catholic Church the Eucharist is reserved in the tabernacle. Usually the tabernacle is a small metal box either in a Blessed Sacrament Chapel or in the sanctuary area. A sanctuary lamp (candle) is usually burning as a sign that Jesus is present.

▲ There are many special devotions to the Blessed Sacrament, including Forty Hours and Benediction, when the sacred host is displayed in a special gold vessel called a monstrance.

▲ As a sign of respect to Christ present in a very real way in the Eucharist, Catholics genuflect or give a reverent bow when entering or leaving church.

Part IV: CHRIST'S ABIDING PRESENCE: THE SACRAMENTS

Section 24 Holy Communion

"Amen, amen, I say to you, whoever believes has eternal life. I am the bread of life. Your ancestors ate the manna in the desert, but they died; this is the bread that comes down from heaven so that one may eat it and not die. I am the living bread that came down from heaven; whoever eats this bread will live forever; and the bread that I will give is my flesh for the life of the world."

The Jews quarreled among themselves, saying, "How can this man give us [his] flesh to eat?" Jesus said to them, "Amen, amen, I say to you, unless you eat the flesh of the Son of Man and drink his blood, you do not have life within you. Whoever eats my flesh and drinks my blood has eternal life, and I will raise [that person] on the last day. For my flesh is true food, and my blood is true drink. Whoever eats my flesh and drinks my blood remains in me and I in [them]. Just as the living Father sent me and I have life because of the Father, so also the one who feeds on me will have life because of me. This is the bread that came down from heaven. Unlike your ancestors who ate and still died, whoever eats this bread will live forever." These things he said while teaching in the synagogue in Capernaum—Jn 6:47-59.

THE PEOPLE WHO KNEW and associated with Jesus were indeed most fortunate and privileged because they actually saw the face of Jesus, heard the voice of Jesus and felt the touch of

Jesus. Yet we today enjoy an even greater intimacy with Christ our Savior. It is true that we cannot look into his face or enjoy the sound of his voice or be comforted by his physical touch, but our privilege today is even greater because we receive his sacred body and blood into our own. This mysterious intimacy is achieved by the precious gift of the Holy Eucharist, which Christ gave to his Church the night before he died. Through the Eucharist Christ is always present among us.

Jesus once told the apostles, *"I will not leave you orphans"*—Jn 14:18. True to his promise, he has indeed remained among us, actually and physically present in the Holy Eucharist.

> What other nation is there so honored as the Christian people? Or what creature under heaven so beloved as a devout soul, to whom God cometh, that he may feed [that person] with his glorious flesh? O unspeakable grace; O wonderful condescension! O infinite love, singularly bestowed on [us].—The Imitation of Christ.

1. What is meant by the expression "Holy Communion"?

"Holy Communion" or "Communion" is the expression used when speaking about receiving the Holy Eucharist.

The expression is very appropriate. It sums up the most important effect of the Holy Eucharist—the strengthening of the union between Jesus and his members and of the union between the members themselves. *The cup of blessing that we bless, is it not a participation in the blood of Christ? The bread that we break, is it not a participation in the body of Christ?—1 Cor 10:16.*

2. Why are bread and wine appropriate material for Holy Communion?

Bread is a staple food in the diet of most people, and wine is the staple drink of many people. Therefore, bread and wine are appropriate material for the Eucharist, which is the food of our soul.

Bread and wine, too, are wonderful symbols. The bread is made of many grains of wheat baked into one wafer; the wine is made up of many grapes, crushed into one draught of wine. This symbolizes the union of all the faithful with each other in Christ.

Bread and wine are also, as we note in the Mass, the "work of human hands." They are the result of human effort to transform natural gifts and therefore symbolize all our daily work that we offer to God.

3. When may we receive Holy Communion?

We may receive Holy Communion every day. The Church encourages everyone to do so. Since Holy Communion is the sacrificial meal, it is most fitting to receive it during the Mass (unless this is impossible because of a person's sickness or the absence of a priest).

4. How often may a person receive Holy Communion?

Ordinarily one would receive Holy Communion only once a day. Even though we have already received Holy Communion, however, we may do so a second time at Masses at Baptisms, first Communions, Confirmations, weddings, funerals, ordinations, and other special occasions.

5. How does Jesus help us through Holy Communion?

Through Holy Communion Jesus gives us:

a) an increase in the divine life of sanctifying grace and consequently a deeper union with God;

b) an increase of faith, hope and love;

c) a closer union with himself and with every member of the Pilgrim People of God;

d) a pledge of our resurrection and our future glory;

e) the forgiveness of our daily sins and the grace to overcome our inclination to sin;

f) the promise of graces to help us love God and others more.

6. How does Holy Communion unite us with our neighbor?

Our Lord gave us Communion in the form of a banquet in which we all eat of the same food. Communion, therefore, both symbolizes and deepens our union with one another in the Mystical Body. It symbolizes our union, because eating and drinking together is a sign of love and friendship. It deepens that union, because it gives us an increase of the divine life and of the power to love one another.

"I pray not only for them, but also for those who will believe in me through their word, so that they may all be one, as you, Father, are in me and I in you, that they also may be in us, that the world may believe that you sent me. And I have given them the glory you gave me, so that they may be one, as we are one"—Jn 17:20-22.

7. What effect does Holy Communion have upon our bodies?

Holy Communion lessens the difficulty we experience in bringing the impulses of the body under control. Frequent and daily Communion is the greatest means we can use to become chaste, temperate, patient, etc.

8. How is Holy Communion a pledge of our future glory?

Jesus promised, *"Whoever eats my flesh and drinks my blood has eternal life, and I will raise [them] up on the last day"—Jn 6:54.*

9. How does Holy Communion remove our daily faults?

Our union with Christ in the Holy Eucharist is a union based on love. Because of this love Christ forgives us our venial sins; the love thus engendered in our hearts merits for us the forgiveness of all or part of the punishment due to sin.

The desire of Jesus Christ and of the Church that all Christians should daily approach the holy banquet is based chiefly on this, that Christians united to God through the sacrament should derive from there the strength to conquer concupiscence, and wash away light faults of daily occurrence, and should forestall more serious ones to which human frailty is exposed—Decree on Frequent Communion

10. What is required in order to receive Holy Communion?

To receive Holy Communion worthily a person must:

a) have a good intention, i.e., the desire to love God more;

b) be free from mortal sin.

11. How can we make our reception of Holy Communion more fruitful?

We can make our reception of Holy Communion more fruitful by a good preparation before and a good thanksgiving after receiving the Eucharist.

Preparation for Holy Communion includes not only an intelligent and active assistance at Mass, which is the immediate preparation for Holy Communion, but also an attempt to practice love of our neighbor in our daily lives.

Thanksgiving includes not only some moments of private prayer and communal singing after Communion but also an attempt to use the graces of the sacrament to increase our practice of the virtue of love.

12. Is it necessary to go to confession before receiving Holy Communion?

It is not necessary to go to confession before receiving Communion unless one has committed a mortal sin. Still, many people who receive Communion daily or weekly go to confession frequently. If someone has committed a mortal sin, however, even though he or she has made a private act of perfect contrition, that person must go to confession before receiving Communion.

13. What kind of sin would it be to receive Holy Communion in the state of mortal sin?

To receive Communion knowingly in the state of mortal sin would be a most serious sin of sacrilege.

14. How does the Eucharist act as Christ's abiding presence among us?

The Eucharist is reserved in the tabernacle of Catholic churches. Jesus is, therefore, actually present in our churches at all times. He is there just as truly as he is in heaven, except that here, under the appearances of bread, he can be seen only with the eyes of faith.

15. Why do we adore the Eucharist?

We adore the Holy Eucharist because Jesus, present in the Eucharist, is truly God. That is why we genuflect or bow whenever we pass in front of the tabernacle. It is an act of adoration of God.

Practice

▲ Catholics are bound under penalty of mortal sin to receive Communion at least once a year during the Easter season, that is, from the first Sunday of Lent until Trinity Sunday. This is called the "Easter Duty."

▲ Catholics may receive Holy Communion either in their hands or on their tongues and in the form of either bread or wine or both.

▲ Many lay people are now asked to be "extraordinary ministers of the Eucharist" and "ministers of care" to help distribute Holy Communion at Mass or to the sick or homebound.

▲ On Good Friday, in order to symbolize that there can be no "business as usual" until the Easter Vigil service, the Church does not celebrate Mass but rather distributes Holy Communion at a special service.

Part IV: CHRIST'S ABIDING PRESENCE: THE SACRAMENTS

Section 25 **The Structure of the Mass**

Now that very day two of them were going to a village seven miles from Jerusalem called Emmaus, and they were conversing about all the things that had occurred. And it happened that while they were conversing and debating, Jesus himself drew near and walked with them, but their eyes were prevented from recognizing him....And it happened that while he was with them at table, he took bread, said the blessing, broke it, and gave it to them. With that their eyes were opened and they recognized him, but he vanished from their sight—
Lk 24:13-16, 30-31.

EVERY IMPORTANT EVENT requires a suitable preparation. The Mass, the most sublime act of worship, is no exception. At the Last Supper, Our Lord surrounded the moment of sacrifice with ceremonies: the supper itself, the washing of feet, a sermon and a hymn. The Church does likewise. The Mass is the ultimate liturgical event. It is filled with prayers, symbols and actions that help us recreate the Last Supper.

The Mass today in the Latin rite is divided into two main parts, the Liturgy of the Word and the Liturgy of the Eucharist. The Liturgy of the Word is composed of an entrance rite, a service of Scripture reading, a homily on the Word of God from Scripture, and the Prayer of the Faithful. The Liturgy of the Word prepares us for the Liturgy of the Eucharist. The Liturgy of the Eucharist is composed of the preparation of gifts, the sacrificial act itself, and the sacrificial meal or Eucharistic banquet.

Each of the two principal parts of the Mass has two related themes. In the Liturgy of the Word, first we speak to God, then God speaks to us. In the Liturgy of the Eucharist, first we give to God, then God gives to us. An understanding of this dynamic in Mass will aid in our appreciation of the Mass itself and will enable us to participate more fully in the liturgy.

1. What is the origin of the Liturgy of the Word?

In the earliest days of the Church the Mass began just as the Last Supper did—with a meal. It was celebrated in the evening in the homes of the people. Later the Mass was separated from the meal and came to be celebrated most often in the morning. In place of the preparatory meal there was substituted an adaptation of the Jewish synagogue service, which the earliest Christians had continued to hold, at first with the Jews in the synagogue and later by themselves. This service of prayer and instruction is the basis of our present Liturgy of the Word. In the course of the centuries other elements of the Liturgy of the Word have been added.

2. What is the structure of the Liturgy of the Word?

a) We speak to God:

• The Entrance Rite. There are various optional ways to begin the Liturgy. The more common form is to sing a hymn while the celebrant enters. Occasionally the congregation is blessed with holy water. We now speak to God our first word, namely we call to mind our sins, express sorrow for them and plead forgiveness.

• The Gloria. Here we express our second word, one of praise. It is addressed to the three persons in the Trinity.

• The Opening Prayer. We express our third and fourth words, those of thanksgiving for past favors and of petition for future favors.

b) God speaks to us:

• The First Reading is usually a reading from one of the books of the Old Testament. We listen to part of the early revelation of God to his chosen people.

• The Responsorial Psalm is a reflective prayer carrying on a theme from the lesson. It is a meditative response to the words of God. It is prayed alternately by the lector and congregation.

• The Second Reading (used only on Sundays and some feast days) is usually from the Letters (or Epistles), the Acts of the Apostles or the Book of Revelation.

• The Gospel Acclamation or Alleluia is the short introduction to the Gospel reading of the day.

• The Gospel Reading reports the actions and very words of our Redeemer, Jesus.

• The Homily is an instruction by the priest based on the Scripture readings of the Mass. God, speaking through the priest, applies the message of Scripture to contemporary times.

• The Creed. We respond to the words of God by an act of faith. This ancient formula of what we believe is a list of the saving actions of God. When praying it we are united to Christians of all ages who have also used it to express the basic tenets of our faith.

• The Prayer of the Faithful is a series of petitions for the needs of the Church, civil government and all humanity.

The various parts of the Liturgy of the Word are not random prayers and readings. Frequently the readings and responses develop a theme or plan for that day. Each part is tied together with the others to teach a special lesson for the assembled Christian community to apply to their daily living.

3. What is the structure of the Liturgy of the Eucharist?

a) We give to God:

• The Preparation of the Gifts begins with a few members of the congregation, representing the entire assembly, bringing gifts of bread and wine and water to the celebrant. Other gifts such as the collection, alms for the poor and symbolic offerings might be included. In addition to the principal gifts of bread, wine and water, we offer ourselves to God the Father. We pledge to strengthen our faith and hope through charitable works. The collection taken up at this time is a part of the procession. We should regard what we offer in the collection as part of our gift to the Christian community.

• The Eucharistic Prayer. This, the most important part of the Mass, is introduced by a song of thanksgiving, called the Preface. During the Eucharistic Prayer, Jesus, through the priest, offers the sacrifice of his body and blood to his Father. Once again he renews the offering he made of his life on the cross. The Consecration occurs in the center of the Eucharistic Prayer. At that time Jesus, through the priest, changes bread and wine into his body and blood. Then the priest invites the assembled congregation to proclaim their faith in the new eucharistic presence of Jesus on the altar.

Before and after the moment of sacrifice the Church prays for various people—the pope, the bishops, the faithful, the living, the dead, sinners, ourselves and for the things of earth we use.

The Eucharistic Prayer has a beautiful ending. Christ, our high priest, mediator between God and all people, drawing all things to himself, presents them to his Father. "Through him, with him, in him, in the unity of the Holy Spirit, all glory and honor is yours, almighty

Father, forever and ever." The people answer, "Amen," which signifies their thankful commitment in faith to the act which Christ has just performed. The "Amen" could mean "I believe."

There are currently four different ordinary Eucharistic Prayers, as well as two for reconciliation and three for children.

b) God gives to us:

• The Lord's Prayer. The communion service begins with the prayer Jesus taught us. We ask for the bread which is Our Lord, and we forgive those who have offended us, as we wish God to forgive us.

• The Rite of Peace. Before approaching the altar to receive Jesus in Holy Communion we should be at peace with our families and our neighbors. We follow the local parish custom and extend some sign of peace to those nearby, symbolizing our peace with all people.

• Holy Communion. The priest, often assisted by ministers of the Eucharist, now gives to us the true bread of life. Through this sacred meal we are intimately united to Jesus and to all others who participate in this holy banquet.

• The Conclusion. We give thanks for what we have received and are sent with the final blessing to live the message of the word and the Eucharist.

4. What is the importance of Communion in the Mass?

Communion is the part of the Mass in which our union with one another and with Christ is most deeply symbolized and increased. The Mass, the Eucharistic Celebration, is a sacrifice-meal. Every member of the assembly is invited to take part in Communion at Mass. Not to do so is to fail to participate fully in the sacrifice and the meal.

5. What is meant by the different roles which are fulfilled in the celebration of Mass?

By the different roles we mean that various actions and prayers are proper to different members of the congregation to perform and say during Mass:

a) The celebrant presides at the assembly. He sums up the petitions of the people in the opening prayer. He preaches the homily after the reading of the Gospel. He prepares the bread and wine. He alone prays the great sacrificial prayer of the Mass, the Eucharistic Prayer, and the words of consecration.

b) The deacon, if there is one, assists the celebrant, reads the Gospel and sometimes gives the homily.

c) The readers proclaim the Word of God to the whole congregation in the Scripture readings.

d) The eucharistic ministers help distribute Communion to the congregation.

e) The leaders of song and the choir assist the whole congregation in singing their parts of the Mass and provide music which helps people pray and meditate.

f) The people sing and pray together the people's parts of the Mass.

g) The servers assist the priest at the altar.

6. What is a concelebrated Mass?

A concelebrated Mass is one at which two or more priests gather at the same altar to offer together—i.e., to con-celebrate—the Eucharist.

7. Why does the priest wear special vestments at Mass?

The garments worn by the priest at Mass are different from

those worn in any contemporary culture. They serve to call to our minds the fact that the ceremony we are witnessing is not ordinary. It is sacred and part of a long tradition.

8. Why are the priest's vestments of different colors?

Vestments of different colors are used to indicate the season of the liturgical year or to commemorate a feast of a particular day. For example, during Lent violet vestments are worn, during the Christmas and Easter season white vestments, on Pentecost red vestments.

9. How does a person prepare for Mass?

When we come to Mass we should thank God for his blessings, ask pardon for our sins and make special requests. In order to be ready to celebrate we should formulate these prayers before coming to church. If we have time we should read the various Scripture passages before Mass so we are more familiar with them.

Practice

▲ We should fully participate in the Eucharistic celebration by enthusiastically fulfilling our appropriate roles.

Mother Church earnestly desires that all the faithful should be led to that full conscious and active participation in liturgical celebrations which is demanded by the very nature of the liturgy. Such participation by the Christian people as *"a chosen race, a royal priesthood, a holy nation, a people of his own"*—*1 Pt 2:9* (cf. 2:4-5), is their right and duty by reason of their baptism.

In the restoration and promotion of the sacred liturgy, this full and active participation by all the people is the aim to be considered before all else; for it is the primary and indispensable source from which the faithful are to derive the true Christian spirit . . . .

Lectors and cantors fulfill their roles by performing these functions reverently and carefully.

Servers, lectors, commentators and members of the choir also exercise a genuine liturgical function. They ought, therefore, to discharge their office with the sincere piety and decorum demanded by so exalted a ministry and rightly expected of them by God's people.

Consequently they must all be deeply imbued with the spirit of the liturgy, each in his [or her] own measure, and they must be trained to perform their functions, in a correct and orderly manner . . . .

The congregation performs its role by listening to the readings and homily with a mind and heart open to the Holy Spirit and by saying and singing their parts of the Mass together in a spirit of prayer.

To promote active participation, the people should be encouraged to take part by means of acclamations, responses, psalmody, antiphons and songs, as well as by actions, gestures and bodily attitudes. And at the proper times all should observe a reverent silence—Constitution on the Sacred Liturgy.

▲ The most basic and important participation in the Eucharistic celebration is taking part in the Eucharistic meal, Holy Communion. We should take part in Communion at Mass as often as we can. We should do so with the realization that we, as members of God's great family, are partaking of God's family meal. Through this meal we are united to each other and to God.

The Church, therefore, earnestly desires that Christ's faithful, when present at this mystery of faith, should not be there as strangers or silent spectators; on the contrary, through a good understanding of the rites and prayers they should take part in the sacred action conscious of what they are doing, with devotion and full collaboration. They should be instructed by God's word and be nourished at the table of the Lord's body; they should give thanks to God; by offering the Immaculate Victim, not only through the hands of the priest, but also with him, they should learn also to offer themselves; through Christ the Mediator, they should be drawn day by day into ever more perfect union with God and with each other, so that finally God may be all in all—Constitution on the Sacred Liturgy.

▲ There are many different forms of music which are suitable for use in liturgical celebrations. Composers have used different forms of music to express religious ideas. While a person may have a preference for one type of music we should try to learn to appreciate different forms. Compositions used in the sacred liturgy should be true music. Texts should present true religious concepts. Tunes should not be chosen for sentimental or nostalgic reasons, but because they help us think of God and our relationship to him.

Part IV: CHRIST'S ABIDING PRESENCE:
THE SACRAMENTS

Section 26 **Reconciliation**

*He entered a boat, made the crossing, and came into his
own town. And there people brought to him a paralytic
lying on a stretcher. When Jesus saw their faith, he said
to the paralytic, "Courage, child, your sins are forgiven." At that, some of the scribes said to themselves,
"This man is blaspheming." Jesus knew what they were
thinking, and said, "Why do you harbor evil thoughts?
Which is easier, to say, 'Your sins are forgiven,' or to
say, 'Rise and walk'? But that you may know that the Son
of Man has authority on earth to forgive sins"—he then
said to the paralytic, "Rise, pick up your stretcher, and
go home." He rose and went home. When the crowds saw
this they were struck with awe and glorified God who had
given such authority to human beings—Mt 9:1-8.*

THE FIRST CHAPTERS of the Book of Genesis describe
how God created everything. Hence all of creation, especially the
human race, was good. But early in human history people
committed the first sin. Therefore, humans, not God, were
responsible for moral evil in the world.

Throughout Old Testament history God frequently sent
special messengers to call all people back to leading a morally
good life. The prophets dramatically preached the need for
repentance and reconciliation. John the Baptist, the last of the
prophets, proclaimed this theme, *"Repent, for the kingdom of
heaven is at hand"—Mt 3:2.*

In the fullness of time God the Father sent his only Son, Jesus, who said, *"Repent, and believe in the gospel"*—Mk 1:15.

Jesus calls every person to live a holy life. In the Sermon on the Mount he admonishes us, *"So be perfect, just as your heavenly Father is perfect"*—Mt 5:48. Consequently a Christian will strive to build his or her life around three basic tenets:

a) to love God above all things with one's whole heart;

b) to love one's neighbor as oneself;

c) to strive to follow God's call to perfection.

Jesus spent almost three years in public teaching. While he denounced sin he manifested great personal love for sinners. God desires not the death of the sinner, but that the sinner be converted and saved (cf. Ez 33:11).

> Then the scribes and the Pharisees brought a woman who had been caught in adultery and made her stand in the middle. They said to him, "Teacher, this woman was caught in the very act of committing adultery. Now in the law, Moses commanded us to stone such women. So what do you say?" They said this to test him, so that they could have some charge to bring against him. Jesus bent down and began to write on the ground with his finger. But when they continued asking him, he straightened up and said to them, "Let the one among you who is without sin be the first to throw a stone at her." Again he bent down and wrote on the ground. And in response, they went away one by one, beginning with the elders. So he was left alone with the woman before him. Then Jesus straightened up and said to her, "Woman, where are they? Has no one condemned you?" She replied, "No one, sir." Then Jesus said, "Neither do I condemn you. Go [and] from now on do not sin any more—Jn 8:3-11.

The story of the woman taken in adultery is only one of the many incidents in the Gospels which give us a glimpse of the love and tenderness of Jesus in his dealings with sinners. Often in the Gospel narrative we see Jesus looking deep into the heart of a man or woman, seeing the frightful condition of that soul after a lifetime of sin and then applying his healing with the words, "Your sins are forgiven." Often the sinners approached Our Lord in the hope of obtaining a cure of their bodily disease. But before healing the body Jesus healed the soul. Sometimes the sinner did not even ask for forgiveness. No matter; Jesus could see what was in the heart and mind, could see not only the sin but the sorrow for sin as well. His unfailing response was, "Your sins are forgiven."

Because of the teachings and actions of Christ, we know that no matter how great or small an offense against our heavenly Father and regardless of how often we have sinned, whenever we approach God begging forgiveness God can and will forgive us all of our sins.

Jesus, who is both human and divine, knows and thoroughly understands human nature. Thus he not only calls for repentance but he gives us a sacrament to make reconciliation possible. The sacrament of Reconciliation should be a joyful experience. In fact, God seems to be unable to resist a humble penitent pleading for mercy. *"I tell you, in just the same way there will be more joy in heaven over one sinner who repents than over ninety-nine righteous people who have no need of repentance"*—Lk 15:7.

1. What are the sacraments of healing?

Through the sacraments of initiation (Baptism, Confirmation and the Eucharist) we come to share in Christ's new life. That new life is received, however, by human persons for whom illness, death and sin are part of their experience. In his life on earth Christ forgave sins and healed both body and spirit. It is Christ's work of healing and forgiveness that is the basis for the sacraments of Reconciliation and Anointing of the Sick. It is for this reason they are known as the sacraments of healing.

2. What is the sacrament of Reconciliation?

Reconciliation is the sacrament by which Jesus, through the absolution of the priest, forgives sins committed after Baptism and brings about reconciliation with God and with the Church.

3. What are the various names for the sacrament of Reconciliation?

The various dimensions of this sacrament are expressed in the way it has been described: "Penance" to express the sinners penitentially turning back to God; "Confession" to express an essential aspect of the sacrament—the confessing of sins to a priest; and "Reconciliation" because in the sacrament the reconciling love of God is celebrated.

4. What is the proper context for understanding the sacrament of Reconciliation?

The proper context for understanding Reconciliation is Jesus' call to conversion, to repent and to believe in his message. Our most fundamental conversion occurs at Baptism at which time all sins are forgiven and we receive the new life of Christ. This call to conversion continues, however, throughout all of our life. Our response to this call is expressed in our ongoing repentance, our turning from sin, that transforms our lives and is the fruit of God's plan.

5. What are the basic elements of the sacrament of Reconciliation?

The sinner's manifestation of sorrow by word or gesture, the sins confessed, the sinner's willingness to make satisfaction and the words of absolution by the priest, "I absolve you from your sins in the name of the Father, and of the Son, and of the Holy Spirit," constitute the essential elements of the sacrament of Reconciliation.

6. How does Jesus Christ help us in the sacrament of Reconciliation?

a) Jesus forgives mortal sin and restores the divine life of sanctifying grace in ever greater abundance.

b) Jesus also forgives all venial sins which we confess with contrition and gives us an increase of the divine life of grace.

c) Jesus gives us a pledge of the graces needed to atone for past sins, to avoid sin in the future, and to live the Christian life.

d) Jesus removes all or part of the temporal punishment due for our sins, depending on the depth of our sorrow and the strength of our purpose of amendment.

7. What must a person coming to Reconciliation do?

There are three aspects to a person's participation in the sacrament of Reconciliation: contrition, confession and satisfaction or penance.

8. What is contrition?

Contrition is sorrow for and hatred of our sins, together with the firm intention of not sinning in the future. Without contrition there can be no forgiveness or reconciliation. God himself cannot forgive a sin if we are not sorry or do not want to give it up.

9. What are the qualities of true contrition?

a) We must mean what we say. We must truly hate sin and there must be a true resolve to reform our lives.

b) Our sorrow must be based on the love, or at least the fear, of God. If we are sorry for our sins only because we are in disgrace, because we are disgusted with ourselves, or for any other merely human reason, our sorrow is not true contrition.

c) We must be sorry for each of our mortal sins. It is not enough to be sorry for one and not another or to detest our sinfulness in general. When we sin mortally we separate ourselves from God. To be reunited with God, we must regret all of our mortal sins and resolve not to commit any of them again.

10. Are there different kinds of contrition?

There are two kinds of contrition, perfect and imperfect. They are different by reason of their motives. In each case we are sorry for our sins because they are an offense against God. In imperfect contrition the motive is fear of the justice of God and of the punishment which our sins deserve. In perfect contrition the motive is the goodness of God, which prompts us to love him above all else for his own sake and to be sorry that we have offended him.

Perfect contrition—even without the sacrament of Reconciliation—removes all sins, even mortal sins. In the sacrament of Reconciliation, however, even imperfect contrition suffices to remove our sins.

11. Why is confession a part of the sacrament of Reconciliation?

Confession is part of the sacrament of Reconciliation because the "confession (or disclosure) of sins, even from a simply human point of view, frees us and facilitates our reconciliation with others"—CCC 1455. Through personal confession to a priest sinners are helped to amend their ways and grow in the love of God.

12. How does confession help the sinner?

a) The urge to confess is natural to us humans. Sorrow or shame is lessened when shared with another.

b) Confession makes us conscious of our sinfulness. It forces us to think of our sins. We cannot bury them and forget about them. We have to face them time and time again. This has the effect of making us conscious of them and helping us to overcome them and to realize how weak we are and how merciful God is.

c) People need reassurance God has actually forgiven them. Sinners are not as apt to have this reassurance if they merely say in their hearts, "I am sorry." When Jesus forgave sins he announced the fact, in order that the sinner would know for sure that he or she was forgiven. In the parable of the Prodigal Son the younger son was sorry for sins. But he knew he had to go to his father and personally admit his guilt. Notice how the father blessed the repentant son for doing so (cf. Lk 15:11-31).

13. What sins must we confess in confession?

There are two levels of seriousness of sin: mortal sin and venial sin. (This is explained more fully in Section 31.)
We must confess all our mortal sins:

a) their number, as nearly as we can remember;

b) their kind, e.g., "I stole $100" (it is not enough to say "I broke the 7th commandment");

c) any circumstances which might change the nature of the sin, e.g., "My spouse has a violent temper and I was afraid."

We are encouraged to confess also our venial sins. However, this is not necessary. The reception of any of the other sacraments, an act of imperfect contrition or any virtuous act also removes venial sins.

If we truly forget to mention a mortal sin when receiving the sacrament of Reconciliation, the sin is forgiven nevertheless. We need not remain away from Communion nor go back to confession immediately. In our next confession we should say, "In my last confession I forgot to mention a serious sin," and then confess it.

14. What is meant by a "bad confession"?

A "bad confession" is one in which the penitent deliberately conceals a mortal sin. This renders the confession invalid and sinful and makes all future confessions invalid and sinful until the sin is confessed.

15. What is meant by a "resolution not to sin again"?

By a resolution not to sin again is meant a sincere intention not to sin again. Even God may not forgive a sin unless the sinner intends not to commit it again. Unless someone is resolved not to repeat an offense he or she can hardly be said to be sorry for it. The resolution to avoid sin in the future, therefore, is necessary for the forgiveness of sin.

In the case of venial sin, unless we are sorry for those we confess and intend not to commit them again we would do better not to confess them, since they are not forgiven. Only those venial sins which we intend to avoid in the future are pardoned.

In the case of mortal sins, unless we are sorry for all our mortal sins and intend not to commit any kind of mortal sin in the future, none of our sins are forgiven.

It is important to remember, however, that all God demands in the way of a resolution is that we truly and firmly intend to do our best. No one may safely say, "I am certain that I shall never commit this sin." All we can say is, "With God's help I shall do my best. I intend never to commit this sin again and shall keep away from anything that would cause me to sin again."

16. What is meant by satisfaction or penance?

Because many of our sins harm our neighbor, if we are truly sorry we must do that which is possible to make amends. For example, if we have stolen, we must make restitution. But all sin harms us and our spiritual lives in some way. In order to recover our spiritual health, therefore, it is necessary to make amends for our sins. This is the reason for the penance that is given by the priest. This penance can take various forms (prayer, works of mercy, voluntary sacrifices). Its purpose is to help us deepen our inner conversion and become truly virtuous people.

17. How do we prepare for the Sacrament of Reconciliation?

We prepare for Reconciliation by placing ourself in the presence of God and making an examination of conscience. An examination of conscience is a reasonable effort to recall the sins committed since our last confession. In examining our consciences, we must avoid two dangers: on the one hand, carelessness and lack of effort to recall our sins; on the other, anxiety and excessive soul-searching.

A good examination of conscience will also be concerned with the performance of good works. A person should ask questions such as, "Did I try to help my neighbor in time of need?" "Did I always speak kindly toward others?" A Christian must not only avoid sin, but must manifest love of God and neighbor in a positive manner. (Failure to do so is sometimes called a "sin of omission.")

18. How do we make an examination of conscience?

First of all, we pray to the Holy Spirit for the wisdom to recognize our sins and for the grace to be sorry for them. Next we call to mind the commandments of God and of the Church and the obligations of our state in life. Then we ask ourselves wherein we have failed to live up to the call of Christ in our lives. If we go to confession frequently we can simply ask ourselves whether we have sinned in thought, word or deed against God, neighbor or self since our last confession.

19. What is to be done if we find that we have no sins to confess or if our confessions become routine?

In the first case, we usually can discover sins and defects in ourselves if we examine our conscience more carefully on the subject of love or one of the other virtues. The holiest people are always well aware of their shortcomings.

In the second case, we should select one or two faults or failings for which we are truly sorry (instead of reciting a whole catalogue of "the usual venial sins") and make an effort to recall the number of times we have committed such sins.

In both cases it will help to seek the advice of our confessor.

20. What is the procedure for the sacrament of Reconciliation?

There are two ways to receive the sacrament of Reconciliation. One way is to make a private preparation and to approach a priest to go to confession.

There are two types of confessionals. One is the traditional confessional in which people are separated from the priest by a screen which makes identification difficult and preserves anonymity for those who desire it. The second way is to go "face to face." This method provides a more personal approach to the sacrament that many find helpful and satisfying.

Another way to celebrate Reconciliation is the communal penance service. Here a number of Christians meet together (usually in a church) and after the reading of the Scriptures make a general examination of conscience. Then they individually approach one of the priests to privately confess their sins and personally receive absolution.

21. What is the purpose of reading Scripture when receiving the sacrament of Reconciliation?

The purpose of Scripture reading is to help the sinner call to mind the mercy of God and to arouse in the person a sincere desire to reform his or her life.

Some people select a specific passage for use in a particular confession, but they also use the passage as a guide for examining their consciences day by day between receptions of this sacrament. For example, you might take the beatitude, *"Blessed are the peacemakers, /for they will be called children of God"—Mt 5:9.*

Using this every day you might ask yourself, "Do I bring peace to my family by the way I treat them? Do I cause hard feelings and disappointment?"

In a communal celebration the Scripture lesson is read by a lector for the benefit of the assembled congregation. In a private reception either the priest or the penitent can select a reading.

22. What is necessary for a worthy reception of the sacrament of Reconciliation?

a) examination of conscience;

b) sorrow for sin;

c) resolution to avoid sin in the future;

d) confession of sins;

e) acceptance of penance.

23. What is meant by "the punishment due to sin"?

The punishment for unrepented mortal sin is eternal separation from God, or hell. *"Then he will say to those on his left, 'Depart from me, you accursed, into the eternal fire prepared for the devil and his angels' "—Mt 25:41.*

Venial sin does not deserve such severe punishment. Yet one who sins venially still should try to make amends for those sins.

24. How does the sacrament of Reconciliation help us grow in the divine life?

a) The sacrament of Reconciliation not only forgives sin; it also develops virtues which make us more Christ-like.

b) Reconciliation is based on a sense of the holiness of God. The realization of the goodness of God must be the basis of all our sorrow. This realization should grow each time we say the act of contrition or go to confession.

c) Reconciliation reminds us of the great love God has for us. Love must engender love; we should grow in the love of God and neighbor each time we receive the sacrament.

d) Reconciliation increases our hope. We realize that even though we are sinners we can obtain from God the help we need to reach heaven.

25. Who is the minister of the Sacrament of Reconciliation?

The bishops and the priests who collaborate in the ministry of the bishop are ministers of the sacrament of Reconciliation. *"Whose sins you forgive are forgiven them, and whose sins you retain are retained—Jn 20:23.*

Practice

▲ We must receive the sacrament of Reconciliation when we are guilty of serious sin because we must become reconciled to God before we may approach the sacrament of the Holy Eucharist. It is not necessary to go to confession each time we receive Communion unless we have committed mortal sin.

▲ Catholics are bound under pain of mortal sin to go to confession at least once a year, but only if we are guilty of serious sin.

▲ You should not wait until the time of your next confession to begin the practice of examining your conscience. It is highly recommended that everyone make an examination of conscience every day. Just before retiring at night is a good time to do so. An effort to recall the sins committed during the day followed by an act of contrition for these as well as all past sins will help you advance spiritually.

▲ When using the open confessional or "face to face" approach, the penitent can receive the sacrament of Reconciliation in a more relaxed manner. This approach encourages in-depth reflection and discussion of the current state of the sinner's relationship with God and neighbor. It invites a dialogue which will lead to a better understanding of the penitent's condition, making it easier for the priest to advise and guide the penitent toward a more grace-filled life.

▲   When going to confession, begin with words like these: "Bless me, Father, for I have sinned. It has been weeks since my last confession. I am married (single, widowed, etc.)" Next, either you or the priest may read a short passage from Scripture. Then, tell your sins. When you have confessed all of them say, "I am sorry for these and all of the sins of my whole life." The priest might then give some spiritual advice before assigning a penance to perform. After the sinner has expressed sorrow by praying an act of contrition the priest gives the sinner absolution. End by saying, "Thank you, Father," and leave the confessional area.

▲   There are special occasions—an emergency situation or the presence of a large number of penitents and a lack of enough confessors; for example—where a priest can give "general absolution" without individual confession. In this case, all sins are forgiven if all the other conditions for forgiveness have been met. It is required, however, that anyone who has committed a mortal sin must confess that sin to a priest in confession at the earliest possible opportunity.

Part IV: CHRIST'S ABIDING PRESENCE:
THE SACRAMENTS

Section 27 **The Anointing of the Sick**

Is anyone among you sick? [You] should summon the presbyters of the church, and they should pray over [you] and anoint [you] with oil in the name of the Lord, and the prayer of faith will save [you], and the Lord will raise [you] up. If [you have] committed any sins, [you] will be forgiven—Jas 5:14-15.

ON ALMOST EVERY PAGE of the Gospels we read of Jesus curing or healing different people from almost every type of disease and physical ailment. Jesus had a deep sympathy and compassion for the sick. He was able to restore health to those with whom he came in contact.

The Church, the new Body of Jesus Christ, shares the same concern for those suffering from all forms of ailments, whether physical, mental or emotional. Thus it is fitting for the Church to have a special sacrament for its members who are suffering from a serious illness.

Throughout history the Church encouraged many of its members to establish hospitals and various institutions for the care of the sick, the diseased and the dying. Many members have joined religious communities of priests, brothers or sisters whose mission is to minister to the sick. Many clergy and laity visit the sick or care for them in their homes on an ongoing basis. Ministers of care regularly take Holy Communion to the sick and homebound in most parishes.

The Church also has the sacrament of the Anointing of the Sick to offer those who are seriously ill. Based on the example and the commands of Jesus himself, the Church uses the special grace of this sacrament to bring strength, consolation, comfort and reassurance to those who are frightened or anxious over serious sickness or imminent death.

1. What is the Anointing of the Sick?

The Anointing of the Sick, along with Reconciliation, is one of the two sacraments of healing. The Anointing of the Sick is the sacrament by which Jesus, through the anointing and prayers of a priest, gives health and strength to a person who is seriously ill.

2. What does Jesus accomplish through the Anointing of the Sick?

Through the Anointing of the Sick, Jesus:

a) increases the divine life in an ill person;

b) sometimes restores health to that person;

c) gives the graces needed to accept the illness;

d) forgives sin and removes the temporal punishment due to sin.

When confession is impossible, Jesus forgives even mortal sin through this sacrament.

3. What is the sign of the Anointing of the Sick ?

The sign of this sacrament is the anointing with a special oil, called the oil of the sick, together with the words of the priest, "Through this holy anointing may the Lord in his love and mercy help you with the grace of the Holy Spirit. May the Lord who frees you from sin save you and raise you up." While praying, the priest anoints the sick person on the forehead and the palms.

4. How is the Anointing of the Sick administered?

It is important to recall that the Anointing of the Sick is both a liturgical and communal celebration. As with the other sacraments it is most appropriately celebrated within the Eucharist. If it is celebrated communally but apart from the Eucharist, a group of seriously ill people gather with their friends and family to receive the anointing in common. Since the sick and elderly should be a special concern to all of the members of the Church it is fitting to show this concern publicly. The ill are thus encouraged and strengthened by the presence of others while those attending the liturgy can begin to see the Christian value of accepting and offering up one's pain and suffering.

The Anointing of the Sick begins with the priest calling to prayer those assembled. They begin with an admission of guilt for sin and prayer for forgiveness. A short service of the Word of God follows. The priest reads passages revealing the healing activity of Jesus. Then he invites those who are witnessing the sacrament to join him in prayer on behalf of the sick.

The priest then silently lays his hand on each sick person. This is an invocation to Jesus to come and cure the illness. If the oil of the sick was not previously blessed by a bishop the priest now blesses it. The actual anointing follows. Those attending the anointing conclude the liturgy by praying together the Lord's Prayer.

5.   Who may receive the Anointing of the Sick?

Anyone who is seriously ill due to sickness or old age may receive this sacrament. Prudent judgment is all that is necessary to determine whether the sickness is serious enough to warrant the sacrament. The sick person need not be in danger of death. For example, an elderly person who is in a weakened condition may be anointed even though no specific serious illness is present. A person undergoing surgery because of a dangerous illness may be anointed. Sick children who have sufficient use of reason to be comforted by this sacrament also may be anointed.

6.   Is the Anointing of the Sick given only to the dying?

Not every seriously sick person dies. In addition, some

illnesses, such as terminal cancer, can last for several months before a person dies. It would be wrong to deny people the consolation of this sacrament and its actual graces until they are on their deathbed.

To accompany the sacrament of the Anointing of the Sick the Church has developed other last rites for the dying. These include holy Viaticum (Communion), the prayers for the dying and the Apostolic Blessing.

In the situation where a person is in a coma the Anointing of the Sick may be given conditionally, that is, the priest will presume that the person truly would like to receive it and proceed on that assumption.

Practice

▲ Those who have the care of a sick person should call a priest as soon as they discover the illness is serious. The person, fortified by the actual graces of this sacrament, can then honestly face life or death, whichever God in his providence has designated.

▲ For a visit by a priest to a sick person provide the following items: a crucifix, the two blessed candles, a glass of water and a spoon. These articles should be on a table which is covered with a white linen cloth.

▲ When the priest comes to a home or hospital or nursing home on a sick call, the members of the family should remain with the sick person, except while the priest is hearing his or her confession.

▲ Catholics should be careful to let their parish priest know whenever there is any serious illness in the family. The priest can judge what ought to be done. In the case of a prolonged illness the priest or a minister of care will bring Communion even when there is no danger of death.

▲ If someone is injured seriously, a priest should be called immediately.

▲ A priest or pastoral minister can be called even though to all appearances death might already have taken place or the person's death may have been declared by a doctor. The prayers offered for the deceased will be a consolation to the departed's family and friends.

Part IV: CHRIST'S ABIDING PRESENCE: THE SACRAMENTS

Section 28 **Holy Orders**

Every high priest . . . is able to deal patiently with the ignorant and erring, for he himself is beset by weakness and so, for this reason, must make sin offerings for himself as well as for the people. No one takes this honor upon himself but only when called by God, just as Aaron was. In the same way, it was not Christ who glorified himself in becoming high priest, but rather the one who said to him:

> *"You are my son;
>   this day I have begotten you"—Heb 5:1-5.*

JESUS CHRIST, mediator between God and humans, is the eternal priest. In the crowning act of his priesthood he offered himself to the Father on the cross for our sake. But Christ was priest not only on the cross; in his very being he is the priest, and his priesthood is an eternal one: *"[Jesus], because he remains forever, has a priesthood that does not pass away. Therefore, he is always able to save those who approach God through him, since he lives forever to make intercession for them"—Heb 7:24-25.*

Jesus is not content to live his priesthood only in heaven. He desires to exercise that priesthood here on earth until the end of time. Jesus, the merciful priest who forgave sinners, the gentle priest who blessed the people, the zealous priest who sought out the lost sheep, the loving priest who offered himself and fed his disciples with his own flesh and blood, still lives and continues his priestly work in the world. He does so in a particular way by means of the sacrament of Holy Orders. Through the sacrament of Holy Orders Jesus gives to human beings the power of changing bread and wine into his body and blood and the power of forgiving sins.

Some people are shocked at the idea that a priest should claim to possess such powers. In reality, however, it is Jesus who continues to perform these wonders. Jesus chooses to forgive sinners, to teach and preach, to give the divine life, to renew his sacrifice on the cross through human beings, those whom he consecrates and empowers as his priests through the sacrament of Holy Orders.

Priests are given these powers so that all the members of the Pilgrim People of God who need these special services will have someone designated to care for their needs. A priest is ordained to provide spiritual services for the members of the Church. A priest is a builder of bridges who brings God to the people and the people to God.

> The priest is like "another Christ" because he is marked with an indelible character, making him, as it were, a living image of our Savior. The priest represents Christ who said, "As the Father has sent me, I also send you; he who hears you hears me"—Encyclical on the Development of Holiness of Priestly Life.

1. What are the sacraments of service?

Through Baptism, Confirmation and Eucharist we are initiated into the Church and come to share as a disciple in the life and mission of the Church. Through the sacraments of Reconciliation and the Anointing of the Sick we are healed and strengthened. In the sacraments of Holy Orders and Matrimony a Christian is commissioned in a special way to the service of others. These two sacraments, therefore, are sometimes called the "sacraments of service."

2. What is the sacrament of Holy Orders?

Holy Orders is best described as "the sacrament of apostolic ministry"—CCC 1536. Through this sacrament the mission that Christ gave to his apostles is continued in the life of the Church.

3. What do we mean when we speak of Christ's priesthood?

Jesus Christ is the high priest whose sacrifice of redemption has brought salvation to the human family. Christ shared his priesthood with the community of believers that is the Church. "Through the sacraments of Baptism and Confirmation the faithful are 'consecrated to be . . . a holy priesthood' "—CCC 1546. While the purpose of the ministerial priesthood differs from the priesthood of the faithful in essence and not only in degree, they remain interrelated. In fact, the purpose of the ministerial priesthood is to serve the priesthood of the faithful so that the mission of the Church might be fully realized.

4. How does the ministerial priesthood serve the Church?

Through the ministry of bishops and priests Christ is present as the head of the Church. The manner in which they participate in this presence is to exercise the sacred power which is given to them as Christ did: as a servant. The ministerial priesthood also acts in the name of the entire Church when it presents the Church's prayers to God.

5. What is the sign of the sacrament of Holy Orders?

The sign of this sacrament is the laying on of the hands by the bishop. When the apostles ordained deacons, priests or bishops they did so by the laying on of hands. *"For this reason, I remind you to stir into flame the gift of God that you have through the imposition of my hands"*—2 Tm 1:6.

6. Who administers Holy Orders?

Only a bishop can administer Holy Orders.

7. What are the "grades" of Holy Orders?

There are three grades or states of ministry which can be conferred through the sacrament of Holy Orders: the episcopacy (bishop), the presbyterate (priest), and diaconate (deacon). The first two grades participate fully in the ministerial priesthood of Christ while the diaconate assists these two.

Like Baptism and Confirmation the sacrament of Holy Orders is permanent because it confers an indelible spiritual character.

First among the Church's ministries is the episcopate or ministry of the bishop. The bishop participates in the fullness of the sacrament of orders and is given the threefold office of teaching, governing and sanctifying. Through ordination and communion with the Bishop of Rome, the pope, a bishop becomes a member of the college of bishops and shares concern and responsibility for the well-being of all the Churches. A diocesan bishop is pastor of a diocese or "local church."

A priest is ordained to collaborate with the bishop in carrying out the mission of the Church. His ministry is exercised in a special way in the celebration of the Eucharist (the Mass). United with the bishop and his brother priests in the presbyterate of a local church he ministers to God's people.

A deacon is ordained for a ministry of service that assists the bishop, especially in the ministry of charitable acts. A deacon may assist a priest or bishop at Mass, preach, distribute Holy Communion, baptize and witness at marriages and officiate at funerals.

8. What is the work of a bishop?

Bishops, as a group, replace the twelve apostles. They have the fullness of the priesthood. Their main work is to govern their diocese and to lead the Pilgrim People of God by teaching, ruling and sanctifying them.

9. What is the work of a priest?

The work of a priest is the work of Christ: teaching, sanctifying and ministering to the members of the Mystical Body of Christ.

a) Some priests are missionaries, carrying the gospel to other lands or doing missionary work in their own country.

b) Some priests are teachers in Catholic schools or chaplains of Catholic students in secular universities.

c) Some priests are engaged in administrative and specialized work.

d) Some priests are in monastic orders, living the life and doing the work which is special to the order or congregation to which they belong.

e) Most priests are working in parishes, as pastors or as associates of a pastor.

The unique function of all priests, whatever their field of special work, is to offer Mass and to pray the Liturgy of the Hours. These functions they perform officially, in the name of the whole Church.

10. What is the work of a priest in a parish?

The work of a priest in a parish is done in collaboration with the staff and other members of the parish. It partakes of something of each of the special fields outlined above.

The parish priest does missionary work. He has the care not only of the healthy members of the parish, but also of those who have fallen away, those who have married outside the Church and those who are lukewarm and weak in their faith. He also works for those who are not Catholics and tries to bring them into contact with the Catholic Church and its teachings.

The parish priest also teaches, instructing those who wish to come into full communion with the Church and teaching religion in the parish school and to children in religious education programs.

The parish priest is to provide spiritual care for the sick within the parish. He visits them in their homes and in the hospitals. He assures that the sick receive Holy Communion and he administers the Anointing of the Sick.

The parish priest baptizes, hears confessions, prepares couples for marriage, assists at weddings and buries the dead.

The parish priest acts as chaplain for various parish organizations. Many parish priests are chaplains of groups who are working in the lay apostolate: the Legion of Mary, Marriage Encounter, Cursillo and many other organizations of men, women and youth.

11. What is the work of a deacon?

There are two kinds of deacons, transitional and permanent. A transitional deacon is a student preparing for ordination to the priesthood. He is ordained a deacon usually near the end of this third year of seminary theology preparation. Most likely he spends part of his last year of training working full-time in a parish.

The permanent deacon is someone ordained to that office with no intention of becoming a priest. He may be married and often continues to hold a secular job. The permanent deacon's role should be primarily one of service in a parish or in some other capacity in a diocese. Some deacons visit the sick and those in prison, help the poor, or work with various service organizations. Others do marriage counseling, marriage preparation, baptisms, etc.

Both types of deaconate have as their responsibility to preach the gospel, serve at the altar and assist in various works of charity.

12. Who can be ordained?

The Church teaches that only a baptized adult male can validly receive the sacrament of Holy Orders. Ordinarily, in the Western or Latin rite only celibate men can be ordained priests or bishops.

Practice

▲ The role of the priest today is a demanding one. A priest must not only be a man of prayer, but also must be educated and well read, an expert organizer and motivator, an efficient administrator and a shrewd businessman. He must also possess the ability to effectively preside at liturgies and should be a good preacher.

▲ A priest is expected to be present at times of crises as well as moments of happiness and joy. A priest's life today is demanding and stressful. Your priest, as well as all priests, need your prayers and support as well as your cooperation and understanding.

▲ The sacrament of Holy Orders, once conferred, can never be undone or revoked. "Once a priest, always a priest." Under very special circumstances, however, a priest may be "laicized," or released from his promises or vows and made part of the laity once again.

Part IV: CHRIST'S ABIDING PRESENCE: THE SACRAMENTS

Section 29 **Marriage**

Be subordinate to one another out of reverence for Christ. Wives should be subordinate to their husbands as to the Lord. For the husband is head of his wife just as Christ is head of the church, he himself the savior of the body. As the church is subordinate to Christ, so wives should be subordinate to their husbands in everything. Husbands, love your wives, even as Christ loved the church and handed himself over for her to sanctify her, cleansing her by the bath of water with the word, that he might present to himself the church in splendor, without spot or wrinkle or any such thing, that she might be holy and without blemish. So [also] husbands should love their wives as their own bodies. He who loves his wife loves himself. For no one hates his own flesh but rather nourishes and cherishes it, even as Christ does the church, because we are members of his body.

> *"For this reason a man shall leave [his] father*
> *and [his] mother*
> *and be joined to his wife,*
> *and the two shall become one flesh."*

This is a great mystery, but I speak in reference to Christ and the church. In any case, each one of you should love his wife as himself, and the wife should respect her husband—Eph 5:21-33.

AFTER READING THIS QUOTATION from St. Paul, some feel that he is degrading women. St. Paul could not and did not mean to do so. What Paul was trying to get at is that the union between a Christian and Jesus is so close as to be similar to a grafting onto each other. Paul sees this same type of union between husband and wife. Two do become one.

Everyone knows that parts of a body cannot be in rebellion or disobedient to the total person. Neither should husband and wife fail to love or be "subject" to each other. Paul sees husband and wife as totally united and working in harmony in the Lord— not engaged in some power struggle with each other.

Within the Mystical Body of Christ each member has his or her function to perform. *"Some people God has designated in the church to be, first, apostles; second, prophets; third, teachers"—1 Cor 12:28.* Certain of the sacraments celebrate our vocation within the Pilgrim People of God and give us the graces to live up to that vocation. It is the sacrament of Marriage that confers the vocation of spouse and parent. Christian husbands and wives, therefore, have a special sacrament which fits them for the very important office which is theirs. The sacrament of Marriage sanctifies the natural love of man and woman, raises it from the natural order to the supernatural and makes it the vehicle of God's grace.

The intimate partnership of married life and love has been established by the Creator and qualified by his love. It is rooted in the conjugal covenant of irrevocable personal consent. Hence, by that human act whereby spouses mutually bestow and accept each other, a relationship arises which by divine will and in the eyes of society, too, is a lasting one. For the good of the spouses and their offspring as well as of society, the existence of this sacred bond no longer depends on human decisions alone.

For God Himself is the author of matrimony, endowed as it is with various benefits and purposes. All of these have a very decisive bearing on the continuation of the human race, on the personal development and eternal destiny of

206

the individual members of a family and on the dignity, stability, peace and prosperity of the family itself and of human society as a whole. By their very nature, the institution of matrimony itself and conjugal love are ordained for the procreation and education of children and find in them their ultimate crown—Dogmatic Constitution on the Church.

1. Who established marriage?

God is the author of marriage, the intimate partnership of life and love of a man and a woman. It is true to say then that the vocation of marriage came from God the Creator and is a reflection of the love that is God, in whose likeness we are created. From the very beginning this marital love is to be a permanent and faithful union. It also is directed to "the begetting and upbringing of children"—Pastoral Constitution on the Church in the Modern World.

2. What is the purpose of marriage?

The purpose of marriage is to bring about both the enrichment and personal fulfillment of the couple and the continuation of the human race by bringing children into the world. It is difficult to separate these two goals because one brings about and strengthens the other. The presence of children causes the continued personal development of the couple as they must adjust and perhaps even sacrifice for the welfare of each other and the children.

3. What is the sacrament of Marriage (or Matrimony)?

The marriage covenant, by which a man and a woman establish between themselves a partnership of their whole lives, is by its nature ordered to the well-being of the spouses and the procreation and upbringing of children. Jesus Christ himself raised the covenant between baptized persons to the dignity of a sacrament.

By his presence at the wedding at Cana Jesus affirmed the goodness of marriage and proclaimed "that thenceforth marriage will be an efficacious sign of Christ's presence"—CCC 1613. For Christians, then, marriage became a sacrament.

4. What is the sign of the sacrament of Marriage?

The sign of the sacrament of Marriage is the expression on the part of the bride and groom of their consent to marriage.

5. When does the sacrament of Marriage occur?

The sacrament of Marriage occurs when a baptized man and a baptized woman freely give their consent to the covenant of marriage. When this consent is consummated by marital intercourse the marriage is said to be indissoluble: i.e., it has been sealed by God and a marital bond is present that can never be dissolved.

6. What are some of the graces of Marriage?

Some of the graces that Jesus pledges to provide throughout the life of a marriage are:

a) the grace of dialogue or communication, which enables spouses to better understand themselves and express their feelings to each other;

b) the grace of unity, which helps a couple solve problems which are divisive;

c) the grace of healing wounds caused by acts of selfishness, uncharitableness, etc., by the spouses;

d) the grace of parenthood, which assists parents in raising and educating their children;

e) the grace of sanctification, which assists spouses in helping each other remove all forms of evil and sin from their home and to acquire virtuous habits and conduct.

The graces of the sacrament of Marriage are given not just

on the day of marriage but continually in the daily life of a Christian husband and wife. They are meant to work in conjunction with, not independently of, the graces of the other sacraments. For example, married people receive the sacraments of Reconciliation and the Holy Eucharist with their vocation in mind—seeking by means of confession to rid themselves of faults which prevent a more perfect marriage union and family life and by means of Communion to grow in love for one another in Christ.

7. What did our Lord teach about the sacrament of Marriage?

The Pharisees approached and asked, "Is it lawful for a husband to divorce his wife?" They were testing him. He said to them in reply, "What did Moses command you?" They replied, "Moses permitted him to write a bill of divorce and dismiss her." But Jesus told them, "Because of the hardness of your hearts he wrote you this commandment. But from the beginning of creation, 'God made them male and female. For this reason a man shall leave his father and mother [and be joined to his wife], and the two shall become one flesh.' So they are no longer two but one flesh. Therefore what God has joined together, no human being must separate." In the house the disciples again questioned him about this. He said to them, "Whoever divorces his wife and marries another commits adultery against her; and if she divorces her husband and marries another, she commits adultery"— Mk 10:2-12.

Jesus taught:

a) that Marriage was instituted by God;

b) that husband and wife find their fulfillment in each other;

c) that Marriage is to last for life;

d) that Marriage must be between one man and one woman.

8. What did Jesus do for Marriage by elevating it to the dignity of a sacrament?

For as God of old made Himself present to His people through a covenant of love and fidelity, so now the Savior of man and the Spouse of the Church comes into the lives of married Christians through the sacrament of Matrimony. He abides with them thereafter so that, just as He loved the Church and handed Himself over on her behalf, the spouses may love each other with perpetual fidelity, through mutual self-bestowal—Pastoral Constitution on the Church in the Modern World.

In making Marriage a sacrament Jesus gave it a new meaning, a new beauty and a new power of sanctifying. Marriage is now not merely the lawful union of husband and wife; it is a source of holiness, a means of a closer union of each spouse with God as well as with each other. The union of husband and wife in Marriage is a mirror or symbol of the union of Christ and his Church.

Finally, by making Marriage a sacrament Jesus gives couples graces which make possible their continued personal growth in comforting and supporting each other.

9. In what way is the union of husband and wife a symbol of the union of Christ and his Church?

The union between Christ and his Church is a vital, life-giving union. The union of husband and wife is a also a vital life-giving union, imparting grace to their souls.

The union between Christ and his Church is an organic union, the union of head and body. The union of husband and wife is a union of two in one flesh and one spirit.

The union between Christ and his Church is a union of infinite love, love which is constant and unwavering, love which is self-sacrificial. The union of husband and wife is also a union of love, love which is exclusively given to one's spouse, love which is unselfish, love which lasts as long as life itself.

It is because of this symbolism that the family born of the sacrament of Marriage is considered to be a "domestic Church," because the family in a unique way carries forward the mission of the Church.

10. Who administers the sacrament of Marriage?

In the Latin rite the bride and groom actually administer this sacrament to each other. Thus, the first gift they give to each other as husband and wife is the gift of the divine life.

A priest or deacon officiates at the wedding ceremony as the official representative of the Church. Along with the wedding party and the rest of the congregation, he witnesses the exchange of the wedding vows.

11. What laws safeguard marriage?

Since marriage was instituted by God, there are divine laws, such as the indissolubility and unity of marriage.

Since marriage was made a sacrament by Jesus, the head of the Church, there are laws made by the Church which protect it. For example, it is the Church law which fixes the age for a valid marriage, sets rules for interfaith marriages, etc.

Since marriage is the basis of human society, the state makes laws governing it. Such laws are those which require a marriage license, blood tests, legal age for marriage, etc.

12. What did Jesus teach about divorce?

Jesus said, *"Therefore what God has joined together, no human being must separate"—Mk 10:9.* He clearly taught, *"Whoever divorces his wife and marries another commits adultery against her"—Mk 10:11.*

In the Old Testament Moses had permitted divorce to the Jews under certain circumstances *"because of the hardness of your hearts"—Mk 10:5.* The Old Law was imperfect in this as well as in other respects. Christ restored Marriage to what God had intended in the beginning, a union of one man and one woman for life. He taught that an attempted marriage following a divorce would be invalid and adulterous.

Divorced Catholics who have not received an annulment are not free to marry again. People in this situation, however, are full members of the Church and free to receive the sacraments.

Anyone considering marrying a divorced person should consult a parish priest for advice.

13. Has the state the power to grant a divorce?

The state has no power to dissolve the spiritual bond of a valid sacramental Marriage. Consequently the Church does not ordinarily recognize the validity of a subsequent marriage of divorced persons. The state may, however, end the civil aspects of a marriage. This is called in civil law a "divorce."

14. Has the Church the power to grant a divorce?

Not even the Church has the power of dissolving a valid, sacramental Marriage which has been consummated. However, because the institution of marriage finds its legal expression in terms of a contract it is appropriate for the Church to examine a failed marriage in order to determine whether there existed a valid contract to begin with. In other words, it is universally understood that certain elements must be present before a contract can be considered valid, and, of course, if a contract was entered into invalidly then that contract is not binding.

For example, if a party agrees to enter a marital contract but agreement was brought about by force or fear or fraud, then the contract is not binding. In such instances a diocesan Marriage Tribunal after a thorough investigation may declare the marital contract invalid, thereby freeing the parties to enter into a subsequent valid union. Therefore, when the Church declares that a Marriage is annulled—i.e., grants an "annulment"—it is merely declaring that something existed at the time of the marriage which rendered it invalid from the very beginning.

Practice

▲ Marriage is a sacred covenant between the spouses and between them and God. A couple should prepare themselves for Marriage by prayer. Shortly before the wedding date couples should also receive the sacrament of Reconciliation.

▲ No one would accept a position from which he or she could never resign without a great deal of thought and investigation. No one would enter a profession without adequate preparation. Yet thousands enter into Marriage with little or no preparation. To remedy this situation most dioceses provide Pre-Cana conferences, Engaged Encounters or other types of Marriage preparation.

▲ Even after many years of marriage couples can derive great benefit from a Marriage Encounter or a Cana conference. In some places these programs are held regularly in various parishes throughout the diocese. They provide an excellent means of stirring up the graces that are in the married couple, in order that their union may become ever more perfect.

▲ Catholics must be married in one of the following ways in order to have a truly valid, sacramental Marriage. They must be married in the presence of a priest or a deacon and in the presence of two other witnesses. If the diocesan bishop grants a dispensation from canonical form, as in the case of a mixed marriage, the wedding can be performed by someone other than a Catholic priest. Catholics not married according to these rules are not considered to have received the sacrament of Marriage.

▲ The Church has set up certain impediments to Marriage— conditions which render a Marriage either unlawful or both unlawful and invalid. For example, the Church prohibits a Catholic from marrying a non-Catholic. When there is a sufficient reason to do so, the diocesan bishop may grant a dispensation from such impediments, provided the impediment does not affect the essence of Marriage.

▲ Couples planning Marriage should consult the parish priest of the bride several months before the wedding. Two Catholics should be married at Mass. Only for a serious reason should a Catholic couple deprive themselves of the great privilege of being married at Mass. At their wedding Mass the new couple may present the gifts of bread and wine and water to the priest. Thus their first action as husband and wife is to make an offering to God, their covenant partner. The couple may select the Scripture texts and certain other optional features for their wedding Mass.

▲ The minister of the non-Catholic party to an interfaith wedding may offer a congratulatory prayer when the wedding is celebrated in a Catholic church. A priest can do the same when a dispensation has been granted for the wedding to take place in a non-Catholic church.

▲ If a couple, because of serious and unresolvable problems, cannot continue to live together, separation and even civil divorce might have to take place. After a civil divorce has been granted, the couple can explore the possibility of annulment with a priest or a representative of the diocesan Marriage Tribunal. If there are no grounds for an annulment, then neither party is free to remarry.

▲ The Church encourages people who are divorced and remarried without an annulment to continue to participate in the life of their parishes. "They are not separated from the Church, but they cannot receive Eucharistic Communion"—CCC 1665. Many dioceses and parishes offer special programs and support groups for divorced or separated Catholics.

Part IV: CHRIST'S ABIDING PRESENCE: THE SACRAMENTS

Section 30 **The Sacramentals**

Then children were brought to him that he might lay his hands on them and pray. The disciples rebuked them, but Jesus said, "Let the children come to me, and do not prevent them; for the kingdom of heaven belongs to such as these." After he placed his hands on them, he went away—Mt 19:13-15.

OUR LORD HAS GIVEN US seven sacraments as signs of his love and by which he sanctifies and strengthens us for our role in his Mystical Body. In imitation of Christ, the Church has given us the sacramentals, which sanctify the ordinary things of life, call down God's blessings upon us and remind us in a practical and vivid way of the truths by which we live. The Church blesses many of the objects which we use in daily life. We need never be out of reach of these blessings. We are never abandoned to our own weakness in any emergency. The Church is constantly at our side, asking God to bless us and the things we use.

1. What are sacramentals?

Sacramentals are "sacred signs which bear a resemblance to the sacraments. They signify effects, particularly of a spiritual nature which are obtained through the intercession of the Church. By them [people] are disposed to receive the chief effect of the sacraments, and various occasions in human life are rendered holy"—CCC 1667.

2. What constitutes a sacramental?

A sacramental includes a prayer and a specific sign appropriate to the purpose of a special ritual. Because all the baptized are called to sanctify life, lay people are able to preside at certain sacramental blessings. The closer such blessings are associated with the sacramental life of the Church, the more likely the administration of them is reserved to a person who has been ordained.

3. How do the sacramentals differ from the sacraments?

Christ instituted the sacraments; the Church the sacramentals. The sacraments were instituted to give grace; the sacramentals to impart a blessing or some special protection and to dispose us to receive grace.

4. What are some of the principal sacramentals?

The ceremonies, actions and prayers which surround the essential act in each sacrament are sacramentals. The anointings in Baptism, the prayers used in the Anointing of the Sick and the nuptial blessing given in Marriage are a few examples of such sacramentals.

The Sign of the Cross, holy water, the Rosary and the Stations of the Cross are examples of sacramentals which are used frequently.

5. What sacramentals are used on certain days during the year?

Candles are blessed and distributed on the feast of the Presentation of our Lord, also known as Candlemas Day, Feb. 2. The blessing of throats is given on St. Blaise Day, Feb. 3. Blessed ashes are placed on our forehead on Ash Wednesday, to remind us of our death and to urge us to do penance during Lent. Blessed palms are distributed on Palm Sunday, as a reminder of Our Lord's triumphal entry into Jerusalem to begin his Passion.

The blessing of fields takes place on August 15. Other sacramentals, such as the blessing of a home or of a mother during pregnancy and a blessing after childbirth, can be given at any time.

6. How should we use the sacramentals?

We should use the sacramentals with faith and reverence, as the Church instructs us to do. We must avoid superstition in our use of medals and other blessed objects, remembering that they, as well as the other sacramentals, produce their effect not automatically but as a result of the prayers of the Church and the devotion they inspire in us.

Practice

▲ Many of the laity wish to associate themselves with various religious orders in order to participate in their prayers and good works of those orders. Originally these lay people were allowed to wear the religious habit of the order with which they were associated. Now they wear the scapular—two small pieces of cloth connected by strings and worn over the shoulders. There are sixteen scapulars in which Catholics may be invested. The oldest and most common of these is the scapular of Our Lady of Mount Carmel, by which the wearer shares in the fruits of the good works and prayers of the Carmelite Order.

▲ In place of the actual scapular one may wear the scapular medal, which has an image of the Sacred Heart on one side and of Our Lady on the other.

▲ Pictures, statues and crucifixes can be an aid in prayer and in keeping us mindful of God and the things of God. Every Catholic home should have a crucifix or some religious picture or statue in a prominent place.

▲ Care should be used in selecting religious objects. They should be in good taste, the kind that inspire devotion rather than mere sentiment. Good religious art is available. Catholics need not be satisfied with anything less.

Part V: LIFE IN CHRIST

Section 31 **Foundations of the Moral Life**

> *When they had finished breakfast, Jesus said to Simon Peter, "Simon, son of John, do you love me more than these?" He said to him, "Yes, Lord, you know that I love you." He said to him, "Feed my lambs." He then said to him a second time, "Simon, son of John, do you love me?" He said to him, "Yes, Lord you know that I love you." He said to him, "Tend my sheep." He said to him the third time, "Simon, son of John, do you love me?" Peter was distressed that he had said to him a third time, "Do you love me?" and he said to him, "Lord, you know everything; you know that I love you." [Jesus] said to him, "Feed my sheep"—Jn 21: 15-17*

TOO OFTEN Catholic moral teaching has been characterized as a series of rules and regulations, the violation of which results in sin. This portrayal has led to at least two unfortunate consequences. On the one hand some have dismissed Catholic moral teaching as too legalistic. On the other hand many Catholics, using the avoidance of sin as their only goal, have been content with observing the minimal requirements of the law.

In fact, the Church itself teaches that any temptation to reduce it's moral teaching to a formula of meeting the external limitations of legal demands must be resisted. For Roman Catholics the moral life flows from our relationship with God. If we truly love and worship the triune God then our thoughts, words, and deeds should be faithful and consistent with our professed love and faith. Anything less reveals our failure to fully understand and live according to our special relationship with God.

Such failure damages the unity God seeks to establish between him and us and between us and his Church. The separation from the divine caused by our freely chosen behavior and attitudes (whether they lead us to acts of commission or omission) is the very essence of sin.

1. Where do Christians get the strength to live a moral life?

Our ability to live of the moral life begins with our being united with Christ in Baptism and becoming temples of the Holy Spirit. It is the Spirit that guides and heals us as we seek to live as disciples of the Lord Jesus.

2. What is the basis of human dignity?

The source of our dignity as human persons is the fact that we are made in the image and likeness of God (cf. Gn 1:27). Gifted with the immortal soul we are meant to enjoy true happiness. We are able to realize this destiny because our human reason can understand God's plan for creation and our free will is able to direct us to seek what is good and true.

3. Why, then, do we sin?

Because of human misuse of free will at the beginning of history humans are all inclined toward evil. The power of this inclination, however, can be overcome by God's gift of divine life, which is grace.

4. How can we determine the morality of our actions?

Traditionally we have said that there are three sources for determining the morality of a human action: the object, or matter, of the action; the intention of the person performing the action; and the circumstance surrounding the action.

5. When is an action morally good?

For an action to be morally good the objective act, the purpose, and the circumstances all must be good. There are some acts, however, that—apart from intention or circumstance—are always morally illicit (e.g., perjury and adultery).

6. How does a person come to know, in a personal way, moral truth?

It is our consciences that call each of us to do good and avoid evil. Our consciences also judge specific moral choices. We are obliged to follow our consciences and have the freedom to do so. Because our consciences can be misguided because of ignorance, however, we are responsible for their proper formation.

7. How does a person form a good conscience?

Because sin primarily offends God we must learn what God expects of us in our moral behavior. Guidelines for moral living are given throughout the sacred Scriptures. Moral theologians under the guidance of the Church have written about moral problems and questions. The Church itself, through its teaching authority (or magisterium), also gives much guidance on the moral life. Once we are aware of these various teachings we are able to make the practical judgments about the goodness or evil of our own personal actions.

8. What is sin?

"Against you alone have I sinned; /I have done such evil in your sight—Ps 51:6. Sin is saying no to God and to God's plan for us. Sin is willful disobedience to God. This disobedience may be an action, a thought, a desire, an intention, or it may be an omission or failure to love.

Sin also offends our neighbor and ourselves. For example, God's seventh commandment forbids us to steal. In the act of theft we offend our neighbors by depriving them of some of their property. We make possible the ruin of our own reputation when our sinful crime becomes public knowledge. Our sins also disrupt the common good of the whole community.

9. How can an internal act be sinful?

Actually, the essence of sin lies in the thought, desire or intention. As soon as we deliberately desire or intend to perform a sinful act we have already offended God. We may lack the courage or the opportunity of putting our desire into action, but that does not change the fact that we have withdrawn our obedience from God. All actions for which we are responsible begin with a sinful thought; the action is merely the carrying out of that desire or intention. This fact explains these words of Christ: *"But I say to you, everyone who looks at a woman with lust has already committed adultery with her in his heart"*—Mt 5:28.

10. What are the different kinds of sins?

The different kinds of sins are:

a) original sin, the sin of our first parents. We suffer from the effects of original sin, but we are not personally guilty of it.

b) actual or personal sin, a sin which we ourselves commit. Personal sin may be mortal or venial.

11. What is mortal sin?

If anyone sees [someone] sinning, if the sin is not deadly, he should pray to God and he will give [the sinner] life. This is only for those whose sin is not deadly. There is such a thing as deadly sin, about which I do not say you should pray. All wrongdoing is sin, but there is sin that is not deadly—1 Jn 5:16-17.

Mortal sin is called deadly because it causes us to lose the divine life of sanctifying grace and consequently God no longer lives in us. Mortal sin is a serious offense against God. In order for a sin to be mortal three conditions must be fulfilled:

  a) The offense in itself must be serious. For example, to tell
     a lie which would seriously injure someone's reputation
     would be a mortal sin; to tell an ordinary lie, which does
     no serious injury, would be a venial sin.

  b) The person who commits the sin must realize what he or
     she is doing and that it is a serious offense against God.
     For example, to kill a person deliberately and unjustly
     would be a mortal sin; to kill accidentally would be no
     sin.

  c) There must be full consent of the will. A person acting
     under any circumstance which deprives the person of
     free will would not be guilty of mortal sin. For example,
     to be forced to commit a sin under threat of violence to
     oneself or another would not be a mortal sin.

12. What are the effects of mortal sin?

  a) Mortal sin destroys our divine life; hence we use the
     word "mortal," meaning "death dealing."

     *But what profit did you get then from the things of
     which you are now ashamed? For the end of those
     things is death. But now that you have been freed
     from sin and have become slaves of God, the benefit
     that you have leads to sanctification, and its end is
     eternal life. For the wages of sin is death, but the gift
     of God is eternal life in Christ Jesus our Lord—Rom
     6:21-23.*

  b) Mortal sin breaks our relationship with God. It causes
     us to turn from doing God's will to doing our own will.

  c) If a person dies in a state of mortal sin, he or she has
     forever alienated himself or herself from God.

223

13. What is venial sin?

Venial sin is a less serious offense against God. Venial sin is a sin which does not sever our relationship with God, but which does weaken our love for God. *"We all fall short in many respects"—Jas 3:2.*

With venial sin, either the offense itself is not a serious matter (e.g., an ordinary lie of excuse, a small theft, a slight disrespect towards God) or else the sinner is not sufficiently aware of the seriousness of his or her action or does not give full consent of the will.

14. Can a sin be fully deliberate and yet be only venial?

Yes. Such a sin is called a deliberate venial sin. Deliberate venial sin weakens the will and paves the way for mortal sin. Deliberate venial sin also lessens the intimacy between us and God. Habitual venial sin brings about a state of spiritual lukewarmness that is very dangerous.

15. How do we know whether an action is sinful?

Our conscience tells us whether an action is right or wrong, a mortal or a venial sin.

16. Can mortal sin be forgiven?

God will forgive any mortal sins and any number of them if the sinner truly repents. God not only forgives the sin but he also restores the divine life and the gifts of faith, hope and love.

17. What happens to one who dies in the state of mortal sin?

One who dies in the state of mortal sin will continue to reject God for all eternity. Such a person will never repent, will never turn back to God. Such a person must, therefore, spend eternity in hell.

18. What is hell?

Hell is a state of eternal damnation. When a person, whose destiny is God, has died rejecting God, the person must spend eternity deprived of God and therefore of all happiness. *"Then he will say to those on his left, 'Depart from me, you accursed, into the eternal fire prepared for the devil and his angels' "*—Mt 25:41.

19. Does the all-merciful God send anyone to hell?

Actually, it is not God but sinners who send themselves to hell. Mortal sin is a rejection of God. Hell is mortal sin carried to its logical and eternal conclusion. God who loves all people certainly desires their salvation and gives them every opportunity to repent and be converted. He alone knows whether anyone actually rejects his merciful overtures.

20. What is purgatory?

Purgatory is a state of purification after death for those who die without repenting of their venial sins. The souls in purgatory possess the divine life and know they are saved; but they do not have the vision of God. They cannot help themselves, but can be helped by the prayers and sacrifices of the faithful on earth and the souls in heaven.

21. What is temptation?

Temptation is an inducement to sin. Deliberate sin, whether mortal or venial, does not "just happen;" it is preceded by an inducement to sin, which is called temptation.

22. What are the sources of temptation?

The sources of temptation are three: the world about us, the devil and our own inclinations to sin. These inclinations are the capital sins.

23. What are the capital sins?

The capital sins are seven: pride, avarice, lust, envy, gluttony, anger and sloth. They are called "capital" sins because they are tendencies or inclinations to a wide variety of specific acts that are sinful.

Practice

▲ Sin by definition has communal consequences. Therefore, whenever we examine our conscience we should attempt to realize how our moral failures contribute to the pain and suffering of our sinful world. Recognizing our own participation in the communal effects of sin we should seek forgiveness through a penance that more effectively brings our cure to a broken world. For example, if we find we are guilty of wastefulness our penance should include some effort to recycle materials we use.

▲ Keep in mind that there are situations that might appear to the objective observer to be a mortal sin but because of subjective influences—such as ignorance, fear or other factors—an individual might be free from moral guilt in a particular case. It is not wise to make these judgements on one's own, however. In case of doubt consult a prudent confessor for advice and counsel.

▲ Catholics are urged to avoid the "near occasions of sin," that is, people, places or things that provide easy temptation to sin. For example, the Church publishes its own movie ratings system that instructs the faithful which films are acceptable for children, teenagers and/or adults and which are morally objectionable for everyone.

Part V: LIFE IN CHRIST

Section 32 **Foundations of the Moral Life (Continued)**

> *"No one who lights a lamp hides it away or places it [under a bushel basket], but on a lampstand so that those who enter might see the light. The lamp of the body is your eye. When your eye is sound, then your whole body is filled with light, but when it is bad, then your body is in darkness. Take care, then, that the light in you not become darkness. If your whole body is full of light, and no part of it is in darkness, then it will be as full of light as a lamp illuminating you with its brightness" —Lk 11:33-36.*

IN A SENSE our vocation as human beings finds its meaning in our capacity to give. Whether it be sharing our skills and talents with others or offering financial and/or emotional support to those in need, we all have numerous opportunities to give something of ourselves to others.

Sometimes, we may feel that the only "others" we need to be concerned with are the members of our family or those who live in our immediate community. This perspective is not wholly consistent with our Christian tradition. Our "light" and "salt" is not only meant to be shared at home but wherever there is need. Certainly our responsibilities are clearer the closer people are to us, but we should never loose sight that Jesus' call to discipleship cannot be limited to concerns defined by proximity.

1. What is the social foundation of the moral life?

Christ has told us that we cannot separate the love of God from the love of neighbor. Made by God to be social in nature, humans live in society. In fact certain social institutions, such as the family and the state, are necessary for the fulfillment of our human vocation.

The purpose of all societal institutions must be to promote the good of the human person. To enable society to achieve this proper purpose some persons are invested with authority, which we are obliged to obey. All authority, including the authority of government, however, must work for the "common good." Authority which acts unjustly or contrary to the moral good need not be obeyed.

2. What is the common good?

Traditional Catholic teaching has described the common good as "the sum total of social conditions enabling groups and individuals to achieve perfection more readily and completely"— Pastoral Constitution on the Church in the Modern World. The common good involves three essential elements: respect for each person, the social well-being and development of the group itself, and the promotion of peace between individuals and groups. It is a primary responsibility of the state to promote the common good.

3. What is the responsibility of individuals to promote the common good?

Because of our individual human dignity it is our personal responsibility, each according to his or her position and role, to promote the common good. This is done at home, at work, and in the public life of our local and national communities.

4. What is social justice?

Social justice is intimately connected to the common good. It is the effort to help individuals and groups realize those conditions under which they can obtain that which they are due.

Social justice involves respecting the dignity of the human person and the rights associated with that dignity. This respect allows us to care for others, especially the disadvantaged, as well as those with whom we disagree. Dignity is the basis for the equality of all persons and for the sense of human solidarity by which material goods are distributed and shared.

5. What is the moral law?

The moral law, whose source is the wisdom of God, lays out for humankind a way of living and acting that allows us to experience the true happiness that God has promised us. The moral law has been expressed in various ways.

6. What is the "natural" moral law?

The natural moral law is the ability given to human beings by God at the time of creation to know what is morally right and what is morally wrong. The moral rules that we come to know through human reason are universal, permanent, and unchangeable. The natural law, though not always easily understood, is the basis for the development of all civil law that protects the dignity of the human person.

7. What are the "Old Law" and the "New Law?"

The "Old Law" or "Law of Moses" was given by God to the chosen people, Israel, and is summed up by the Ten Commandments. The Old Law is imperfect because it merely tells us what is contrary to the love of God and neighbor but does not offer the grace to live the law of love fully.

The "New Law," given by Christ and expressed in the Beatitudes, fulfills the moral prescriptions of the Old Law and "releases their hidden potential and has new demands arise from them"—CCC 1968. The New Law of Christ calls for a true reform of the human heart.

8. How do we come to know moral truth?

In addition to what we can know by human reason, we also can learn about moral truth from the pastors of the Church: the pope and bishops. In the authentic teaching of the Church, which we call the magisterium, "the 'deposit' of Christian moral teaching has been handed on, a deposit composed of a characteristic body of rules, commandments, and virtues proceeding from faith in Christ and animated by charity"—CCC 2033. This teaching of the magisterium is to be observed and respected by all who seek to live a moral life.

9. Why does the Church create its own laws?

The laws (or precepts) of the Church are designed to help us live moral lives. Like Jesus himself, however, the Church emphasizes that changing our hearts and loving our neighbors is much more important than fulfilling the minimum requirements of the law (cf. Mk 2:23-28).

10. What are the laws or precepts of the Church?

The precepts of the Church are laws given to us by Church authorities and provide the minimal basis for a prayerful moral life. The precepts are now described in the following manner:

The first precept, "You shall attend Mass on Sundays and holy days of obligation," requires the faithful to participate in the Eucharistic celebration when the Christian community gathers together on the day commemorating the Resurrection of the Lord.

The second precept, "You shall confess your sins at least once a year," ensures fitting preparation for the Eucharist by the reception of the sacrament of Reconciliation, which continues Baptism's work of conversion and forgiveness.

The third precept, "You shall humbly receive your Creator in Holy Communion at least during the Easter season," guarantees as a minimum the reception of the Lord's body and blood in connection with the Paschal feast, the origin and center of the Christian liturgy.

The fourth precept, "You shall keep holy the holy days of obligation," completes the Sunday observance by participation in the principal liturgical feasts which honor the mysteries of the Lord, the Virgin Mary, and the saints.

The fifth precept, "You shall observe the prescribed days of fasting and abstinence," assures times of asceses and penance which prepare us for liturgical feasts; they help us acquire mastery over our instincts and freedom of heart.

The faithful also have the duty of providing for the support of the material needs of the Church each according to his [or her] abilities—CCC 2042-2043.

Practice

▲ The Church in every country names certain feasts "holy days of obligations." Catholics are required to attend Mass on those days on the same basis as Sundays. The holy days of obligation in the United States are the Solemnity of Mary (January 1), the Ascension of Our Lord (forty days after Easter), the Assumption of Our Lady (August 15), All Saints (November 1) the Immaculate Conception (December 8) and Christmas (December 25).

▲ The Church has developed laws of fast and abstinence that oblige us to limit the quality and/or quantity of food we eat on certain days. Fasting limits the quantity of food; abstinence forbids the eating of meat.

On days of fast, only one full meal is allowed for anyone over 18 but not yet 59 years of age. Two other meatless meals, sufficient to maintain strength, may be taken according to one's needs. Eating between meals is not permitted, but liquids including milk and fruit juices are allowed. Everyone over 14 years of age is bound to observe the law of abstinence, which means that no meat at all is to be eaten.

Current Church rules require only two days of fasting and abstinence—Ash Wednesday and Good Friday. The Church does, however, recommend we pick several other days of our own choice for either fasting or abstinence. Fridays throughout the year and all weekdays of Lent are good days for observing these salutary practices, which both give praise to God and help us develop discipline in our lives.

▲ In some instances one is automatically excused from a law of the Church. For example, someone who has diabetes is excused from the requirement to fast. In other cases, where keeping a particular law of the Church would be unusually difficult or cause a special hardship, it might be prudent to ask for a dispensation from a priest. This can be done either in person or even over the telephone.

▲ A recent development in the Catholic Church is the growth of the concept of stewardship. Initially seen as a helpful means of increasing parish revenues, stewardship's expectation that we give of our time, talent and treasure has also had a positive impact on individual moral life. The more people are willing to share what God has given, the more they understand what it means to be truly Catholic.

▲ There are several Catholic organizations that work for social justice, including the Campaign for Human Development and Catholic Charities. Catholics are also involved in a variety of social justice efforts, including local community organizations, labor unions, peace and justice groups and pro-life and environmental movements.

▲ The primary way that Catholics work for social justice is through their daily work on their jobs, with their families and in their communities.

Part V: LIFE IN CHRIST

Section 33 **Faith, Hope and Love**

Beloved, let us love one another, because love is of God; everyone who loves is begotten by God and knows God. Whoever is without love does not know God, for God is love. In this way the love of God was revealed to us: God sent his only Son into the world so that we might have life through him. In this is love: not that we have loved God, but that he loved us and sent his Son as expiation for our sins. Beloved, if God so loved us, we also must love one another—1 Jn 4:7-11.

THE MOST IMPORTANT FACT of our human existence is that we each possess a soul. The soul is both the means and symbol of our unique and special fellowship with God. The dignity of our relationship with God is then raised to the status of God's children through the life-giving waters of Baptism.

Since in Baptism we have received a new life from Christ we must live a life consistent with the dignity of a Christian. The Christian life is beautifully illustrated and defined by the word "love." The Christian life is a life of love.

We would not be able to live this new life without three special gifts from God. These gifts are the power to believe God, the power to hope in God and the power to love God and all the children of God. We call these three gifts the virtues of faith, hope and love.

These gifts, together with the gifts of the Holy Spirit and the other helps which God gives us, enable us to live according to the new life which is ours as members of the Mystical Body of Christ.

1. Why do we receive the divine life here on earth?

We receive the divine life here on earth because God wants us to be born again and begin to share his life here and now. The more like God we become, the greater glory we give God.

2. How do we receive the divine life?

The ordinary way of receiving the divine life is through Baptism, to which we are led by faith. *"Whoever believes and is baptized will be saved"*—Mk 16:16.

3. How does the divine life grow within us?

When God gives us the divine life he also gives us new powers which enable us to act and grow in that life. These new powers are the virtues of faith, hope and charity; the moral virtues of prudence, justice, temperance and fortitude; and the gifts of the Holy Spirit.

4. What is faith?

Faith is the power given us by God which enables us to believe God in whatever he has told us. Our minds cannot fully understand the mysteries which God has revealed to us. But faith makes us certain of the truth of everything God has said, more certain than we are about things we see or hear, because faith rests on the authority of God himself. Finally, faith is a responsive obedience to God's revelation.

5. Can we earn the gift of faith?

We receive faith from God as a free gift. There is nothing we can do to earn it. But God, who *"wills everyone to be saved and to come to knowledge of the truth"*—1 Tm 2:4, offers the gift of faith to all.

6. What is an act of faith?

An act of faith is an expression we give to the gift of faith.

An act of faith is a great act of humility; it demands that we submit our minds to God and accept his word for something we cannot see for ourselves. *"Amen, I say to you, whoever does not accept the kingdom of God like a child will not enter it"*—Lk 18:17.

7. How do we live by faith?

We live by faith by acting according to what we believe rather than according to what the world tells us. To live by faith means also to strive for a deeper faith and to desire the will of God rather than our own.

> *What good is it, my [friends], if someone says he has faith but does not have works? Can that faith save him? If a brother or sister has nothing to wear and has no food for the day, and one of you says to them, "Go in peace, keep warm, and eat well," but you do not give them the necessities of the body, what good is it? So also faith of itself, if it does not have works, is dead.*

> *Indeed someone might say, "You have faith and I have works." Demonstrate your faith to me without works, and I will demonstrate my faith to you from my works . . . .*

> *For just as a body without a spirit is dead, so also faith without works is dead—Jas 2:14-18, 26.*

8. What is hope?

Hope is the power given us by God that enables us to have confidence in the forgiveness of sins and eternal life. Hope also includes a desire for the rewards which God has promised those who love him.

> *You who fear the LORD, wait for his mercy,*
> *   turn not away lest you fall.*
> *You who fear the LORD, trust him,*
> *   and your reward will not be lost.*
> *You who fear the LORD, hope for good things,*
> *   for lasting joy and mercy.*

Study the generations long past and understand;
    has anyone hoped in the LORD and been disappointed?
Has anyone persevered in his fear and been forsaken?
    has anyone called upon him and been rebuffed?
Compassionate and merciful is the LORD;
    he forgives sins, he saves in time of trouble.

—Sir 2:7-11.

9. What is an act of hope?

An act of hope is an expression we give to the gift of hope. Like the act of faith it is a great act of humility. Left to ourselves we have no right to hope for forgiveness or to aspire to heaven. But clinging to Christ, our Savior, who has paid the price of our salvation, we rely on the goodness of God, who has promised to save us if we cooperate with the help he gives.

10. What is love?

Love is the gift given by God that enables us to love him above all things for his own sake and to love ourselves and all people as children of God.

11. How are faith, hope and love increased within us?

Faith, hope and love are increased within us by their use. The more we exercise faith the stronger becomes our faith; the more we hope and love the greater become our hope; the more we love the easier it becomes to love.

12. What are the moral virtues?

The moral virtues are:

a) prudence, the virtue which inclines us to form right judgments about what we should or should not do;

b) justice, the virtue which inclines us to give to all persons whatever is due to them;

c) temperance, the virtue which inclines us to govern our appetite according to what is right and pleasing to God

d) fortitude, the virtue which inclines us to do what God desires, even when it is hard and disagreeable.

13. What are the gifts of the Holy Spirit?

The gifts of the Holy Spirit are:

a) wisdom, the gift which moves us to judge all things, human and divine, as God sees them and to have a relish for the things of God;

b) understanding, the gift which moves us to a deeper insight into the truths that God has revealed to us;

c) right judgment, the gift which moves us to act with prudence, especially in difficult cases;

d) courage, the gift which moves us to do great things for God joyfully and without fear of difficulties and obstacles;

e) knowledge, the gift which moves us to see the things of this world in their true perspective, in their relation to God;

f) piety, the gift which moves us to love God as our Father and to have affection for all persons and things consecrated to him;

g) fear of the Lord, the gift which moves us to fear offending God and being separated from him whom we love.

All the gifts of the Holy Spirit make us receptive to the guidance of God and the graces he sends us, and so enable us to act quickly and easily in the performance of his will.

14. How can we express our love for God?

As children of God we can express our love for our Father:

a) by offering him ourselves and everything we do. *"So whether you eat or drink, or whatever you do, do everything for the glory of God"*—1 Cor 10:31.

b) by doing his will. *"In this way we know that we love the children of God when we love God and obey his commandments. For the love of God is this, that we keep his commandments. And his commandments are not burdensome"*—1 Jn 5:2-3.

c) by imitating Christ, whom God has sent not only as our Savior but also as our model. *"[L]earn from me, for I am meek and humble of heart . . ."*—Mt 11:29.

d) by uniting ourselves to Christ by eating his flesh and drinking his blood in the Eucharist. *"(T)he one who feeds on me will have life because of me"*—Jn 6:57.

e) by recalling God's mercy to us. *"So I tell you, her many sins have been forgiven; hence, she has shown great love. But the one to whom little is forgiven, loves little"*—Lk 7:47.

f) by praying. *"With all prayer and supplication, pray at every opportunity in the Spirit"*—Eph 6:18.

g) by loving others. *"If someone who has worldly means sees a brother [or sister] in need and refuses . . . compassion, how can the love of God remain in [that person]?"*—1 Jn 3:17.

15. How do we show love for all people?

We show our love for all people by treating them with the reverence which is due them as children of God. This means much more than "not bothering" people or refraining from insulting or injuring them. We must treat persons as Jesus himself would. We must practice the works of mercy. Jesus tells us that at the last judgment he will say to us:

"Come, you who are blessed by my Father. Inherit the kingdom prepared for you from the foundation of the

world. For I was hungry and you gave me food, I was thirsty and you gave me drink, a stranger and you welcomed me, naked and you clothed me, ill and you cared for me, in prison and you visited me." Then the righteous will answer him and say, "Lord, when did we see you hungry and feed you, or thirsty and give you drink? When did we see you a stranger and welcome you, or naked and clothe you? When did we see you ill or in prison, and visit you?" And the king will say to them in reply, "Amen, I say to you, whatever you did for one of these least [sisters or] brothers of mine, you did for me"—Mt 25:34-40.

16. What are the works of mercy?

The works of mercy are: to feed the hungry, to admonish the sinner, to give drink to the thirsty, to instruct the ignorant, to clothe the naked, to counsel the doubtful, to visit those in prison, to comfort the sorrowful, to shelter the homeless, to bear wrongs patiently, to visit the sick, to forgive all injuries, to bury the dead, to pray for the living and the dead.

Often we fail to see opportunities to practice the works of mercy because we fail to understand them properly. "The naked" are not only those who have no clothes at all but also those who do not have enough clothes. "The homeless" are not only displaced persons but also families who cannot find a decent place to live because landlords refuse to rent to couples with children or to people of certain races.

The words of St. John, *"If someone who has worldly means sees a brother [or sister] in need and refuses ... compassion, how can the love of God remain in [that person]?"—1 Jn 3:17,* apply to nations as well as to individuals. Yet today there are countries where abject poverty is so widespread as to be the rule, countries which need financial and technical aid in order to feed and clothe their people. Christians, mindful of these words of St. John, may not close their eyes to such conditions nor condone a policy of apathy or opposition to measures which would help those in need in these countries.

17. Why do we have to love all people?

When Jesus was asked the question, "Who is my neighbor?" he replied by telling the story of the good Samaritan, which teaches us that our neighbor is everyone, not only those who belong to our race, our country, our religion (cf Lk 10:29-37) Even those who hate us and injure us must be included in our love. Jesus tells us in the Sermon on the Mount: *"But I say to you, love your enemies, and pray for those who persecute you, that you may be children of your heavenly Father, for he makes his sun rise on the bad and the good, and causes rain to fall on the just and the unjust"—Mt 5:44-45.*

Practice

▲ Every Catholic should be concerned with practicing works of mercy. Most parishes will offer numerous organizations and ministries in which you can participate and by doing so perform works of mercy. For example, you can volunteer as a minister of care and bring the Eucharist to the homebound, or you can offer to participate in the parish's social concern group or plan a food drive at Christmas and Easter. Usually, every parish can use an extra religion teacher or someone who is willing to act as an aid to a catechist. Become involved with the St. Vincent de Paul Society, or volunteer to serve on a parish bereavement team and help others to cope with the loss of a loved one. These are only a few ways that you can practice works of mercy regularly within your own community.

▲ In your examination of conscience check as to whether you are actually sharing with others the knowledge you are acquiring about God and his Church.

▲ Are there any sick friends or acquaintances whom you have not visited lately? Are there any newcomers in the neighborhood whom you might welcome by a visit?

Part V: LIFE IN CHRIST

Section 34 **The First Three Commandments**

Now someone approached him and said, "Teacher, what good must I do to gain everlasting life?" He answered him, "Why do you ask me about the good? There is only One who is good. If you wish to enter into life, keep the commandments." He asked him, "Which ones?" And Jesus replied, " 'You shall not kill; you shall not commit adultery; you shall not steal; you shall not bear false witness; honor your father and your mother;' and 'you shall love your neighbor as yourself—Mt 19:16-19.

THE GREAT COMMANDMENT of love requires of us that we act towards God as his sons and daughters and that we act towards other people as children of the same Father, members of the Body of Christ.

While these two commandments are broad and can be implemented in various ways, God also gave us the Ten Commandments where we find our minimal duties towards God and neighbor set forth in clear terms.

If we love God we will keep the first three commandments; they tell us our duties towards God. If we love ourselves and our neighbor we will keep the other seven commandments; they tell us our duties towards ourselves and our neighbor.

The Ten Commandments are not laws which were enacted to establish order or to test our obedience. They flow from our very nature as human beings. Because we were created by God and depend on him completely we must, as intelligent responsible beings, acknowledge that dependence. We must praise God, love him, believe him and show reverence for his name. Because all of us human beings have certain rights that we receive from God, we must respect those rights in others.

In studying the Ten Commandments, therefore, we are studying the laws which tell us how we must act because we are human beings—how we must act towards God and how we must act towards other people. But, more than that, in studying the Ten Commandments we are studying the laws which help us fulfill the great law of love.

1. What is the significance of the Ten Commandments?

"You shall love the Lord, your God, with all your heart, with all your soul, and with all your mind. This is the greatest and the first commandment. The second is like it: You shall love your neighbor as yourself"—Mt 22:37-39.

The Ten Commandments must be understood in the context of Christ's command to love God and neighbor with all of our heart, mind, and soul. They flow from the covenant that exists between God and his people. The commandments express how we should live in response to God's love with God and our neighbor. In their basic content, they must be obeyed.

2. What is the first commandment?

"I the LORD, am your God, who brought you out of the land of Egypt, that place of slavery. You shall not have other gods besides me"—Ex 20:2-3.

The first commandment binds us to believe in everything which God has revealed, to worship him, to trust him and to love him above all things. In other words, the first commandment commands us to practice faith, hope and love.

3. How do we practice faith, hope and love?

a) We practice faith by believing all the truths which the Church teaches as revealed to us by God, by professing our faith and never under any circumstances denying it.

b) We practice hope by relying on God's mercy, never doubting that he will forgive our sins if we are truly sorry for them and believing that he will give us all the help we need to reach heaven.

c) We practice love by keeping all the commandments and doing the works of mercy. *"If you love me, you will keep my commandments"—Jn 14:15.*

4. How serious are sins against faith?

Sins against faith are most serious, because they strike at the very foundation of our relationship to God.

5. What are the sins against faith?

The sins against faith are:

a) the denial of all or any of the truths which God teaches through the Church;

b) deliberate doubt about any truth of faith;

c) failure to profess the faith when obliged to do so;

d) failure to obtain necessary religious instruction;

e) reading books dangerous to our faith;

f) refusal to accept the authority of the pope as visible head of the Church;

g) the worship of some created thing instead of the true God;

h) superstition;

i) attendance at spiritualistic seances or the consultation of mediums.

6. What are the sins against hope?

The sins against hope are presumption and despair.

7. How does one sin by presumption?

One sins by presumption by assuming that salvation can be obtained by one's own efforts without God's help or by God's action without one's own cooperation.

8. What is despair?

Despair is a refusal to trust that God will forgive our sins and give us the means of salvation.

9. What are the sins against love?

All sins are in some way sins against love. Specific sins against love are treated under the fifth commandment.

10. What is the second commandment?

"You shall not take the name of the LORD, *your God, in vain"—Ex 20:7.*

We keep the second commandment by showing reverence to God, and especially to his holy name.

11. What are the sins against the second commandment?

The sins against the second commandment are:

a) blasphemy, i.e., mocking, ridiculing, despising God, his Church, the saints or holy objects (this is one of the most serious of sins);

b) irreverence in using the name of God, Jesus or the saints (this sin is usually venial);

c) cursing, i.e., calling down evil upon another (cursing would be a mortal sin if the person were serious; ordinarily he or she is not);

d) swearing, i.e., calling upon God to witness the truth of what we are saying, when what we are saying is not true or when there is no sufficient reason to call upon God (perjury, i.e., lying while under oath, can be a mortal sin);

e) breaking a vow, i.e., a deliberate promise made to God to do something which is particularly pleasing to him (to break a vow would be a mortal or venial sin depending on how one is bound by the vow).

12. What is the third commandment?

"Remember to keep holy the sabbath day. Six days you may labor and do all your work, but the seventh day is the sabbath of the LORD, your God"—Ex 20:8-9.

We keep the third commandment by worshiping God in a special way and refraining from unnecessary work on Sunday.

13. Why did the Church change the Sabbath from Saturday to Sunday?

The Church, using the power of binding and loosing which Christ gave to the pope, changed the Sabbath for Catholics from Saturday (when the Jews celebrate it) to Sunday because it was on Sunday (the first day of the week) that Christ rose from the dead and that the Holy Spirit descended upon the apostles.

The bishops of many dioceses have obtained permission from the pope to anticipate the Sunday masses of obligation on Saturday evenings. This is based on the biblical notion that one day ends at sundown and the next one begins at dusk.

14. How are we obliged to worship God on Sundays and holy days of obligation?

The law of God does not specify the amount of worship required. But there is a Church law which binds us to assist at Mass on Sundays and holy days. By observing this law of the Church we are observing also the divine law of worship on the Lord's Day.

15. Is our attendance and participation in the Sunday Mass an obligation?

We are obliged to attend and participate in the Sunday liturgy unless excused by a serious inconvenience. We should prefer, however, to consider the Sunday Mass as an opportunity, which it truly is. At Mass we meet with and pray with others who share our religious convictions. To be absent from the Sunday Mass would be to miss an opportunity to be with God and the local Christian community.

16. Is assistance at Mass all that is required on Sundays and holy days?

Assistance at Mass on these days is all that is required under pain of sin. But the spirit of the law requires a real sanctification of the whole day.

> Let the public and private observance of the feasts of the Church, which are in a special way dedicated and consecrated to God, be kept inviolable: and especially the Lord's day which the apostles, under the guidance of the Holy [Spirit], substituted for the Sabbath. . . . Sundays and Holy Days, then, must be made holy by divine worship, which gives homage to God and heavenly food to the soul—Encyclical on the Sacred Liturgy.

17. What kind of work is forbidden on Sunday?

Unnecessary work is the type of work forbidden on Sunday. Changing social and economic factors have changed the concept of work. Therefore, it is difficult to give principles with clear-cut applications to any and all situations.

18. What kind of work is permitted on Sunday?

Such work which is necessary for the common good is permitted on Sundays. For example, sometimes it is necessary for police, railroad workers, drugstore and medical workers, etc., to work on Sundays.

Some work is necessary for other reasons, (for example, cooking and dishwashing in the home). Some work becomes necessary because of an emergency or in an unusual situation. In the latter case, if there is any doubt, one should ask one's confessor. Conducting business which is not necessary for the common good does not give honor to the Lord's day. A helpful guide to our behavior is found in the Code of Canon Law which says we should "Abstain from any work or enterprise that inhibits the worship due to God, the joy proper to the Lord's day, works of mercy and necessary relaxation of mind and body."

Practice

▲ We cannot love someone we do not know. God has told us of himself in order that we might love him. Because we are God's children we know our Father far better than do those who have not the gift of faith. But we can never know God well enough. Our love for our Father should prompt us to seek more and more knowledge of him commensurate with our age, our intelligence and our education.

▲ All people are called to know, love and worship God. The Church is obliged to make known to all people the presence of God and how the one, true religion abides in the Catholic Church. At the same time there exists a right to religious freedom that is grounded in the dignity of the human person.

▲ Difficulties about matters of faith are not the same as doubts. Difficulties are questions which occur because of an inquiring mind, the need of further knowledge or mistaken information.

▲ Superstitions can include believing in astrology, consulting fortune tellers, even gambling. It also can underlie supposedly "religious" practices such as burying statues of St. Joseph in order to sell a house. While most superstitions may be harmless and might normally be venial sins, to guide one's life by superstitions is very serious and could be a mortal sin.

▲ When an individual takes a formal oath to tell the truth, the whole truth, and nothing but the truth "so help me God," he or she is required under the second commandment (as well as the eighth) not to lie, even by withholding information by means of a "mental reservation."

▲ Keeping holy the Sabbath means not only doing something special on Sundays but also living the rest of the week in a way that does not contradict or bring shame on that which we profess and worship on Sunday.

Part V: LIFE IN CHRIST

Section 35 **The Fourth Commandment**

My son, take care of your father when he is old; /grieve him not as long as he lives. /Even if his mind fail, be considerate with him; /revile him not in the fullness of your strength. /For kindness to a father will not be forgotten, /it will serve as a sin offering—it will take lasting root. /In time of tribulation it will be recalled to your advantage, /like warmth upon frost it will melt away your sins. /A blasphemer is he who despises his father; /accursed of his Creator, he who angers his mother—Sir 3:12-16.

WHEN GOD SENT HIS SON into the world he sent him as a member of a family. Jesus had a human mother and a human foster-father and chose to be subject to them. By so doing he taught us the importance God places on the family. By his life at Nazareth as a member of the Holy Family Christ has sanctified family life and given us an example of what that life should be. He taught us the dignity of parenthood by the reverence he showed to Mary and Joseph, whom he treated as the representatives of his Father.

By the fourth commandment God reminds us that as his children we must respect authority within the family by honoring and obeying our parents. He reminds us, too, that we must respect and obey his other representatives who exercise lawful authority over us in the larger family of God.

1. What is the significance of the family?

A couple (husband and wife) united in marriage and their children form a family whose members are equal in dignity. It is a natural society and as such is to be preserved and protected by civil society and government.

2. What is the fourth commandment?

"Honor your father and your mother, that you may have a long life in the land the Lord, your God, is giving to you"—Ex 20:12.

Everyone is obliged by this commandment to obey all lawful authority and to exercise it conscientiously.

Parents keep this commandment by providing for the spiritual as well as the material needs of their children; by giving them affection, protection, discipline, education and good example; and by preparing them to live as children of God in this world and so attain eternal union with God.

Sons and daughters keep this commandment by obeying, honoring and respecting their parents, and by providing for them in their old age.

3. Whom must we obey?

a) Children who are under age and still dependent on their parents must obey them in everything which is not in opposition to the laws of God.

b) We must obey the Church. Christ acts through the pope and through the spiritual ruler of the diocese, the bishop.

"And so I say to you, you are Peter, and upon this rock I will build my church, and the gates of the netherworld shall not prevail against it. I will give you the keys to the kingdom of heaven. Whatever you bind on earth shall be bound in heaven; and whatever you loose on earth shall be loosed in heaven"—Mt 16:18-19.

c) We must obey the civil government unless a law contradicts the laws of God. Whether a law binds us under sin or merely compels our obedience under the threat of a penalty depends on the specific circumstances.

4. Does the fourth commandment oblige us to love our country?

The fourth commandment obliges us to fulfill our duties as citizens of our country, to respect its laws and institutions, to cooperate for the common good and to love and defend our country when the cause and the means it uses are just.

5. Are there limits to this obligation?

"The citizen is obliged in conscience not to follow the directives of civil authorities when they are contrary to the demands of the moral order, to the fundamental rights of persons or the teachings of the Gospel"—CCC 2242.

Practice

▲ The right and duty of educating their children belongs to the parents. Parents, therefore, may not leave the religious education entirely to the school or the religious education program. The religious education is meant to assist the parents, not supplant them in this important duty.

The family . . . holds directly from the Creator the mission and hence the right to educate the offspring, a right inalienable because inseparably joined to the strict obligation, a right anterior to any right whatever of civil society and of the State, and therefore inviolable on the part of any power on earth—Encyclical on the Christian Education of Youth.

▲ Parents have a great responsibility towards their children in the matter of giving good example. It is unrealistic to suppose that children will develop right attitudes in regard to respect for law, the use of money, respect for others, tolerance, etc., if their parents display the fact that they themselves have un-Christian attitudes towards these things.

▲ The good or harm which a parent can do by way of example is most evident in the matter of prayer and the sacraments. Parents who are never seen to pray, who miss Mass or who rarely receive Holy Communion can hardly expect their children to develop good habits in regard to prayer and the sacraments. On the other hand, parents who do pray and teach their children to pray and who receive Holy Communion every time they assist at Mass are giving their children excellent example and are in a position to encourage their children to do likewise.

▲ One of the duties we have as citizens of our country is that of voting and of doing so intelligently. Nowadays there are organizations which can give us information on candidates for office. A good Christian should take his privilege of voting seriously and exercise it wisely. Remembering that Our Lord called us "the salt of the earth" and "the light of the world," good Christians should take an interest in and participate in civic affairs. Only thus can we expect to carry the principles of Christ into our communities.

▲ Parents should respect their children's choice of vocation. Parents are frequently wrong in encouraging their children too strongly to follow pursuits which are merely lucrative rather than those which contribute to society, e.g., teaching, nursing or religious life.

Part V: LIFE IN CHRIST

Section 36 **The Fifth Commandment**

"You have heard that it was said to your ancestors, 'You shall not kill; and whoever kills will be liable to judgment.' But I say to you, whoever is angry with [another] will be liable to judgment, and whoever says to [another], 'Raqa, will be answerable to the Sanhedrin, and whoever says, 'You fool,' will be liable to fiery Gehenna. Therefore, if you bring your gift to the altar, and there recall that [another] has anything against you, leave your gift there at the altar, go first and be reconciled with [that person], and then come and offer your gift. Settle with your opponent quickly while on the way to court. . . . Otherwise your opponent will hand you over to the judge, and the judge will hand you over to the guard, and you will be thrown into prison. Amen, I say to you, you will not be released until you have paid the last penny—Mt 5:21-26.

AS MEMBERS OF THE FAMILY of God we must treat all people as our brothers and sisters in Christ and assist them in their journey through life back to the Father. We must, therefore, respect the rights of every person.

The fifth commandment reminds us that we must live a life of Christian love and concern within the family of God and must injure neither the body nor the soul of our neighbor. The fifth commandment reminds us, too, that we must acknowledge that our own lives belong to God and that we must preserve our own health and well-being and refrain from risking it rashly or needlessly.

1. What is the fifth commandment?

"You shall not kill"—Ex 20:13.

We keep the fifth commandment by preserving our own life and by respecting our neighbor's right to life. The basis of this commandment is in the fact that God is the origin and destiny of all human life. Therefore, all human life is sacred. It is for this reason that it is sinful to directly harm the life or health of another person.

2. What are the sins against the fifth commandment?

The sins against the fifth commandment are:

a) murder;

b) abortion;

c) mercy killing;

d) suicide;

e) mutilation of one's body;

f) risking one's life without a sufficient reason;

g) excessive eating and drinking (gluttony);

h) unjust anger, which leads to hatred, revenge, fighting and quarreling;

i) abuse of the body and mind by drugs or alcohol.

3. Is it ever permitted to take the life of another?

To kill in legitimate self-defense is not sinful.

4. Why are abortion and "mercy killing" against the fifth commandment?

The Church teaches in no uncertain terms that from the moment of conception the rights of an unborn person—especially the right to life itself—are to be respected. This is also true of those who are sick, weak, elderly, handicapped or dying. Consequently, all forms of abortion, euthanasia and assisted suicide are morally unacceptable. Civil society and government, as well as individuals, are obliged to respect and recognize these rights.

5. How are we obliged to preserve our own lives and health?

Because both physical life and health have been given to us by God as gifts, we are obliged to use every ordinary means in preserving them. We may not, therefore, risk our lives except for a sufficient reason, for example, to rescue another. Nor may we allow our body to be mutilated or deprived of an important function unless it be necessary to save the body itself, e.g., an amputation or hysterectomy in cancer cases.

On the other hand, we are not required to use extraordinary means to preserve life when those means would be futile or unduly burdensome. The decision to refuse medical help for oneself or one's loved one in this situation, however, should only be taken after much prayer and reflection and consultation with others.

6. How serious a sin is it to mutilate the body unnecessarily, to deprive it of an important function or to shorten one's life?

Sterilization, except in the case of legitimate removal of a diseased organ, is very wrong because it closes off the possibility of new life being formed. The use or trafficking in illegal narcotics is likewise morally illicit because of the grave harm it does to self or others. Suicide, or even shortening one's life knowingly, can be a mortal sin.

7. Is it permissible to participate in medical experiments or to donate organs?

If medical experiments contribute to healing of individuals and the improvement of public health, if they do not involve disproportionate or avoidable risks to the subject, and if the subject has given informed consent, then they are morally acceptable. This is also true of organ donation.

8. What is hatred?

Hatred is wishing evil to another. It is a matter of the will, not of feelings. We are not guilty of sin because we feel an aversion to certain people, as long as we do not encourage or manifest such a feeling. We are obliged to love our neighbor, not to like him or her. Liking is a matter of the feelings and is not always under the control of the will. Nor is the inability to like someone incompatible with loving that person.

9. Is war morally acceptable?

Peace is the necessary context for the dignity of human persons and society to be preserved and enhanced. For peace to prevail the demands of justice must be met. Because of the evils associated with war, we are obliged to work for peace. It is possible, however, once all efforts at peace have been exhausted for a government to engage in legitimate self-defense by military force. The conditions necessary for use of military force are contained in what has been called the "just-war" theory. According to that theory, at one and the same time:

a) the damage inflicted by the aggressor to the nation or community of nations would be lasting, serious and certain;

b) all other means of putting an end to it must have been shown to be impractical or ineffective;

c) all serious conditions for success must be present;

d) the use of arms must not involve more serious evils and disorders than those to be eliminated. (The power of modern weapons of destruction weighs heavily on the evaluation of this condition.)

Once war has been initiated, the moral law—including the fifth commandment—still remains in effect and must be observed.

10. Is a Christian obliged to serve in the military?

The state, in order to protect a nation's common good and to insure peace, may impose the obligation on its citizens of serving the military. At the same time, provision must be made for those who, because of reasons of conscience, indicate they cannot bear arms. Those who so object are obliged, however, to serve the nation in some other way.

11. Are religious and racial prejudice against the fifth commandment?

Prejudice is an unreasonable emotion and always opposed to charity. To judge and condemn any person because that person happens to belong to a certain religious group, nationality or race injures that person. To manifest prejudice by our actions hurt the feelings of our neighbor and is therefore a sin against charity. To deny any person her or his rights is a sin against justice as well as charity. This is particularly true in the case of joining an organization (such as the Nazi Party or the Ku Klux Klan) which promotes racial, ethnic or religious hatred.

12. May we seek revenge or refuse to forgive injuries?

Jesus insisted that our sins will not be forgiven by God unless we forgive others offenses against us. *"If you forgive others their transgressions, your heavenly Father will forgive you. But if you do not forgive others, neither will your Father forgive your transgressions"—Mt 6:14-15.*

13. What is scandal?

Scandal is any evil action, or one which has the appearance of evil, that does spiritual harm to another. Bad example is frequently scandalous, since it may easily lead another into the same sin.

Scandal given to the young is particularly serious. *"Whoever causes one of these little ones who believe [in me] to sin, it would be better for him if a great millstone were put around his neck and he were thrown into the sea—Mk 9:42.*

14. How serious are sins of hatred, scandal, cooperation in sin and uncharitable words and actions?

The seriousness of such sins is determined by the seriousness of the harm done to our neighbor. To wish serious evil to another, to cooperate with someone in a serious sin, to give serious scandal or to talk or act against our neighbor in such a way as to injure someone seriously can be mortal sins against the fifth commandment.

Practice

▲ In the field of race relations Christians have a great opportunity for giving the world an example of justice and charity. It would be a shocking thing if the behavior of Christians in regard to segregation and other injustices were no different from that of others. We must never forget that Our Lord said, *"This is how all will know that you are my disciples, if you have love for one another"—Jn 13:35.*

▲ Changes in knowledge or circumstances can deepen our understanding of the moral law. Regarding the morality of the death penalty, for example, Pope John Paul II recently stated, "On this matter there is a growing tendency, both in the church and in civil society, to demand that it be applied in a very limited way or even that it be abolished completely. . . . As a result of steady improvements in the penal system, such cases [where the death penalty is morally allowed] are very rare, if not practically nonexistent"—*Encyclical on the Gospel of Life.*

Part V: LIFE IN CHRIST

Section 37 **The Sixth and Ninth Commandments**

Do you not know that your body is a temple of the holy Spirit within you, whom you have from God, and that you are not your own? For you have been purchased at a price. Therefore glorify God in your body—1 Cor 6:19-20.

OUR FATHER HAS GIVEN US a world in which human skill and artistry can add to the order and beauty of his creation. But God was not content to allow us to share in his creation merely as workers and artists. He desired to give men and women a share in the power of divine love and in the creation of new human beings who are destined to share in the divine life. Thus he gave to human beings the wonderful gift of sexuality.

Human sexuality is something deeply mysterious and beautiful. Sexual intercourse is the means whereby a married couple with God's blessing give themselves to one another in love and thereby find their fulfillment in one another and a closer union with God through one another. It is also the means by which they bring new life into the world.

Among all the powers that we possess the power of human sexuality is unique. It is the only gift we have which we may not use for our own sake. The power of our five senses we use in order to bring the outside world into our mind. Our power of nourishing ourselves we use in order to build up our own body. But the power of human sexuality we possess only in order that we might give ourselves to another in a union of body and soul that is to last a lifetime and can (and sometimes does) result in the creation of new life.

Love always expresses itself by an attempt to give. We give gifts to those we love, the gift of attention, interest, time. We give presents to those we love—the deeper the love the more precious and personal the present.

Our sexuality is in some mysterious way peculiarly, deeply ourselves. The very words "intimate, private, personal" applied to the sexual faculty give evidence of this fact. Thus sex is the means whereby husband and wife can give themselves to one another in a special and unique way.

Sexual activity, therefore, is not merely a means of obtaining pleasure, although it certainly is that when it is done in a loving and mutually sensitive manner. Sex is something sacred—the ultimate way that a husband and wife say "I love you" to each other.

It is only the misuse of sex that is shameful, all the more shameful because it is the misuse of something sacred. The sixth and ninth commandments are a prohibition against the misuse of sex either by act or by thought. They teach us that sex in human beings may never be divorced from love. The misuse of sex is a sin against love, not only against divine love—as is every sin— but against human love as well.

1. How are we to understand human sexuality?

Our understanding of human sexuality begins with God, who is love, and in whose image and likeness we are made. The triune God "lives a mystery of personal loving communion" and "inscribed in the humanity of man and woman the vocation, and thus the capacity and responsibility, of love and communion"— Encyclical on the Family. It was this same creative action of God which created us as male and female. In fact, because the human person is a unity of body and soul, "sexuality affects all aspects of the human person . . . . It especially concerns affectivity, the capacity to love and to procreate, and in a more general way the aptitude for forming bonds of communion with others"—CCC 2332.

Such a view of sexuality implies both equal personal dignity and complementarity between men and women.

2. What are the sixth and ninth commandments?

"You shall not commit adultery. . . .
"You shall not covet your neighbor's wife"—Ex 20:14, 17.

These two commandments call upon us to respect human sexuality and to use it in the way intended by God. They call us to lives of chastity, fruitfulness and fidelity in all our personal relationships.

3. What is chastity?

Chastity is the integration of our sexuality with all other aspects of our personhood. It is achieved by using our human freedom to achieve self-control that is informed by the virtue of temperance and responds to the sexual challenges encountered at various stages of life. Chastity is a characteristic of all persons, each in accord with their state in life, whether single, married or vowed religious.

4. What are the sins against the sixth and ninth commandments?

Anything which is opposed to the virtue of chastity is a sin against the sixth or the ninth commandment. Such sins include lust, masturbation, fornication, adultery, homosexual acts, pornography, prostitution, rape and incest.

Do you not know that the unjust will not inherit the kingdom of God? Do not be deceived; neither fornicators nor idolaters nor adulterers nor boy prostitutes nor practicing homosexuals nor thieves nor the greedy nor drunkards nor slanderers nor robbers will inherit the kingdom of God. That is what some of you used to be; but now you have had yourselves washed, you were sanctified, you were justified in the name of the Lord Jesus Christ and in the Spirit of our God—1 Cor 6:9-11 (cf. also Gal 5:19-24, Eph 5:5).

5. Why is artificial birth control morally wrong?

The use of artificial birth control—whether a drug or a mechanical device—is condemned by the Church because it separates the sexual act from the procreative act and is thus a sin against the virtue of chastity, even when used by married couples.

6. What is Natural Family Planning?

The Church teaches that being responsible in the procreation of children is not only legitimate but necessary. Health problems—both physical and psychological—finances, even overpopulation can all be reasons for couples to decide to limit the number or to space the births of their children. During the past few years scientists and doctors have learned how to help couples identify and recognize very reliable signs of a woman's time of fertility. Couples wishing to have children can then make love during those times, while those wishing to avoid pregnancy can do so by refraining from sexual relations. Natural Family Planning (N.F.P.) works in accord with and in cooperation with normal bodily functions and is approved by the Church.

7. Are demonstrations of affection between unmarried persons against the virtue of chastity?

Demonstrations of affection between unmarried persons are right and good as long as they are true demonstrations of affection and do not lead to unchaste thoughts or acts.

8. Why are thoughts and desires against chastity sinful?

Any deliberate desire to commit a sinful act is in itself sinful. If the act we desire to perform would be a mortal sin, the deliberate desire to commit it would be in itself a mortal sin (cf. Mt 5:27-28).

Thoughts or fantasies of a sexual nature can easily arouse sexual feelings, especially in the young. For an unmarried person, who has no right to the use of sex, to consent to such feelings would be a sin.

Pornography is another moral problem because sexually stimulating materials can easily cause persons to sinfully desire or even enter into sinful actions either alone or with others.

Some people have an inclination to sin with another person of the same sex. Such inclinations must be brought under control before causing moral harm to oneself or others. That being said, it should be noted that persons who are homosexual do not choose their condition. As human persons they are to be treated with all human respect and unjust discrimination against them is forbidden by Jesus' law of love.

9. What is the virtue of modesty?

The virtue of modesty is the virtue which protects chastity by inclining us to guard our senses so as not to invite temptation and to be considerate in our dress and behavior so as not to cause temptation to others. We humans naturally have curiosity about the opposite sex. This is not sinful unless it leads to sinful desires or actions. Looks, reading and other such actions which are opposed to the virtue of modesty can be sinful according to the circumstances.

10. Is masturbation a sin?

Masturbation is sinful because it is contrary to the purpose of sexuality. It does not involve the mutual self-giving of marital love nor is it open to human procreation.

11. Why is the sixth commandment sometimes called "the difficult commandment"?

Because of the effects of original sin the desire to experience sexual pleasure outside of marriage is easily aroused in us. Our eyes, our ears, our sense of touch, even our imaginations can bring us into contact with people or situations which stimulate our sexual drives. Yet for people who are not married to each other, since they have not the right to the use of sex, there can be no deliberate acquiescence to such stimulation—much less a seeking of it—without serious sin.

12. How do we preserve our chastity?

We preserve our chastity:

a) by the habit of prayer and prayer in time of temptation;

b) by cultivating devotion to our Blessed Mother;

c) by the frequent reception of the sacraments of Reconciliation and the Holy Eucharist;

d) by avoiding near occasions of sin, such as certain types of books, pictures, entertainments and companions.

Practice

▲ Our present society has little regard for the virtue of chastity. Therefore, parents and teachers should take special care to inculcate in the young an appreciation of this important virtue. Chastity should be presented not as a repression of human instincts but as a positive virtue which is essential to full manliness and womanliness. Above all, they should stress the fact that sex is something good and holy, that there is nothing evil about any part of the body, that the body—good by nature—has been made a temple of the Holy Spirit. If sex is presented as good and sacred and its importance in marriage explained, it can easily be pointed out why any misuse of sex is a tragic misfortune rather than a daring adventure.

▲ Couples experiencing difficulties grappling with the question of birth control should follow the advice of Pope Paul VI and Pope John Paul II and pray for help in responding to the Church's teaching on this delicate and serious issue. The popes urge such couples to continue to receive the sacraments of Reconciliation and Holy Communion because they will provide the graces each couple needs.

▲ Sexual abuse and harassment—in the workplace and in the home—are sins against the sixth and ninth commandments. Catholics should be exemplary in their respect for members of the opposite sex and their commitment never to use sex as an oppressive or degrading force.

▲ Adultery is an especially grievous sin in part because of the impact it has on the spouses and children of both parties.

Part V: LIFE IN CHRIST

Section 38 **The Seventh and Tenth Commandments**

Then God said: "Let us make [humans] in our image, after our likeness. Let them have dominion over the fish of the sea, the birds of the air, and the cattle, and over all the wild animals and all the creatures that crawl on the ground."

God created [humans] in his image;
in the divine image he created [them];
male and female he created them.

God blessed them, saying: "Be fertile and multiply; fill the earth and subdue it. Have dominion over the fish of the sea, the birds of the air, and all the living things that move on the earth." God also said: "See, I give you every seed-bearing plant all over the earth and every tree that has seed-bearing fruit on it to be your food; and to all animals of the land, all the birds of the air, and all the living creatures that crawl on the ground, I give all the green plants for food." And so it happened—Gn 1:26-30.

OUR LORD TAUGHT US to be poor in spirit. This means that we are neither too attached to nor desirous of material things. *"What profit would there be for one to gain the whole world and forfeit [one's] life? Or what can one give in exchange for [one's] life?"—Mt 16:26.*

Material possessions can distract us in our efforts to reach heaven. On the other hand, the Church tells us that it is good for men and women to provide for themselves and their dependents, to be paid a fair or just wage and to have the right to private property. In fact, the Church constantly calls for a better distribution of wealth in the world.

The seventh and tenth commandments, however, regulate the possession and use of the things God has entrusted to us and to others.

There is much injustice in the world today on the part of individuals, groups and governments. Some people are avaricious and greedy. Some governments still deny the right of individuals to own productive property. The person who steals (whether as a thief, an employer or a worker), the state which unjustly deprives people of what is theirs, the child who damages property, all these offend against the right order which God has established between his children and the things he has given them for their use.

1. What are the seventh and tenth commandments?

"You shall not steal. . . .

"You shall not covet your neighbor's. . . . ox or ass, nor anything else that belongs to [your neighbor]"—Ex 20:15, 17.

We keep the seventh and tenth commandments:

a) by respecting the property of others;

b) by paying our just debts;

c) by dealing honestly in business;

d) by paying a living wage to our employees;

e) by doing a full day's work for a full day's pay;

f) by living up to our agreements and contracts;

g) by returning things we have found;

2. What are the sins against the seventh and tenth commandments?

The sins against the seventh and tenth commandments are:

a) stealing

b) cheating;

c) vandalism;

d) acceptance of bribes;

e) use of false weights and measures;

f) charging exorbitant prices;

g) wasting time;

h) careless work;

i) violation of contracts and agreements;

j) envy of another's possessions.

3. How is the seriousness of sins against the seventh commandment determined?

The seriousness of sins against the seventh commandment is determined by the seriousness of the harm done either to the individual or to the community. Ordinarily it is considered serious if the injustice is equivalent to one day's wages for the injured party. In most cases, taking a considerable amount from even a wealthy person or corporation would constitute a serious sin against justice.

4. When is there an obligation of making restitution?

Whenever there has been a violation of justice, one is bound to make full restitution. One guilty of injustice is bound in conscience to restore the object unjustly possessed, withheld or destroyed. This restitution should be equal to the value it had at the time, together with any natural increase that value might have experienced.

The sincere intention to restore the value of the goods stolen is necessary before a sin against justice can be forgiven. If one who is guilty of an injustice can no longer find the owner or the owner's heirs, the guilty person is obliged to give the stolen goods or their value to the poor or to use them for some charitable cause.

5. What does the Church say about the right to private property?

The Church says that the right to private property is a natural right, one that may not be taken away. This does not mean, however, that persons may do with their property whatever they please. This is because the goods which come to us from creation have as their purpose the well-being of the entire human family. Therefore, it is wrong to waste or misuse property or misuse it in way that will be harmful to others. Then, too, the good of society may dictate that someone give up the ownership of some particular property, but only when that person is justly compensated for it.

> At the same time a [person's] superfluous income is not left entirely to [one's] own discretion. We speak of that portion of [that] income which [the person] does not need in order to live as becomes his [or her] station. On the contrary the grave obligations of charity, beneficence and liberality which rest upon the wealthy, are constantly insisted upon in telling words by Holy Scripture and the Fathers of the Church—Encyclical on Restructuring the Social Order.

Finally, our respect for the integrity of creation requires that animals, plants and inanimate beings be afforded the proper moral respect and used in a fashion that will truly further the quality of all life today and in the future.

6. Is justice between two individuals the only form of justice about which Christians should be concerned?

Christians must be concerned about all forms of justice and injustice. A decent and humane social order is vitally necessary if people are to be able to seek God with their whole beings.

. . . with respect to the fundamental rights of the person, every type of discrimination, whether social or cultural, whether based on sex, race, color, social condition, language or religion is to be overcome and eradicated as contrary to God's intent. . . .

Moreover, although rightful differences exist between [people], the equal dignity of persons demands that a more humane and just condition of life be brought about. For excessive economic and social differences between the members of the one human family or population groups cause scandal, and militate against social justice, equity, the dignity of the human person, as well as social and international peace.

Human institutions, both private and public, must labor to minister to the dignity and purpose of [all humanity]. At the same time let them put up a stubborn fight against any kind of slavery, whether social or political, and safeguard the basic rights of [all] under every political system. Indeed human institutions themselves must be accommodated by degrees to the highest of all realities, spiritual ones, even though meanwhile, a long enough time will be required before they arrive at the desired goal—Pastoral Constitution on the Church in the Modern World.

7. Why is concern for justice a religious concern?

Concern for justice is a religious concern because it was a concern for Jesus:

a) Jesus came to free all men and women from sin and the effects of sin. Injustice, war, discrimination are all effects of sin. Jesus wants to overcome them. People who are not free because of political, economic or social conditions, people who suffer from war and aggression need to experience the freeing concern and love of Jesus in the actions of the members of Jesus' body, the Church.

b) Jesus came to unite all men and women. Any form of

discrimination or injustice separates them.

c) Jesus came to establish the Kingdom of God here on this earth. The Kingdom will reach completion in the next life, but it has begun now and it embraces every aspect of people's lives. It embraces work, politics, education, recreation as well as prayer and religious beliefs.

8.   What does the Church say about justice?

In the past one hundred years the popes and the bishops have spoken time and time again about social problems. They have outlined the principles of justice against which an individual and a society should judge its norms. A person who truly wishes to live out a baptismal commitment will become familiar with recent Catholic social teaching as contained in such documents as:

a) Mater et Magistra: Christianity and Social Progress (1961);

b) Pacem in Terris: Peace on Earth (1963);

c) Gaudium et Spes: Pastoral Constitution on the Church in the Modern World (1965);

d) Dignitas Humanae: Declaration on Human Freedom (1965);

e) Populorum Progressio: On the Development of Peoples (1967);

f) Economic Justice for All (1986);

g) Laborem Exercens: On Human Work (1981);

h) Sollicitudo Rei Socialis: On Social Concern (1987);

i) Centessimus Annus: On the 100th Anniversary of Rerum Novarum (1991).

j) Evangelium Vitae: The Gospel of Life (1995).

These, as well as many shorter documents and speeches of the popes and bishops, demonstrate the obligation of Christians to be involved in the search for justice, the right of the Church to speak on these matters and guidelines to help people form their consciences in these matters.

Practice

▲ The Church upholds the right of workers to join trade unions. It urges workers to take an active part in unions, not only for the workers' protection but also for the establishment of an economic order characterized by justice, tranquility and order. To this end the Church also encourages associations among employers that will likewise work for justice, tranquility and order.

▲ The Church's social teachings remind us that the purpose of economic activity is to serve individuals and the entire human family, that human labor can be a means of sanctification, that the state has a proper but nuanced role in economic matters, that a solidarity should exist among nations and that we are called to have a preferential love for the poor.

▲ The Church's moral tradition reminds us of the evil associated with greed and envy and of the proper role of a spirit of detachment from material goods that allows us to focus on our ultimate destiny.

▲ The ideal wage is one paid with the family in mind. Pope Pius XI said: "The wage paid to the [worker] must be sufficient for the support of the [person] and the [person's] family"—Encyclical on Restructuring the Social Order.

▲ The prevalence of certain unjust practices does not alter the fact that they are sins against justice. Among such practices would be business deals which are based on the slogan, "Let the buyer beware." To sell a defective article—the defects of which are carefully camouflaged—is unjust and therefore un-Christian.

▲ To steal from the government or from a great many people is as sinful as stealing from an individual. The cynical excuse, "everyone does it," is unworthy of a Christian.

▲ The tenth commandment contains the seeds of its own punishment. Coveting our neighbors goods leads to a dissatisfaction with our own blessings and therefore a general unhappiness with our own lives.

Section 39 **The Eighth Commandment**

*[W]e all fall short in many respects. If anyone does not
fall short in speech, he [or she] is a perfect [person],
able to bridle [the] whole body also. If we put bits into
the mouths of horses to make them obey us, we also
guide their whole bodies. It is the same with ships: even
though they are so large and driven by fierce winds, they
are steered by a very small rudder wherever the pilot's
inclination wishes. In the same way the tongue is a small
member and yet has great pretensions.*

*Consider how small a fire can set a whole forest ablaze.
The tongue is also a fire. It exists among our members as
a world of malice, defiling the whole body and setting
the entire course of our lives on fire, itself set on fire by
Gehenna. For every kind of beast and bird, of reptile and
sea creature, can be tamed and has been tamed by the
human species, but no human being can tame the tongue.
It is a restless evil, full of deadly poison. With it we bless
the Lord and Father, and with it we curse human beings
who are made in the likeness of God. From the same
mouth come blessing and cursing. This need not be
so. . . . Does a spring gush forth from the same opening
both pure and brackish water? Can a fig tree . . .
produce olives, or a grapevine figs? Neither can salt
water yield fresh—Jas 3:2-12.*

JESUS CHRIST IS THE WAY, the truth and the life.
Because he is truth itself, he detests lying and hypocrisy. Our Lord

always dealt gently with sinners; but the lying, hypocritical Pharisees he sternly denounced time and time again. Christ expects us to love the truth as he loves it.

The eighth commandment reminds us that, as members of Christ, we must refrain from lying, deceit and hypocrisy. Such things come from the devil, *"a liar and the father of lies"—Jn 8:44;* they have no place in the family of God.

As members of Christ, we must also be solicitous to protect the good names of others. We must imitate the example which Jesus gave us at the Last Supper, when, with the utmost delicacy, he let Judas know that he was aware of his betrayal but nevertheless did not name him as the traitor before the other apostles.

1. What is the eighth commandment?

"You shall not bear false witness against your neighbor"—Ex 20:16.

We keep the eighth commandment by speaking the truth and by being careful not to injure the good names of others.

2. What are the sins against the eighth commandment?

The sins against the eighth commandment are:
a) lying;
b) calumny;
c) detraction;
d) revealing certain secrets;
e) perjury.

3. What is a lie?

A lie is the expression of something which we know to be untrue, made with the intention to deceive.

4. How serious is it to tell a lie?

To tell a lie is ordinarily a venial sin. If a lie injures someone seriously or is told while under oath (perjury), it can be a mortal sin.

5. Is it ever permissible to tell a lie?

It is never permissible to tell a lie, even to avoid evil or to accomplish good. When there is sufficient reason, however, we may use what is called a "mental reservation."

6. What is a mental reservation?

A mental reservation is either the use of an expression which may be taken in two ways or the act of leaving something unspoken. In social and business life there are many commonly used mental reservations. For example, "Mrs. Smith is not at home," may mean that the lady of the house is actually out, or it may be an accepted polite way of saying that she does not wish to see the caller.

Mental reservations can be much more serious—for example, the failure to tell a customer about a defective product. In any case, mental reservations may only be made when there is sufficient reason and no one is harmed by their use.

7. What is calumny?

Calumny is lying about someone in such a way as to injure that person's good name.

8. What is detraction?

Detraction is the unnecessary revelation of something about a person which is true but which injures that person's good name.

9. How serious are the sins of calumny and detraction?

Both calumny and detraction can be mortal sins if the statement made about another person is seriously damaging to that person's reputation. They are venial sins if what is said about the other person is not serious. Gossip, when it constitutes calumny or detraction, is sinful.

One who has committed either calumny or detraction must make whatever effort is required to restore the good name of the injured person. The resolution to make such restitution is necessary in order to obtain forgiveness of these sins.

10. How serious is the obligation of keeping a secret?

The seriousness of the obligation of keeping a secret is determined by the importance of the secret to the person who confided it.

The secrecy of the confessional may never be violated by the priest for any reason whatsoever, even at the cost of his life.

Practice

▲ Gossip columnists and magazines enjoy such prestige today that we are apt to forget the fact that the unnecessary revelation of the sins and crimes of others is unjustifiable and can be seriously sinful. The Christian should refrain from supporting defamatory magazines which specializes in innuendo, scandal and detraction.

▲ An exaggeration can be a lie. This fact should be remembered not only in social life but in business as well. There is no justification for making exaggerated claims for a product in order to make a sale. Catholics should remember that honesty in speech ought to be one of our hallmarks both in social life and in business dealings.

▲ It is very easy to criticize and complain about others, to discuss their faults needlessly and to pass judgment on their actions—especially in their absence. Catholics should, rather, bring out the good points of a person under discussion and defend the person as we would want ourselves defended.

▲ One of the worst sins against the eighth commandment is hypocrisy. Christ ordered us to live out what we say we believe. *"Not everyone who says to me, 'Lord, Lord,' will enter the kingdom of heaven, but only the one who does the will of my Father in heaven"*—Mt 7:21.

Part V: LIFE IN CHRIST

Section 40 **Life Everlasting**

*Then I saw a new heaven and a new earth. The former
heaven and the former earth had passed away, and the
sea was no more. I also saw the holy city, a new Jerusalem, coming down out of heaven from God, prepared as a
bride adorned for her husband. I heard a loud voice from
the throne saying, "Behold, God's dwelling is with the
human race. He will dwell with them and they will be his
people and God himself will always be with them [as their
God]. He will wipe every tear from their eyes, and there
shall be no more death or mourning, wailing or pain,
[for] the old order has passed away"—Rev 21:1-4.*

WHEN THE SON OF GOD came into this world he came
as a helpless infant. Jesus Christ lived a life of poverty. He was
rejected by the very people he came to save. Yet his death on the
cross, an apparent failure and humiliation, was actually a glorious
triumph.

While among us, Jesus prophesied that he would return to
earth one day, no longer in poverty and humiliation, but to judge
the living and the dead as "Lord of the cosmos and of history"—
CCC 668.

Belief in the second coming of Christ sustained the early
Church even in its darkest hours when persecution threatened to
overwhelm the struggling Christian community. No matter how
bleak their situation, the early Christians never ceased believing
that the final victory would be Christ's.

The believed that they were already at *"the last hour"—1 Jn 2:18*. As we understand this phrase today, we mean that final age of the world has already begun although it has not yet been completed.

While acknowledging this is the time of the Holy Spirit we are also aware that ours is a time of trial which effects the Church and all of humanity. Today we face powerful and subtle forms of evil which permeate our personal and social lives. We should not be dismayed by this fact. Our Lord warned us that such things would happen.

While we spare neither effort nor prayer in extending the kingdom (or reign) of God on this earth, we should also remember that—however powerful his enemies—the final victory will be Christ's. He will return in glory and triumph. His enemies will be forever vanquished, and those who are united to him and share his life will share in his eternal victory.

1. Will the work of the Church ever end?

The Church's mission of proclamation and sanctification will cease when the world comes to an end; but its work of praising and glorifying God will continue forever in heaven.

2. What will the happiness of heaven be like?

While heaven surpasses human understanding Scripture provides us with some insight into the mystery:

a) We believe that in heaven we shall be happy in a way far greater than any of us has ever been happy, even in our happiest moments on earth. There will be no sorrow, no pain, no hardship, no want.

"He will wipe every tear from their eyes, and there shall be no more death or mourning, wailing or pain, for the old order has passed away"—Rev. 21:4.

Those whom the LORD has ransomed will return /and enter Zion singing. /crowned with everlasting joy; /They will meet with joy and gladness, /sorrow and mourning will flee—Is 35:10.

But the souls of the just are in the hand of God, /and no torment shall touch them. /They seemed, in the view of the foolish, to be dead; /and their passing away was thought an affliction /and their going forth from us, utter destruction. /But they are in peace— Wis 3:1-3.

b) There will be perfect rest— not the rest of inactivity, but the rest which is the perfect satisfaction of all longing, the rest which the heart finds in the contentment of perfect love. As we say in the Mass offered at funerals:

"May the angels take you into paradise: may the martyrs come to welcome you on your way, and lead you into the holy city, Jerusalem. May the choir of angels welcome you, and with Lazarus, who once was poor, may you have everlasting rest."

c) There will be final and complete union with God, the source of all joy and happiness. In this world we can know God only by faith. In heaven we shall see God as he is, face to face, and we shall be overwhelmed by his beauty and goodness. *"At present we see indistinctly, as in a mirror, but then face to face. At present I know partially; then I shall know fully, as I am fully known— 1 Cor 13:12.*

d) There will be complete ease and familiarity in our conversation with God. Prayer, which is frequently difficult here on earth, requiring great application and effort, will be a supreme joy in heaven. Our conversation with God will be infinitely more delightful than any we have had, even with those whose company we have enjoyed most on earth.

e) There will be companionship with all the members of our Father's great family, the angels and the saints and all those we have known and loved in this world. There will be no farewells, no separation, no end of the love, peace and joy which will prevail among the children of God.

f) Whatever we find pleasant, beautiful or desirable in this world attracts us because it is a faint reflection of God. We have moments of exaltation, periods of joy and contentment here on earth; but they never last. They cannot satisfy us because they cannot and do not last. If such hints of the beauty and lovableness of God can delight us here, we can only begin to imagine what happiness will be ours when we behold the reality of God himself, the inexhaustible source of all happiness, for all eternity.

3. Will the world ever end?

The world as we know it will end some day. However, there will be *"a new heaven and a new earth"—Rev 21:1*, the details of which are still veiled in mystery.

4. When will the world end?

Only God knows the day and the hour. Our Lord spoke of the end of the world several times; but because his words are prophecies they are mysterious and are capable now of being interpreted in various ways.

> *As he was sitting on the Mount of Olives, the disciples approached him privately and said, "Tell us, when will this happen, and what sign will there be of your coming, and of the end of the age?" Jesus said to them in reply, "See that no one deceives you. For many will come in my name, saying, 'I am the Messiah,' and they will deceive many. You will hear of wars and reports of wars; see that you are not alarmed, for these things must happen, but it will not yet be the end. Nation will rise against nation, and kingdom against kingdom; there will be famines and earthquakes from place to place. All these are the beginning of the labor pains. Then they will hand you over to persecution, and they will kill you. You will be hated by all nations because of my name. And then many will be led into sin; they will betray and hate one another.*

Many false prophets will arise and deceive many; and because of the increase of evildoing, the love of many will grow cold. But the one who perseveres to the end will be saved. And this gospel of the kingdom will be preached throughout the world as a witness to all nations, and then the end will come"—Mt 24:3-14.

"If anyone says to you then, 'Look, here is the Messiah!' or, 'There he is!' do not believe it. False messiahs and false prophets will arise, and they will perform signs and wonders so great as to deceive, if that were possible, even the elect. Behold, I have told it to you beforehand. So if they say to you, 'He is in the desert,' do not go out there; if they say, 'He is in the inner rooms,' do not believe it. For just as lightning comes from the east and is seen as far as the west, so will the coming of the Son of Man be. Wherever the corpse is, there the vultures will gather.

"Immediately after the tribulation of those days,
    the sun will be darkened,
      and the moon will not give its light,
    and the stars will fall from the sky,
      and the powers of the heavens will be shaken.

"And then the sign of the Son of Man will appear in heaven, and all the tribes of the earth will mourn, and they will see the Son of Man coming upon the clouds of heaven with power and great glory. And he will send out his angels with a trumpet blast, and they will gather his elect from the four winds, from one end of the heavens to the other"—Mt 24:23-31.

"Therefore, stay awake! For you do not know on which day your Lord will come" —Mt 24:42.

5. How did the early Christians interpret these prophecies?

Some early Christians apparently expected the end of the

world in their own lifetime, even though they had been warned by St. Peter:

> Know this first of all, that in the last days scoffers will come [to] scoff, living according to their own desires and saying, "Where is the promise of his coming? From the time when our ancestors fell asleep, everything has remained as it was from the beginning of creation." They deliberately ignore the fact that the heavens existed of old and earth was formed out of water and through water by the word of God; through these the world that then existed was destroyed, deluged with water. The present heavens and earth have been reserved by the same word for fire, kept for the day of judgment and of destruction of the godless.

> But do not ignore this one fact, beloved, that with the Lord one day is like a thousand years and a thousand years like one day. The Lord does not delay his promise, as some regard "delay," but he is patient with you, not wishing that any should perish but that all should come to repentance. But the day of the Lord will come like a thief. . . .

> But according to his promise we await new heavens and a new earth in which righteousness dwells.

> Therefore, beloved, since you await these things, be eager to be found without spot or blemish before him, at peace.

> Therefore, beloved, since you are forewarned, be on your guard not to be led into the error of the unprincipled and to fall from your own stability—2 Pet 3:3-10, 13-14, 17.

However, it is also clear that even those Christians throughout the ages who did not expect the second coming of Christ before they died tried to live in such a way as to be prepared for it. They looked forward with eagerness to the second coming of Christ as the final and glorious fulfillment of all that a Christian should hope for.

6. What will be the great event at the end of the world?

The great event will be the return of Christ to this world. Christ's work on earth will not be finished until he returns in glory to reveal his triumph to all people. He himself describes this scene:

"When the Son of Man comes in his glory, and all the angels with him, he will sit upon his glorious throne, and all the nations will be assembled before him. And he will separate them one from another, as a shepherd separates the sheep from the goats. He will place the sheep on his right and the goats on his left. Then the king will say to those on his right, 'Come, you who are blessed by my Father. Inherit the kingdom prepared for you from the foundation of the world. For I was hungry and you gave me food, I was thirsty and you gave me drink, a stranger and you welcomed me, naked and you clothed me, ill and you cared for me, in prison and you visited me.' Then the righteous will answer him and say, 'Lord, when did we see you hungry and feed you, or thirsty and give you drink? When did we see you a stranger and welcome you, or naked and clothe you? When did we see you ill or in prison, and visit you?' And the king will say to them in reply, 'Amen, I say to you, whatever you did for one of these least . . . of mine, you did for me. Then he will say to those on his left, 'Depart from me, you accursed, into the eternal fire prepared for the devil and his angels. For I was hungry and you gave me no food, I was thirsty and you gave me no drink, a stranger and you gave me no welcome, naked and you gave me no clothing, ill and in prison, and you did not care for me.' Then they will answer and say, 'Lord, when did we see you hungry or thirsty or a stranger or naked or ill or in prison, and not minister to your needs?' He will answer them, 'Amen, I say to you, what you did not do for one of these least ones, you did not do for me.' And these will go off to eternal punishment, but the righteous to eternal life"—Mt 25:31-46.

7. Will the judgment which Christ makes at the end of the world be a real judgment?

It will not be a real judgment in the sense that Christ will be rendering a decision. At death everyone immediately receives the consequence of his or her acceptance or rejection of God's grace during life. Each of us will participate in the blessedness of everlasting life, either immediately or after a time of purification (purgatory), or "can even condemn oneself for all eternity by rejecting the Spirit of love"—CCC 679.

Nothing decided at this "particular judgment" will be changed in the final judgment at the end of time. The damned will still be in hell and the saved in heaven. Christ will merely announce who has been saved and who has been damned.

8. What do we mean by the resurrection of the dead?

At the end of the world the bodies of the dead will arise. St. Paul, speaking of the bodies of the just after the resurrection says: *"For that which is corruptible must clothe itself with incorruptibility, and that which is mortal must clothe itself with immortality"—1 Cor 15:53.*

Our bodies after the resurrection will be spiritualized. The beauty of the soul will shine forth. In a word, our bodies will be beautiful, as Christ's was at the Transfiguration, and will possess all the qualities of Christ's body after the Resurrection.

9. How should we prepare for the second coming of Christ?

Our preparation for the end of the world and the second coming of Christ should be positive rather than negative. Instead of dreading the end of the world and anxiously looking for signs and portents, we should prepare ourselves to meet our Savior by endeavoring to lead a holy life and doing our part in spreading the kingdom (or reign) of God. With these words of expectation, St. John ended the Book of Revelation, the last book of the Scriptures:

The one who gives this testimony says, "Yes, I am coming soon." Amen! Come, Lord Jesus!

The grace of the Lord Jesus be with all—Rev 22:20-21.

Practice

▲ It is heartening to remember that the final victory will be Christ's and that we shall share in that victory if we remain in union with our Savior. But before the final victory there is much to be done. The Church's mission compels us to constantly proclaim Christ's message of love and forgiveness and to work for the transformation of the world. The final triumph is assured, but in the meantime God requires our cooperation. There are others— our relatives, friends and acquaintances—who may come to love Christ more, perhaps even become members of his Church, provided our example and our efforts are what they ought to be. Others should be able to see that our lives have been enormously enriched because we have been joined to the Body of Christ. They should be able to see in our lives evidence of that deepest union with God which comes from prayer. They should be able to see that we live by faith, that we are sustained by hope, that we practice love of God and our neighbor in our daily life.

▲ All the means which will enable us to live up to the great challenge of living the Christian life are at our disposal. God sustains us in our efforts. No prayer goes unanswered. Aid from our brothers and sisters in the great family of God is forthcoming if we give ourselves to the communion of saints.

▲ The life-giving sacraments are there to give us holiness and strength. We should receive them often. Above all, the great source of grace and love, the Eucharist, is there for us. If we wish to be more deeply united to Christ and our neighbor we should make daily Mass and Communion our ideal.

▲ Help and encouragement comes to us from association with our fellow members in the community of faith. The more deeply we enter into the life of the parish, the more effective we shall be as Catholics. We should take our part in the parish life and its organizations.

▲ Finally, we should remembers always the words of Pope Pius XII:

> For nothing more glorious, nothing nobler, nothing surely more honorable can be imagined than to belong to the holy, Catholic, apostolic and Roman church, in which we become members of one Body as venerable as it is unique; are guided by one supreme Head; are filled with one divine Spirit; are nourished during our earthly exile by one doctrine and one heavenly Bread, until at last we enter into the one, unending blessedness of heaven— Encyclical on the Mystical Body.

Catholic Prayers

Pray without ceasing—1 Th 5:17.

1.   What is prayer?

St. Therese of Lisieux, the Little Flower, perhaps said it best: "For me prayer means launching out of the heart towards God; it means lifting up one's eyes, quite simply, to heaven, a cry of grateful love, from the crest of joy or the trough of despair."

2.   Why do we pray?

The origin of all prayer is to be found in God's movement toward us, in God's invitation to the encounter with him. We pray in response to that invitation.

3.   Where can we learn about prayer?

We learn about prayer first from the world of nature. Nature almost insists that we raise our voices in praise and thanksgiving to its creator.

We can learn about prayer from the experiences of prayer we find in the Hebrew Scriptures. The prayers of Jesus found in the Christian Scriptures are also powerful instructions, as are the prayers of Mary. Likewise, the liturgy of the Church and the prayers of its saints are teachers of prayer.

4)   What are the various kinds of prayer?

From the earliest days of the Church five different forms of prayer have been recognized:

a) adoration. We acknowledge the greatness of the triune God; we bless God for having blessed us.

b) petition. Acknowledging our sinfulness and our dependency as creatures we petition for the coming of God's Kingdom and then for that which is necessary for that coming to be realized.

c) intercession. Like Jesus, we raise up our hearts and minds to God out of concern for others.

d) thanksgiving. Every event and need we have become the occasion for offering thanks to God.

e) praise. The other forms of prayer are drawn together as we proclaim the glory of God.

5. To whom do we pray?

The primary focus of our prayer is God the Father, but it can also be directed to Jesus, who is God incarnate, and to the Spirit, who draws us into prayer. We can also direct prayers to Mary, the Mother of Jesus, and to the saints and angels.

6. How can prayer be expressed?

Prayer can be expressed in a variety of ways:

a) vocal prayer. Our heart is expressed in spoken words, our own or those of others.

b) meditation. All of our human faculties are engaged in a search to understand the true meaning of the Christian life.

c) contemplation or mental prayer. An unspoken "conversation" in which one comes into communion with the very mystery that is God.

7. Is prayer easy?

Prayer is not always easy. In prayer we can encounter our own lack of belief, can be distracted by other concerns, and even fear that our prayer is not effective. Humility—that is, true trust in God and the courage to persevere—open us to the love of God that can overcome these difficulties.

SIGN OF THE CROSS

In the name of the Father, and of the Son, and of the Holy Spirit.   Amen.

OUR FATHER

Our Father, who art in heaven, hallowed be thy name; thy Kingdom come, Thy will be done on earth as it is in heaven. Give us this day our daily bread; and forgive us our trespasses as we forgive those who trespass against us; and lead us not into temptation but deliver us from evil. Amen.

HAIL MARY

Hail Mary, full of grace; the Lord is with thee; blessed art thou among women, and blessed is the fruit of thy womb, Jesus.

Holy Mary, Mother of God, pray for us sinners, now and at the hour of our death.   Amen.

GLORY BE

Glory be to the Father, and to the Son, and to the Holy Spirit. As it was in the beginning, is now and ever shall be, world without end.   Amen.

THE APOSTLES' CREED

I believe in God, the Father Almighty, Creator of heaven and earth; and in Jesus Christ, his only Son, Our Lord; who was conceived by the Holy Spirit, born of the Virgin Mary, suffered under Pontius Pilate, was crucified, died, and was buried. He descended into hell, the third day he arose from the dead. He ascended into heaven, sits at the right hand of God, the Father Almighty; from thence he shall come to judge the living and the dead.

I believe in the Holy Spirit, the Holy Catholic Church, the Communion of Saints, the forgiveness of sins, the resurrection of the body, and life everlasting.   Amen.

NICENE CREED

We believe in one God, the Father, the Almighty, maker of heaven and earth, of all that is seen and unseen.

We believe in one Lord, Jesus Christ, the only Son of God, eternally begotten of the Father, God from God, Light from Light, true God from true God, begotten, not made, one in Being with the Father.

For us and for our salvation he came down from heaven; by the power of the Holy Spirit he was born of the Virgin Mary, and became man.

For our sake he was crucified under Pontius Pilate; he suffered, died and was buried.

On the third day he rose again in fulfillment of the Scriptures; he ascended into heaven and is seated at the right hand of the Father. He will come again in glory to judge the living and the dead, and his kingdom will have no end.

We believe in the Holy Spirit, the Lord, the giver of life, who proceeds from the Father and the Son. With the Father and the Son he is worshipped and glorified. He has spoken through the Prophets. We believe in one, holy, Catholic, and apostolic Church. We acknowledge one baptism for the forgiveness of sins. We look for the resurrection of the dead, and the life of the world to come. Amen.

PRAYER TO THE HOLY SPIRIT

Come, Holy Spirit, fill my heart with your holy gifts. Let my weakness be penetrated with your strength this very day that I may fulfill all the duties of my state conscientiously, that I may do what is right and just.

Let my charity be such as to offend no one, and hurt no one's feelings; so generous as to pardon sincerely any wrong done to me.

Assist me, O Holy Spirit, in all my trials of life,
enlighten me in my ignorance, advise me in my doubts,
strengthen me in my weakness, help me in all my needs,
protect me in temptations and console me in afflictions.

Graciously hear me, O Holy Spirit, and pour your light
into my heart, my soul, and my mind.

Assist me to live a holy life and to grow in goodness and
grace. Amen.

THE DIVINE PRAISES

Blessed be God.

Blessed be his Holy Name.

Blessed be Jesus Christ, true God and true man.

Blessed be the name of Jesus.

Blessed be his most Sacred Heart.

Blessed be Jesus in the most Holy Sacrament of the Altar.

Blessed be the Holy Spirit, the Paraclete.

Blessed be the great Mother of God, Mary most holy.

Blessed be her holy and Immaculate Conception.

Blessed be her glorious Assumption.

Blessed be the name of Mary, Virgin and Mother.

Blessed be St. Joseph, her most chaste spouse.

Blessed be God in his angels and in his saints.

May the heart of Jesus, in the Most Blessed Sacrament,
be praised, adored, and loved with grateful affection, at
every moment, in all the tabernacles of the world, even to
the end of time. Amen.

PRAYER TO THE BLESSED TRINITY

The Father is my hope. The Son is my refuge. The Holy Spirit is my protector. Glory to the holy and undivided Trinity, now and for ever.

Let us praise the Father, the Son and the Holy Spirit; let us bless and exalt God above all for ever!

Almighty and everlasting God, to whom we owe the grace of professing the true faith, grant that while acknowledging the glory of the eternal Trinity and adoring its unity, we may, through your majestic power, be confirmed in this faith and defended against all adversities; through Jesus Christ our Lord, who lives and reigns with you in the unity of the Holy Spirit, one God, for ever and ever. Amen.

PRAYER BEFORE RECONCILIATION

Come, Holy Spirit, into my soul. Enlighten my mind that I may know the sins I ought to confess, and grant me your grace to confess them fully, humbly, and with contrite heart. Help me to firmly resolve not to commit them again.

O Blessed Virgin, Mother of my Redeemer, mirror of innocence and sanctity, and refuge of penitent sinners, intercede for me through the Passion of your Son, that I may obtain the grace to make a good confession.

All you blessed angels and saints of God, pray for me, a most miserable sinner, that I may repent from my evil ways, that my heart may henceforth be forever united with yours in eternal love. Amen.

ACT OF CONTRITION

O my God, I am sorry for having offended you. I detest all my sins because they offend you, my God, who are all good and deserving of all my love. I firmly resolve, with the help of your grace, to sin no more and to avoid whatever leads me to sin. Amen.

PRAYER BEFORE HOLY COMMUNION

Come, O Blessed Savior, and nourish my soul with heavenly Food, the Food which contains every sweetness and every delight. Come, Bread of Angels, and satisfy the hunger of my soul.

Come, glowing Furnace of Charity, and enkindle in my heart the flame of divine love.

Come, Light of the World, and enlighten the darkness of my mind.

Come, King of Kings, and make me obedient to your holy will.

Come, loving Savior, and make me meek and humble.

Come, Friend of the Sick, and heal the infirmities of my body and weakness of my soul.

Come, Good Shepherd, my God and my All, and take me to yourself. O most holy Mother, Mary Immaculate, prepare my heart to receive my Savior. Amen.

PRAYER AFTER HOLY COMMUNION

Dear Lord, help me to remove from my mind every thought or opinion which you would not sanction, every feeling from my heart which you would not approve.

Grant that I may spend the hours of the day gladly working with you according to your will.

Help me just for today and be with me in it. In the long hours of work, that I may not grow weary or slack in serving you.

In conversations that they may not be to me occasions of uncharitableness.

In the day's worries and disappointments, that I may be patient with myself and with those around me.

In moments of fatigue and illness, that I may be mindful of theirs rather than of myself.

In temptations, that I may be generous and loyal, so that when the day is over I may lay it at your feet, with its successes which are all yours, and its failures which are all my own, and feel that life is real and peaceful, and blessed when spent with you as the Guest of my soul. Amen.

PRAYER TO JESUS IN THE EUCHARIST

Soul of Christ, make me holy.

Body of Christ, save me.

Blood of Christ, fill me with love.

Water from Christ's side, wash me.

Passion of Christ, strengthen me.

Good Jesus, hear me.

Within your wounds, hide me.

Never let me be parted from you.

From the evil enemy, protect me.

At the hour of my death, call me.

And in eternal life always keep me. Amen.

MORNING OFFERING

O Jesus, through the Immaculate Heart of Mary, I offer you my prayers, works, joys and sufferings of this day in union with the Holy Sacrifice of the Mass throughout the world.

I offer them for the intentions of our Bishops and for all our associates, and in particular for those recommended by our Holy Father this month. Amen.

GRACE (BEFORE AND AFTER MEALS)

Bless us, O Lord, and these your gifts which we are about to receive from your bounty through Christ Our Lord. Amen.

We give you thanks for all your benefits, Almighty God, who lives and reigns forever. May the souls of the faithful departed, through the mercy of God, rest in peace. Amen

EVENING PRAYER

O my God, another day is ending and I call out to you once more.

I praise you for your love and goodness shown to me throughout this day.

Help me follow your will and strive to become what you intend me to be.

Watch over my loved ones and keep them close to you.

Let me wake tomorrow refreshed in body and spirit, grateful for another day in your grace.   Amen.

HAIL HOLY QUEEN

Hail, Holy Queen, Mother of mercy, our life, our sweetness and our hope.

To you do we cry, poor banished children of Eve, to you do we send up our sighs, mourning and weeping in this vale of tears.

Turn, then, most gracious advocate, your eyes of mercy toward us; after this our exile, show unto us the blessed fruit of your womb, Jesus.

O clement, O loving, O sweet Virgin Mary.

Pray for us, O holy Mother of God, that we may be made worth of the promises of Christ.

Almighty and everlasting God, who by the cooperation of the Holy Spirit prepared the body and soul of the glorious Virgin Mother Mary to be a fit dwelling for your Son, grant that we who rejoice in her memory may be freed by her kindly prayers both from present ills and from eternal death; through the same Christ our Lord. Amen.

MEMORARE

Remember, O most gracious Virgin Mary, that never was it known that anyone who fled to your protection, implored your help, or sought your intercession, was left unaided.

Inspired by this confidence, I fly to you, O Virgin of Virgins my Mother. To you I come, before you I stand, sinful and sorrowful.

O Mother of the Word Incarnate, despise not my petitions, but in your mercy hear and answer me.   Amen.

LITANY OF THE SAINTS

Lord, have mercy on us.　　　　*Lord, have mercy on us.*
Christ, have mercy on us.　　　*Christ, have mercy on us.*
Lord, have mercy on us.　　　　*Lord, have mercy on us.*

Holy Mary, Mother of God,　　　　　*Pray for us*
St. Michael,
Holy Angels of God,
St. Joseph,
St. John the Baptist,
St. Peter and St. Paul,
St. Andrew,
St. John,
St. Mary Magdalene,
St. Stephen,
St. Ignatius,
St. Lawrence,
St. Perpetua and St. Felicity,
St. Agnes,
St. Gregory,
St. Augustine,

St. Athanasius,

St. Basil,

St. Martin,

St. Benedict,

St. Francis and St. Dominic,

St. Francis Xavier,

St. John Vianney,

St. Catherine,

St. Theresa,

All you saints of God,

Lord, be merciful,   *Lord, save us*

From all harm,

From every sin,

From all temptations,

From everlasting death,

By your coming among us,

By your death and rising to a new life,

By your gift of the Holy Spirit,

Be merciful to us sinners,   *Lord, hear our prayer*

Guide and protect your
   Holy Church,

Keep our Pope and all the clergy
   in faithful service to your Church,

Bring all people together
   in trust and peace,

Strengthen us in your service,

PRAYER TO OUR GUARDIAN ANGEL

Angel of God, my Guardian Dear, to whom God's love commits me here, ever this day be at my side, to light and guard, to rule and guide. Amen.

PRAYER FOR LIFE

Loving God, Creator of all life, you have known us from all eternity. Before you ever formed us in our mother's womb you knew us.

Teach us to foster proper attitudes about all of your creation, the unborn, the elderly, the handicapped, the terminally ill.

Help us to see anew the miracle and sacredness of all life and give us a greater awareness of our responsibility toward this gift from you.

We ask this through Christ our Lord. Amen.

PRAYER FOR THOSE WHO HAVE DIED

May the souls of the faithfully departed, through the mercy of God, rest in peace.

Eternal rest grant unto them O Lord, and let perpetual light shine upon them. Amen.

PRAYER FOR VOCATIONS

Oh God, you have called us to salvation and have sent your Son to establish the Church for this purpose and you have provided the sacred ministers. The harvest is ever ready but the laborers are scarce. Inspire our youth to follow Jesus in the priesthood and religious life. Amen.

PRAYER FOR THE POPE

Father, we pray for your protection and guidance over our Holy Father, (name). Give him strength and wisdom to stand as a prophet for our times. May he be a light in darkness around which we gather in hope.

We ask you to bring about reconciliation through his faithful teaching of peace and justice. Grant him compassion and care to live the Gospel in love and service to all people.

Let him follow in the path of Peter and Paul who, filled with the Holy Spirit, preached that the Lord saves all who call upon his name. Amen.

A PRIEST'S PRAYER

Lord God, you willed that priests should come forth from the community in order to serve your people. We, like everyone else, are sinners and must trust in your mercy. We're not always right and are often wrong. We strive for perfection but often fail. We are called to preach the truth but are often untrue. Our task is to heal but we too often wound.

With all the expectations and demands placed on us we often forget that we are just human—struggling to live up to our sacred call. We forget that our strength is not in our skills and cleverness but in submission to your will and faith in your unabiding love.

Lord God, help me and all priests to put you before our self-interest and comfort. Give us the Holy Spirit's power to avoid pride, stubbornness, and desire for self-glory. Help us be holy and teach us to forgive those who unjustly criticize and hurt us. Forgive us our many failings and lead us to joyfully live our priestly lives with understanding and compassion. Amen.

PRAYER OF ST. FRANCIS

Lord, make me an instrument of your peace.
Where there is hatred, let me sow love;
where there is injury, pardon,
where there is doubt, faith,
where there is despair, hope,
where there is darkness, light,
and where there is sadness, joy.

O Divine Master, grant that I may not so much seek to be consoled as to console; to be understood as to understand, to be loved as to love; for it is in giving that we receive, it is in pardoning that we are pardoned, and it is in dying that we are born to eternal life.

ACT OF FAITH

O my God! I firmly believe that you are one God in three Divine Persons, Father, Son and Holy Spirit. I believe that your Divine Son became human and died for our sins, and that he will come to judge the living and the dead. I believe these and all the truths which the holy Catholic Church teaches because you have revealed them, who can neither deceive nor be deceived.

ACT OF HOPE

O my God! relying on your infinite goodness and promises, I hope to obtain pardon of my sins, the help of your grace and life everlasting, through the merits of Jesus Christ, my Lord and Redeemer.

ACT OF LOVE

O my God! I love you above all things with my whole heart and soul because you are all-good and worthy of all love. I love my neighbor as myself for the love of you. I forgive all who have injured me, and ask pardon of all whom I have injured.

List of References Quoted

Catechism of the Catholic Church (CCC) (Libreria Editrice Vatican, 1994) 4, 82, 87, 97, 116, 132, 135, 138, 154, 182, 199, 214, 215, 229, 230, 231, 251, 260

Code of Canon Law (Libreria Editrice Vatican, 1983) 106, 247

Constitution on the Sacred Liturgy (Second Vatican Council, 1963) 123, 124, 174, 175

Declaration on the Relation of the Church to Non-Christian Religions (Second Vatican Council, 1965) 74

Decree on Ecumenism (Second Vatican Council, 1964) 96

Decree on Frequent Communion (Pius X, 1905) 163

Dogmatic Constitution on the Church (Second Vatican Council, 1964) 146

Encyclical on Restructuring the Social Order (Pius XI, 1931) 270

Encyclical on the Christian Education of Youth (Pius XI, 1929) 251

Encyclical on the Development of Holiness of Priestly Life (Pius XI, 1935) 198

Encyclical on the Family (John Paul II, 1981) 260

Encyclical on the Gospel of Life (John Paul II, 1995) 258

Encyclical on the Mystical Body (Pius XII, 1943) 288

Encyclical on the Sacred Liturgy (Pius XII, 1947) 246

Imitation of Christ (Thomas a Kempis, 1486) 160

Ineffabilis Dei (Apostolic Constitution of Pope Pius IX defining the Dogma of the Immaculate Conception, 1854) 119

Munificentissium Deus (Apostolic Constitution of Pius XII defining the Dogma of the Assumption, 1950) 119

Pastoral Constitution on the Church in the Modern World (Second Vatican Council, 1965) 207, 210, 228

Index